ADULTERY

IN THE UNITED STATES

ADULTERY
IN THE UNITED STATES

STATES

CLOSE ENCOUNTERS
OF THE SIXTH
(OR SEVENTH) KIND

EDITED BY PHILIP E. LAMPE

PROMETHEUS BOOKS

Buffalo, New York

90 89 88 87   4 3 2 1

Library of Congress Cataloging-in-Publication Data

Lampe, Philip E.
    Adultery in the United States.

    Includes bibliographies.
    1. Adultery—United States. I. Title.
HQ806.L38 1987   306.7′36   87-9641
ISBN 0-87975-375-7

CONTENTS

ADULTERY
IN THE UNITED
STATES

INTRODUCTION

Sexual behavior is a common and necessary part of nature. It is, of course, not unique to humans. However, there appear to be important differences between the sex drive of animals and that of humans. For example, the female of most animal species is sexually receptive only during a seasonal estrous period. Often, this is the only time when males and females continue in a close association. In contrast, humans share with the anthropoids the biological phenomenon of continuous sexuality whereby females are not limited to seasonal sexual receptivity. This may be seen as an aid, if not a guarantee, to continuous association between the sexes. Some species of animals mate for life and are completely faithful to their mate; other species mate only momentarily with any and all members of the opposite sex. Both practices can be found among humans. On the one hand, humans exhibit a desire for enduring sexual relationships; this is a basis for marriage. On the other hand, humans reveal a desire for sexual variety; this is a basis for adultery. Finally, in the animal world each species has a specific mating pattern which is found among virtually all of its members. Such is not the case among humans. Although humans constitute a single genus and species, *Homo sapiens,* a wide variety of mating practices is found.

All aspects of human sexual feelings and behavior are culturally patterned, and a wide range of differences exist (Horton and Hunt, 1980: 128). Some people are monogamous and have a single life-long mate, while others are polygamous and have two or more mates simultaneously. Many people's marital experience is somewhere between these two poles, having only one mate at a time but, because of death or divorce followed by remarriage, having two or more mates over a lifetime. This practice has been referred to as both "serial monogamy" and "progressive polygamy." Polygamy may take one of three forms. A female may have several permanent mates, as in the case of polyandry or, as more frequently occurs, a male may have several permanent mates, as in the case of polygyny. In a relatively few instances there may even be a permanent arrangement of several males and females being common mates, such as in the case of group marriage. Were these alternative forms of marriage based entirely on biological drive or strictly individual choice, one might expect to find them randomly distributed throughout the world's cultures. Such is not the case. What one finds instead, however, is that each culture has a dominant form of marriage which is supported by both prescriptions and proscriptions.

In the United States, for example, as in virtually all of the Judeo-Christian world, monogamy is the only socially approved and legally sanctioned form of marriage, and the spouse is considered to be the exclusive and permanent sexual partner. However, as with other social norms, there is a good deal of deviant behavior and not all sexual behavior is, in fact, limited to one's spouse. The persistence of these deviations seems to indicate that, as many previous writers have stated, man is not by nature monogamous. However, it must be pointed out that this same evidence also does not prove that man is naturally polygamous. While human biology establishes the possible *range* of our sexual activity, monogamy and polygamy—as well as adultery—can best be explained in socio-cultural and psychosocial terms.

Virtually every society for which data are available has at least some established guidelines regarding sexual behavior. Although societies differ as to the extent and scope, as well as the specific content, of such guidelines, most societies do regulate, in the form of prescriptions and/or proscriptions, certain types of sexual behavior that may be seen as in some way affecting the well-being of the community. Two of the most universally prohibited types of sexual behavior are incest and adultery. Incest taboos, which prohibit sexual intercourse between persons too closely related to be legally married, may be viewed as an attempt by a society to increase and extend group unity by forcing members of one family to establish close ties with other families through the bond of marriage. The prohibitions of adultery may be seen as an attempt to preserve group unity by preventing divisive conflicts from arising between families, because of unacceptable sexual relationships. It is this latter category of sexual behavior, adultery, which is of particular interest to us here.

ORIGINS OF ADULTERY

Adultery has often been perceived as an extension and exercise of property rights, wherein females are viewed as part of a male's possessions. In a sense, this possessiveness of females found a model in the animal world. Charles Darwin, in *The Descent of Man,* noted that in species in which a male animal collects a number of females, the male dominates his collection of mates and jealously guards them from all possible male rivals. Even his own male offspring will be expelled from the group when they get older. Mating privileges are often something to be fought for and earned, with only dominant males enjoying the rewards.

Similar attitudes appear to be present in man. Speaking of primitive man, MacCulloch (1928) wrote that "woman being conceived as belonging to man, any interference with her would immediately outrage man's instinctive sense of property, and would at once arouse jealousy." A man thus aroused, he wrote, may be expected to attack the male transgressor in order to recover his property, the woman, and to punish him in a way that would serve as a warning to all others. However, since the woman is a sentient being, and therefore to some extent a consenting party to the transgression, the man may also vent his anger on her. MacCulloch concluded, "Thus it must be admitted that, at the earliest stage of human history, adultery could have been nothing but a breach of proprietary rights, to be followed, when discovered, by a more or less savage act of private revenge upon both the culprits" (1928: 122). Concerns over adultery, therefore, are often seen as originating in feelings of jealousy which are aroused and/or a preoccupation with property rights where wives are considered to belong to their husbands.

RELATIONSHIP OF MARRIAGE AND ADULTERY

Where there is no marriage there can be no adultery. This is not to say that marriage is responsible for adultery. Rather, it is meant to point out that where marriage and marital rights and obligations are defined differently, interpretations of and reactions to adultery may also differ. What may appear to a member of one society as adulterous behavior may not be so interpreted by the members of another. When this occurs the reactions of the individuals involved are not, in fact, reactions to adultery. In general, therefore, the statement appears to be correct that "Throughout history most societies have been concerned with adultery, treating it variously as a crime, a moral wrong, a private matter, an infringement of the husband's rights, or a threat to family stability and orderly succession" (Nichols, 1979: 192).

An extensive cross-cultural study by the anthropologist George P. Murdock revealed that of the 148 societies, past and present, for which adequate data was available, in only 5 was adultery freely allowed. Another 19 societies conditionally permitted it and four more disapproved of adultery without strictly forbidding it.

However, it must be noted that "these figures apply only to sex relations with an unrelated or distantly related person" (1949: 265). Murdock stated that most societies appear to permit extramarital relations with certain affinal relatives under at least some circumstances. These individuals are usually those who may be viewed as a possible marital replacement in case of the death of the spouse. Relevant to this is the earlier observation of the sociologist Kingsley Davis (1939) that a sexual custom is accepted by a society to the degree that it is perceived as supporting the social institutions of marriage and family. The renowned anthropologist Bronislaw Malinowski was of the opinion that "prenuptial license and the relaxation of the matrimonial bonds must not be regarded as a denial of marriage, as its abrogation, but rather as its complement. The function of license is not to upset but rather to maintain marriage" (1928: 104).

REACTIONS TO ADULTERY

It has been stated that adultery has had few rivals as a cause of murder and misery (Diamond, 1985: 177), however this statement may be misleading. There appears to be no single universal reaction to adultery. Cross-cultural data reveal a wide variety of beliefs and practices. Acceptance, at least in certain situations, is found in some parts of the world. In some societies a husband has the right to lend his wife to a male visitor. An example of this custom, sometimes called "wife hospitality," is found among certain Eskimo groups. In these same societies, however, a wife does not have the right to volunteer herself to a male. Such an act would result in the punishment of both the wife and her partner by the husband. Among the Kaka in Cameroon it is socially acceptable for a man to have sexual relations with the wives of certain of his relatives. A man who commits adultery among the Konyagas may be forced to become a second husband to the woman. As such he can have free sexual access to the wife but he pays a price for this right: he must also work for the benefit of the household and obey the original husband. Marriage does not imply exclusive sexual privileges for the spouses among the Arunta of Australia. Therefore a certain amount of sexual license is allowed for both husbands and wives, especially during a major ceremony or on other special occasions. The foregoing are but a few historical examples of what might be seen as an approving or tolerant attitude toward adultery.

Severe sanctions against adultery, however, have been found to prevail in other parts of the world. In West Africa the traditional Senoufo and Bambara tribes have allowed the wronged husband to kill his adulterous wife—as well as her male partner—as a way of preserving his honor. Under Muslim law the husband of a wife discovered in the act of adultery has also been allowed to kill his wife with impunity. Similarly, among the Wotjobaluk of Victoria, Australia, the husband has had the right to kill both the wife and her lover, while among the Yerkla mining peoples of South Australia, the adulterous wife was branded with a firestick for her first offense, speared in the leg for her second offense, and if subsequently discovered to have engaged in adultery, was killed. Among some tribes of native Australians the prescribed punishment for an adulterous wife was to be handed over to any males who wanted to have sexual intercourse with her. And in parts of Pre-Columbian Mexico an adulterous wife could have her nose and ears cut off, after which she might be stoned to death.

Among the Indians in North America a variety of attitudes were also exhibited toward adultery, ranging from acceptance to rejection. Among the Columbian Indians men sometimes bartered their wives among themselves as a sign of friendship. The Pueblo Indians accepted adultery as long as it was done discreetly and was kept a secret. The Cheyenne Indians considered it to be a private matter, whereas among the Comanches the husband was forced by group opinion to chastise his adulterous wife and secure reparations from her male partner. Some tribes even recognized the marital rights of females. Thus an Omaha Indian wife could seek revenge on both her husband and his paramour for an adulterous affair, and wives in the Sioux and Dakota tribes could leave a husband because of his infidelity.

At times the reaction adultery has evoked has depended upon the social status of one or both of the sexual partners involved. For example, the Hebrews considered a married woman to be guilty of adultery if she had sexual intercourse with any male other than her own husband while a married man was guilty of adultery only if he had intercourse with another man's wife. Among the Bantu of equitorial and southern Africa, a man who engaged in adultery with the wife of a commoner received a fine; adultery with the wife of the king brought him the death penalty. Thus, some of the differences between societies may be explained by the respective society's view of marriage and/or the relative worth of individuals involved.

PROOF OF AND PROTECTION AGAINST ADULTERY

Just as attitudes towards and treatment of adultery, often so different from our own so as to be virtually incomprehensible, show a surprising diversity, so too are the methods various cultures have used to prove adultery, and to protect against it. Perhaps the most interesting "proof" is the birth of twins. Some cultures have believed that a man can be father of no more than one child at a time. Twins were, therefore, evidence of two different fathers. In such cases the supposed adultery may be viewed as having occurred with a divinity or spirit, as in the Greek myths of Alemene and Leda, or it may be judged as having occurred with a human lover. Such a belief has been reported among some South American tribes and the Melanesians.

To protect their own wife or wives from engaging in adultery, and thus preserve themselves from the ridicule reserved for the cuckold, men have employed a number of techniques. The most common are the establishment of social norms and punishment under religious, civil, and criminal laws. In addition to these regulatory measures, some societies have adopted more concrete measures which rely less on the acceptance and conformity of individuals. Examples would include the physical separation of the sexes and/or the use of clothing and veils to completely cover the woman from view. Such practices are still found in some parts of the Muslim world. Another common tactic, especially in Hispanic countries, has been the utilization of a chaperone. For the more affluent members of some societies, such as those found in ancient Persia and China, there was the practice of employing a eunuch to guard the wives. And the medieval European husband who was going off to a war could have his wife locked into a chastity belt, a large, spiked device designed to discourage amorous males from "getting too close." Thus, while some societies seemed to operate on the principle "out of sight, out of mind," others appeared to be thinking "look but don't touch!"

Both approaches attempt to restrict undesirable sexual behavior by imposing external controls. Additional external controls include fines, imprisonment and even death. Other approaches rely on internal controls which are developed during the socialization process. The two most commonly recognized internal controls are guilt and shame. Guilt, which is identified with the conscience, is an internal discomfort ranging from mild to unbearable which results from violating one's own internalized standard of behavior, whereas shame is an internal discomfort which is a reaction to others' real or imagined criticism of one's behavior. The United States is one of the societies which relies heavily on guilt to restrict adulterous behavior, although the anthropologist Ruth Benedict (1946) expressed the opinion that it was in the process of moving from a guilt culture to a shame culture. One of the reasons given for this change was a relaxation of morals.

PLAN OF THE BOOK

As can be seen, a universal study of adultery would be fascinating but would also be an awesome task. This book is much more limited in scope. We will examine, in some detail, adultery in the United States from colonial times to the present. Such a study is important for several reasons. First, it will help illustrate the difference between the ideal culture, that which is supposed to be, and the real culture, that which is. Such a discrepancy has always existed in the United Sates, as it has in all societies. Behavior which diverges greatly from what is expected is generally referred to as deviant behavior and is subject to negative social sanctions. Second, it will provide the basis for a better understanding of American society and the process of social change. It has often occurred that a social deviant of one age is looked upon as a social reformer in another age, and what was once condemned will be praised. Third, it will provide an integrated perspective of a form of behavior which has often been considered to be a social problem. Thus, the reader will be able to appreciate the complexity and variety of factors which are involved in social behavior and social norms.

The book will utilize a general historical or developmental approach as it examines adulterous behavior from five separate perspectives: legal, religious, literary, philosophical, and social scientific. An attempt will be made to remain objective and avoid the temptation to interject personal opinions and evaluations regarding the behavior we are examining. After a brief overview of the historical antecedents of the United States culture as they relate to adultery, each of the five perspectives will be developed in a separate chapter by professionals in the field. The final chapter will attempt to integrate the ideas presented in these various perspectives and in so doing comment on the possible future status of adultery in the United States.

Finally, the title not only indicates the topic of concern, but also recognizes the pluralistic nature of society. The United States is a religiously pluralistic society which was founded as a Christian country. While the Ten Commandments are a common element of the Judeo-Christian religions, there is some difference in the specific enumeration of each commandment. The discrepancy in enumeration derived from two sources: the particular translation used, and whether the translation was based on Exodus or Deuteronomy. The title of this book recognizes the difference. However, in the following chapters reference will be made to the sixth (Catholic and Jewish version) rather than the seventh (Protestant version) commandment since it is the older tradition. Similarly, the commandment "Thou shalt not steal" will be referred to as the seventh and "thou shalt not covet thy neighbor's wife" as the ninth.

REFERENCES

Benedict, Ruth. 1946. *The Chrysanthemum and the Sword.* New York: Houghton Mifflin.

Darwin, Charles. 1904. *The Descent of Man.* New York: A. A. Hill.

Davis, Kingsley. 1939. "Illegitimacy and the Social Structure," *American Journal of Sociology,* 45 (September): 215-233.

Diamond, Jared. 1985. "Everything *Else* You Always Wanted to Know About Sex," *Discovery,* 6 (April): 70-82.

Horton, Paul, and Chester Hunt. 1980. *Sociology.* New York: McGraw-Hill.

MacCulloch, J. A. 1928. "Adultery." In *Encyclopedia of Religion and Ethics.* edited by J. Hastings, 122-126. New York: Charles Scribner's Sons.

Malinowski, Bronislaw. 1928. "The Anthropological Study of Sex." *Verhandlungen des I International Kongresses fur Sexualforschung,* edited by McMarcuse, vol. 5, (1928): 92-108.

Murdock, George P. 1949. *Social Structure.* New York: Macmillan.

Nichols, William. 1979. "Adultery." *Encyclopedia Americana,* p. 192. Danbury, Conn.: Grolier.

Philip E. Lampe
ROOTS OF THE
UNITED STATES HERITAGE

Webster's New World Dictionary defines adultery as "Sexual intercourse between a married man and a woman not his wife, or between a married woman and a man not her husband."

Down through the ages adultery has been a major and recurrent theme in the story of human relations. It has had repercussions not only on the individual level but also on the social level. This becomes evident when the written record of human civilizations is examined. Therefore, not only individuals but also societies have had to deal with the reality of adultery. The ways in which this has been accomplished are revealed in the law, religion, mythology/literature, and philosophy of the peoples who have produced them. A brief perusal of each of these sources at different periods of time may be beneficial to form a background against which to examine adultery in the United States in greater detail.

Since the present concern is with tracing the roots of the American tradition, attention will be largely limited to those cultures which have contributed most significantly to our heritage. Much of the ancient world, including the more advanced civilizations in China and India, viewed sexual behavior in a positive way. In the Middle East there were also sex-positive cultures. However, these cultures were not as influential as the Hebrews, Greeks, and Romans in shaping the sexual attitudes of our Western heritage. The Hebrews, founders of Judaism, had a strong influence on Western moral thinking, including sexual attitudes. Greeks were even more influential, especially through their literary, medical, and philosophical teachings. And the Romans passed on a rich tradition of legal principles, and contributed much sexual terminology that is still in use, such as "cunnilingus," "felatio," "masturbation," and "prostitute" (Bullough, 1976).

EARLY LAW

Although adultery has been interpreted and evaluated in a number of ways by different societies down through the centuries, it is noteworthy that one tendency found in most cultures is that more attention appears to be given to an errant wife than to an errant husband. According to the Code of Hammurabi, in Babylonia (c. 1790 BC), long thought to be the oldest legal code ever written, punishment of death by drowning was provided for adultery. Because the code viewed adultery primarily as an offense against the husband, the husband was permitted to waive or mitigate the punishment against his wife should he so desire. The unfaithful wife could be permitted to take an oath in the temple and then return to her husband (Stone, 1976: 59). What is now believed to be an even older law in Eshnunna, Sumer (c. 2000 BC), stated that if a soldier's wife had a child by another man while the husband was away at war, she should be taken back by the husband upon his return; the law made no mention of punishment (Stone, 1976: 59).

A similar mentality is found in the laws of ancient Greece. According to a provision in a criminal law by Draco (c. 620 BC), it was the husband's right to slay the adulterer with impunity if he was caught "in the act," and it was the husband's duty to divorce his adulterous wife. Furthermore, the aggrieved husband did not have to return the dowry, as was cutomary in the case of divorce. A law of Solon (c. 590 BC) stated that such an adultress could not wear any ornaments and was forbidden to attend public sacrifices so as not to corrupt decent women (Toumbouros, 1959: 32-40). In Roman law the offending female spouse could be killed, but males were generally not severely punished.

EARLY RELIGION

For at least 2000 years before the birth of Jesus there was a widespread acceptance of the mother goddess throughout what is now the Near and Middle East (Stone, 1976). This deity was considered to be the Mother of the world and was known under a variety of names, including Isis, Astarte, Nut, Innin, Istar, and Hathor, to name but a few. Women commonly enjoyed greater social and sexual freedom in those societies which followed the goddess. According to the Biblical archaeologist William Albright, sacred prostitution was almost always found in connection with the Goddess cult of Phoenicia and Syria. He expressed the opinion that the erotic aspect of this cult became very sordid, according to Western standards (Albright, 1953: 75-76). It seems safe to assume that at least some of the worshippers were married. Thus, under certain conditions, adultery was viewed as socially and morally acceptable behavior.

A reaction to this practice may be seen in the Old Testament. At various times the goddess worship appeared among segments of the Hebrew nation. Images of the goddess Asherah began to be carved and worshipped (1 Kings 15: 2-14), bringing condemnation from the prophets and other faithful followers of Yahweh. Jewish concern over adultery, however, may have been occasioned as much by economic as by religious concern. Extramarital sexual intercourse of a married man, for example, was not *per se* a crime in either Biblical or later Jewish law. The distinction made between the culpability of a husband and a wife apparently stems from the economic aspect of Israelite marriage. The wife, or an engaged woman for whom the bride price had already been paid, was the husband's possession, and adultery constituted a violation of his exclusive right to her. As a possession of the husband, however, the wife had no such corresponding right; his extra-marital sexual actions did not violate *her* property rights. (Exod. 20: 17, Deut. 5: 21; 22: 22-29; Lev. 20: 10).

In a society which was both matriarchal and matrilineal where females exercised power and inheritance was passed on through the mother—practices often associated with worship of the mother goddess—paternity was not as important as it was for the Hebrews, who were both patriarchal and patrilineal (Stone, 1976). In Hebrew society inheritance was passed on from father to son. Under such an arrangement it was necessary to ensure that a husband's property did not pass on to the offspring of another man. Thus the concern for protecting the virginity of the unmarried women and the virtue of the married may have been, at least in part, economically motivated.

Such a claim, of course, no matter how appealing it may be to the more pragmatic-minded, must be largely conjectural. Moreover, there are arguments against a strictly economic explanation. Laws against adultery may be placed in a broader context of other Hebrew laws including those which forbade rape and protected orphans, widows, and strangers. What is fact and not speculation is that the Hebrews were certainly very much concerned with the matter of adultery. It is referred to 43 times in the Old Testament[1] (Hartdegen, 1977). Not all of the references pertain to misconduct by a husband or wife, however. The prophets, from Hosea on, were wont to compare Israel's bond to Yahweh with the marital union, so many references refer to the conduct of the entire Hebrew nation—a population of "chosen people" who had entered into a covenant with Yahweh but who had turned away from Him to follow foreign gods. This behavior, like that of a spouse who turns to another person for sexual pleasure, was looked upon as a case of infidelity. As is illustrated by the Biblical story of Susanna, who was falsely accused of committing adultery in a secluded garden with an unidentified youth, infidelity was sufficient reason to receive the death penalty (Dan. 13: 19-43). Stoning, a punishment often prescribed for crimes which were felt to threaten the well-being of the nation was a common form of execution (Deut. 22: 24), as was burning (Gen. 38: 24). When Moses discovered members of the chosen people worshipping the golden calf, he had them put to the sword; religious infidelity was also grounds for execution (Exod. 32: 26-28).

In the Old Testament extramarital intercourse is often equated with prostitution. A woman who had sexual relations outside of marriage was often referred to as a harlot. In certain Biblical warnings against adultery, fornication and prostitution are woven together, indicating they are in some way comparable (Sir. 9: 3-9). Indeed, adultery is one of the transgressions singled out in the Ten Commandments; the sixth commandment is, "thou shall not commit adultery." So serious, in fact, was this behavior considered to be that another commandment, the ninth, prohibits the very thought or desire to engage in an adulterous relationship: "thou shall not covet thy neighbor's wife."

A continuation of this same condemnation of adultery exhibited in the Old Testament is found in the New Testament, where the term adultery is used 26 times[2] (Hartdegen, 1977). There is, however, a notable difference in the specific use of such references. Whereas the Old Testament often uses the term as a metaphorical way to refer to religious infidelity, the New Testament uses the term only in the literal sense of marital infidelity.

Jesus explicitly extended the meaning of adultery to include thoughts as well as actions: "You have heard it said by them of old time; 'Thou shall not commit adultery.' But I say to you that whoever looks on a woman to lust after her already committed adultery with her in his heart" (Matt. 5: 27-28). And Jesus made two further modifications. Whereas the Old Testament authorized the execution of an adulteress, Jesus directed that she be forgiven for her wrong-doing (John 8: 9). The second modification derives from the declaration that, "The Creator from the beginning made them male and female and that He said: 'This is why man must leave father and mother and cling to his wife, and the two become one body.' They are no longer two, therefore, but one body. So then, what God has united, man must not divide" (Matt. 19: 5-6). Thus in Jesus's view, since divorce does not end the marriage bond, "Anyone who divorces his wife and marries another woman commits adultery against his former wife, and if a woman divorces her husband and marries another man, she is an adulteress" (Mark 10: 11-12).

As Christianity developed among the followers of Jesus, and over the centuries became the dominant religion and a driving force in the Western world, Christians were taught that abstinence from sex may facilitate salvation. A preference for sexual asceticism did not originate with early Christianity. There existed in the classical world in which Christianity developed a strong countercurrent to the more sexually-positive traditions found in the Islamic, Hindu, Taoist, and Buddhist parts of the world. According to Bullough (1976) negative attitudes towards sexual behavior in Christianity are derived more from paganism than from Judaism. The emphasis on celibacy found in the Greek philosophies of Epicureanism, Cynicism, and Stoicism, is more striking than what is found in the Gospels. The sex-negative attitude of the pagans did much to reinforce the prohibition on adultery which did derive from Judaism and the Gospels.

EARLY LITERATURE

Ancient literature often speaks of adultery, although not necessarily by name. In Homer's *Iliad,* for example, Paris flees with the beautiful Helen, wife of King Menelaus, in an action that launches the proverbial thousand ships and ultimately results in death and destruction. In Homer's *Odyssey,* when the wandering Ulysses is seduced by the sorceress Circe as he attempts to return to his beleagured wife and son at home in Ithaca, he forgets all of his obligations and, as a consequence, his men are turned into swine.

Love, seduction, and adultery were common occurrences in Greek myth. These often served as the cause or catalyst for the eventual development of tragedy. In part this can be traced to the high esteem in which the home and family were held, together with the acceptance of private vengeance as an integral element in the system of justice. The play *Agamemnon,* by Aeschylus, illustrates these cultural values. In this play Thyestes seduces his brother, Atreus's wife. To avenge this adultery, Atreus secretly kills his brother's children and serves their flesh to their adulterous father at a feast.

In Greek and Roman mythology adultery was not limited to mortals. At times the gods became accomplices and would aid mortals in their adulterous plans, while at other times the gods themselves were sexual partners. An example of a god as accomplice is to be found in the story of Paris and Helen. In this myth, which according to Harvey (1955: 306) was apparently unknown to Homer, Paris acted as a judge in a beauty contest between the goddesses Hera, Athene, and Aphrodite. Although each of the goddesses offered bribes, he selected Aphrodite as the fairest in return for her promise to help him gain the love of the most beautiful woman in the world. This, as it turned out, was Helen, wife of King Menelaus of Sparta. After Helen went away with Paris, Menelaus and his chiefs set out to recover her. As a result of the adulterous action a war was fought, the city of Troy was destroyed and Paris himself was mortally wounded.

Adultery by the gods was of two kinds: adultery between a god and a mortal, and adultery between two gods. Zeus provides us with an example of the first type. In Greek mythology he is the supreme deity, a position he achieved by the overthrow of his father Cronus. Popularly identified as the god of the sky, Zeus was considered to be the husband of Hera, to whom he was often unfaithful. One of Zeus's illicit lovers was the mortal Semele, who consequently gave birth to Dionysus. Semele was inadvertently killed by a thunderbolt from Zeus after his jealous wife, Hera, convinced Semele to beseech her lover to show off his celestial might.

Gods also had adulterous affairs with other gods. Aphrodite, the Greek goddess of love, was the wife of the god Hephaestus, but she was often unfaithful to him. When Hephaestus became aware of an affair Aphrodite was having with the god Ares, he set a trap for the lovers, catching them in a net while in love's embrace. While thus entwined, they were put on display and exposed to the ridicule of the assembled gods.

A more consistently light-hearted, often farcical approach to adultery is found in the works of the pre-Christian Roman poet Publius Ovidius Naso, better known as Ovid. His poem "The Art of Love" is a parody of the technical treaties of his time which dealt with love-making. Another work, "The Cure of Love," explains how a lover could terminate an affair once he or she lost interest in it. His "Amours" is a personal account of some of his own insights and experiences in the art of love. As his words illustrate, Ovid held physical love in high regard even though he frequently spoke of it as though it were a game or battle:

> Tacticians recommend the night attack,
> use of the spearhead, catching the foe asleep.
> These tactics wiped out Rhesus and his Thracians,
> capturing the famous horses.
> Lovers use them too—to exploit a sleeping husband,
> thrusting hard while the enemy snores. (Amours, 4: 21-26)

Evidently this competitive view of love was shared by others. We have the account of the Roman Emperor and historian Claudius of his adulterous wife, Messalina, referred to by the Roman historian Juvenalis as the "whore-empress" (Grant, 1975: 145), who once challenged the leading professional whore to a contest to determine who could sexually accomodate the most men successively without tiring. As befits an empress, she proved herself to be superior to a common prostitute.[3] There have been so many accounts of Messalina's sexual exploits that historian Grant commented that if only one-tenth of the stories were true "she was phenomenally over-sexed" (1975: 145).

Ovid had a more reflective side. After speaking of Cupid's commissions and offering advice to his own lover on how she should behave in the event he may encounter her with her husband at a party, he goes on to say that he realizes she may need other lovers but these should be kept secret. Love should be a private affair to be enjoyed behind closed doors. He continues:

> But when you dress put on your moral make-up too
> and wear the negative look of virtue.
> Take whomever you please—provided you take me in.
> Don't enlighten me. Let me keep my illusions
> Need I see those notes coming and going?
> That double hollow in the bed?
> Your hair in sleepless disarray?
> Those love-bites on your neck?
> You'll soon be committing adultery before my very eyes.
> Destroy your good name if you must, but spare my feelings.
> These endless confessions bring me out in a cold sweat—
> Honestly, they're killing me.
> My love becomes frustrated hate for what I can't help loving.
> I'd gladly die—if only you'd die with me.
> I'll ask no questions, I promise, and ferret out no secrets
> If you'll do me the simple favor of deceit. (*Amours* 3:27-42).

In his more pensive moments, Ovid recognized that adultery could be an enjoyable game, but a game which had its losers. Ovid himself was married three times, the first two marriages ending in divorce—an example of an era of Roman society in which the institution of marriage was eroding. By the fourth century of the Christian era both pre-marital and extra-marital sexual relations had become so common in Rome that concerned officials imposed fines on offenders. This action appears to have been ineffective, however, for according to the historian Livy, "The Romans were able to build a temple to Venus out of the fines paid by adulteresses" (Bardis, 1963).

EARLY PHILOSOPHY

In the realm of philosophy we find that ancient Greeks developed two concepts of love: *Eros,* which embodied a carnal, physical kind of love; and *Agape,* which described a spiritual or intellectual love. It was assumed that most men would eventually marry because of the necessity for procreation, but it was not assumed that the wife would be the exclusive, or even the primary, lover in the husband's life. The husband was allowed to have extramarital sexual relations with other males or with females, including the educated entertainer-women of Athens called the *Hetaerae.* Neither kind of sexual liaison was considered to be a serious threat to the stability of the marital relationship (Tavuchis and Goode, 1975: 16).

In Plato's dialogue *The Symposium,* love is said to derive from Aphrodite, the goddess of love. Since Aphrodite has the two aspects of pandemus (common) and uranian (celestial), love also is seen as being of two types: comman and celestial. Common love may be either homosexual or heterosexual; it is always concerned primarily with bodily pleasures. Celestial love, he wrote, is homosexual, and focuses chiefly, but not exclusively, on intellectual and spiritual union. The most ideal union is formed by an older man and a youth. While Plato considered celestial love to be more noble, common love was not condemned. His distinction helps illustrate the point made in the dialogue that in and of itself an action is neither good nor bad. It is how the deed is done, whether nobly and properly or not, which makes the difference. In addition, love is singled out as an especially powerful and acceptable motivation for actions, which if undertaken for a baser reason would be socially ridiculed or rejected.

Plato's student Aristotle had, in contrast, a harsh view of infidelity. In his *Politics,* he describes marriage as a complete community of life between the spouses. For an unfaithful husband who kept *hetaerae,* Aristotle recommended the penalty of death, breaking with the Greek tradition that had earlier concerned itself solely with the infidelity of the wife and left the husband free to pursue his own sexual pleasures.

While Aristotle's views were largely incorporated into the teachings of the Christian church, the ideas of both Ovid and Plato provided the seeds for the "courtly love" tradition which reached full bloom in medieval Europe. It was this latter tradition which, in turn, influenced modern Western ideas of romantic love.

LATER INFLUENCES FROM THE WEST

In the centuries following the birth of Jesus the cultural developments which took place in the West would become far more important for the future development of the as-yet-undiscovered New World than those which took place in the East. Three Western European countries in particular were to contribute greatly to the cultural formation of the United States: England, France, and Spain. These countries not only became leading world powers but, more importantly for our analysis, they became colonial powers in the New World. Therefore, their cultures were not only readily available to the people colonizing the newly discovered continent, but at certain times and in certain places were also even forced upon them.

Other cultures, such as those of Germany and Italy, also had an influence on the legal, moral, literary, and philosophical development of the United States. Although they were not North American colonial powers as were the other three countries mentioned above, these two Western European countries also have left their mark on the American society. This was largely by way of contributing to what is commonly known as the Western Heritage to which the United States is a legitimate heir.

LAW

This Western Heritage includes the laws developed over the centuries in leading Western European civilizations. Adultery was legally proscribed behavior in all of these countries. In England, the country which is generally considered to have had the greatest influence on our legal system, the ecclesiastical courts were allowed to exercise wide disciplinary control over the moral life of the members of the Church from around 1475 until 1640, when Oliver Cromwell ascended to power. Adultery was dealt with in such a court, along with other moral and legal transactions such as procuration, in-continency, and incest (Holdsworth, 1952: 619). In ecclesiastical law men as well as women were held accountable for their part in adul-terous behavior; hence both were liable to punishment. Trials could take any one of several forms: 1) an inquisition in which the judge was the accuser; 2) accusation of some individual who was said to "promote the office of judge"; or 3) denunciation by some other individual (Holdsworth, Vol. 1, 1952: 619-620).

In Western society women have traditionally been treated more severely than men for adultery. Both the Mosaic code and Roman law defined adultery as a criminal offense only when committed by a married woman. This tradition was followed by English common law, which held only the woman culpable of adultery. However, ex-cept for a brief period during Cromwell's reign when adultery could be punishable by death, marital infidelity was generally not con-sidered an indictable crime to be pursued by the State. In civil court a charge could be brought against a man who had sexual relations with another man's wife. The husband's interest in his wife's consor-tium was considered to be sufficiently proprietary to support an action of "trespass." It was the incapacity of the wife to legally give her consent that was the principle upon which the husband was allowed to bring the particular charge of trespass, also called the action of "criminal conversation," against one who had committed adultery with his wife (Holdsworth, Vol. VIII, 1952: 430). It is inter-esting to note that in 1800 Lord Auchland proposed to make it illegal for an adulterer, should he divorce his wife, to subsequently marry the guilty lady with whom he had committed adultery. He also recommended that adultery be made a common law misde-meanor. These proposals were debated in both Houses of Parliament but were never acted upon (Holdsworth, Vol. XIII, 1952: 268).

In medieval Germany a husband had virtually complete control over his wife, who was considered his chattel, much as his servants were. Since a wife was considered as part of a husband's property, she could not legally charge her husband with the crime of adultery. As for a wife's illicit lover, he was charged with committing an un-lawful interference with the husband's rights. The wronged husband had the right to exercise many options: he could lock his unfaithful wife in a room and not give her food; he could sell her; or he could drive her with curses from his house and dissolve the marriage. The offended husband was even entitled to kill his wife should he so desire (Huebner, 1918: 617–618).

Early Roman law did not protect the marital unions between slaves. This situation was later changed under Lombard law which even protected the conjugal rights of slaves against their masters. A master who committed adultery with a slave's wife suffered the loss of his ownership in addition to the [ordinary] penalties which may be levied. The reason given for this law was that it is God's law that none shall sin with another's wife (Calisse, 1928: 330-331). A man could also be fined and lose authority over his wife if he took a concubine into his house (Calisse, 1928: 319). One other consequence of the adultery was the *faida,* a penalty attaching to private interests and left for execution to the injured party. In other words, the husband of an unfaithful wife was allowed to seek revenge on the offending male, possibly beginning a feud that would cross generational lines and be passed on to male heirs (Calisse, 1928: 272).

Relevant to this brief perusal of Western legal traditions regarding adultery are the practices of "Droit de seigneur" and "Jus primae noctis." This first French phrase refers to the right of a feudal overlord to spend the wedding night in bed with the bride of any of his tenants who married. The latter Latin phrase literally translated means the "law of the first night," and, again, refers to the right or claim of the feudal lord to terminate the virginity of the bride of his vassal on their wedding night. Basically both concepts are understood to refer to the socially approved and/or prescribed defloration of a new bride by someone other than the husband (see Foras, 1886; Schmidt, 1881). The idea that the landowner has such a right may have derived from the practice of culagium, which was a request for permission to marry. Since marriage entailed the movement of the bride to the abode of her husband, and sometimes from the jurisdiction of one landlord to that of another, a fine had to be paid. In some dioceses a fine was also required by the bishop for a dispensation for the couple to consummate the marriage on their wedding night. The Church urged newly married couples to practice sexual abstinence for the first several days as an act of mortification (Westermarck, 1922). The historical authenticity of this legally adulterous practice is sometimes questioned, although there appears to be some evidence that it was practiced at least in Scotland (MacKechnie, 1930). However, one commentator was of the opinion that the "Droit du seigneur" may have been understood as *God's* right, and applied to the religious counsel of practicing continence on the wedding night (Guinagh, 1965: 139-140).

RELIGION

Since Western religious heritage is Judeo-Christian, it has been influenced by the commandment prohibiting adultery. Because of the previously noted relationship between marriage and adultery, it is desirable to examine the development of marriage in our religious heritage more closely. In the Christian Church marriage was not always considered to be a sacrament in the same way that communion and penance were, for example. The ceremony was neither initiated by Jesus nor commanded or explicitly endorsed by Him for His followers. The early Church, therefore, allowed the government to continue to regulate marriage and divorce. Indeed, there was no official and standard Christian wedding ceremony until the 11th century.

At the beginning of the Christian era there was disagreement among the Jews regarding divorce. Followers of Rabbi Shammai believed divorce could be obtained only because of some serious misconduct such as adultery on the part of the wife, whereas those who followed Rabbi Hillel held that a husband could divorce his wife for any conduct which displeased him. Christians were also less than unanimous. The problem stemmed from the difference in wording between the Gospel of Mark (10: 11-12), which equates all divorce and remarriage with adultery, and those of Luke (16: 18), which labels as adultery the remarriage of a wife, and Matthew (5: 32, 19: 9), which seems to allow divorce in the case of adultery. As a result, adultery was usually accepted as grounds for divorce and, often, as a justification for remarriage. Husbands who divorced an unfaithful wife were commonly allowed to remarry. Wives, in contrast, while they were often allowed to divorce an unfaithful husband, were not usually allowed to remarry. These disagreements were resolved when the standard Church ceremony was developed and marriage became recognized as a sacrament instituted by Jesus. As a result, marital sex became more acceptable and remarriage became unacceptable for all divorced Christians (Martos, 1981).

Meanwhile, there was an even more fundamental dispute regarding marriage itself. When did the legally binding marriage occur? Under Roman law the couple was married when they gave their mutual consent. German law, however, decreed that the couple was not married until the marriage was sexually consummated. This question had important implications for both divorce and adultery. The issue was finally resolved in the 12th century when Pope Alexander III decided that it was the free mutual consent of the man and woman which was the basis for marriage. It was also decided the Church could annul any marriage which had not been consummated.

Until the 16th century Reformation, Western Europe was overwhelmingly Roman Christian, or what was to be subsequently designated Roman Catholic. Within this Christian tradition there appears to have always existed an influential strain of antisexual sentiment by apologists whose arguments can be traced back at least to those of St. Paul. Representatives of this group viewed sexual intercourse as basically undesirable and/or evil, although perhaps a necessary evil. Such anti-sexual attitudes were reinforced by the rival theologies of the Manicheans and other Gnostic sects. The 4th century sinner-turned-saint Augustine of Hippo, a former follower of Manichaenism, became a leading figure in Christian thought on matters pertaining to marriage. He was the first and only patristic writer to deal extensively with sex and marriage. Augustine believed that marriage was a sacrament, and therefore good, but he also thought that sex was essentially evil. One reason for this conclusion was his belief that original sin (from the fall of Adam and Eve) was passed on from generation to generation through sexual intercourse of the parents. Indeed, sexual desire was itself a consequence of original sin; had Adam and Eve not sinned God would have found some other way to populate the earth. Augustine accepted that sex was now part of God's plan, but he indicated that the only completely acceptable justification for sexual intercourse, even between spouses, is procreation. He wrote, "The intercourse necessary for generation is without fault and it alone belongs to marriage. The intercourse that goes beyond this necessity no longer obeys reason, but passion. Still, not to demand this intercourse but to render it to a spouse, lest he sin by fornication, concerns the married person. But if both are subject to such concupiscence, they do something that manifestly does not belong to marriage" (Firth, 1981: 42).

Adherents of this tradition have seen virginity and celibacy as more acceptable and pleasing to God. They arrived at some interesting conclusions regarding intercourse and adultery. St. Jerome, a contemporary of Augustine, wrote: "It is disgraceful to love another man's wife at all, or one's own too much. A wise man ought to love his wife with judgment not with passion. Let a man govern his voluptuous impulses, and not rush headlong into intercourse. . . . He who too ardently loves his own wife is an adulterer" (Hunt, 1959: 115). Augustine echoed this sentiment: "A man who is too ardent a lover of his wife is an adulterer, if the pleasure he finds in her is sought for its own sake" (Against Julian, II, 7). These statements imply that the essence of adultery is concupiscence, rather than unfaithfulness as in the Old Testament. Therefore under certain conditions, such as unbridled sexual passion, a person could commit adultery with his or her own spouse.

An even earlier church father, Origen, had questioned whether or not the sin of adultery could even be forgiven through penance and the sacrament of confession. In his treatise *On Prayer,* Origen stated, "There are some, who I know not how, arrogate to themselves a power exceeding that of the priests presumably because they know nothing of sacerdotal science; they boast that they can forgive the sin of idolatry, adultery and fornication, as if their prayer over such criminals could pardon mortal sins" (Quasten, 1953: 84-85). Gregory of Nyssa stated that adultery was not only a sin of lust, but also treachery, and a sin against the spouse. Thus, adulterers should receive twice the penalty fornication did, an analysis to which St. Basil concurred (Bullough, 1976: 196).

A different opinion was expressed by the 15th century scholastic theologian Gabriel Biel, a thinker who influenced the originator of the Protestant Reformation, Martin Luther. Biel believed that adultery was bad not because its objective essence was opposed to the form and essence of man and therefore necessarily against the attainment of man's final end, which is union with God, but rather because it is forbidden by the command of the divine will (Davitt, 1951: 55-64). Hence, viewing adultery as evil is based on an act of faith in God and his revealed Word. Martin Luther also believed adultery violated God's will. It clearly was a violation of the sixth commandment and was also against the spirit, if not the letter, of the seventh commandment, "Thou shalt not steal," since the adulterer took what belonged to another (Althaus, 1972). In addition, adultery was seen as violating the highest social calling, marriage. A quote sometimes attributed to Luther: "if you will not (fulfill the conjugal duty), another will; the maid will come if the wife will not," has been open to misinterpretation. This old proverb was not an endorsement of adultery; it was a warning to a wife that if she didn't sexually please her husband, she could lose her marriage (Lehmann, 1962).

Another leader of the Protestant Reformation, and a contemporary of Luther, was John Calvin. Calvin established a logical system of belief for Protestantism much as Thomas Aquinas did for Catholicism. Like Luther, Calvin spoke out against adultery and recognized it as grounds for divorce. In addition, he agreed with the treatment offered adulterers in the Old Testament and tried to convince the civil authorities in Geneva to adopt the death penalty for adultery (Bullough, 1976: 506).

During the patristic and medieval periods adultery was considered by the church to be a very serious sin. In part, this view was related to the generally negative view of sexual intercourse espoused by Origen and Augustine. The sin of adultery could be forgiven only by confession and subsequent penance, often public, and the offending individuals could be restricted from receiving the Eucharist for a period of time up to five years (Firth, 1981).

Theologians in the late medieval and early modern periods discussed the possibility of three distinct but perhaps interrelated motives for marital intercourse: procreation, avoidance of fornication, and pleasure. The first was viewed as unquestionably legitimate while the other two were questionable but possibly valid as a concession to man's fallen nature (Hitchcock, 1981: 53-66).

Approximately 10 percent of Christian canon law texts between the twelfth and fourteenth centuries dealt with sexual matters, as opposed to 6 percent of civil law texts. Fornication, which may be viewed as primarily a personal matter, was of much more concern to canon law than to civil law. Adultery, however, which has obvious implications for property and public order, was almost as much a concern of civil law as of canon law (Brundage, 1982a). The canonists drew upon a large body of earlier Roman jurisprudence for many of their doctrines regarding adultery. Nevertheless, there were some important differences. Roman law never specifically defined adultery. Canon law simply defined it as sexual relations between a married person and someone other than his or her own spouse. One of the most important differences between Roman and Canon law was in their interpretation of parity of the sexes. Whereas in Roman law adultery was treated as the married woman's offense, Canon law treated it as an offense by both the man and woman. Canonists elaborated a systematic hierarchy of sexual crimes, with adultery being considered much more serious than fornication or bigamy. Finally, whereas Roman law allowed the wronged husband to kill his adulterous wife, the Church rejected this on the grounds that it violated the principles of Christian ethics. The Church did, however, accept adultery as grounds for judicial separation (Brundage, 1982b).

LITERATURE

Western literature has a rich tradition of dealing with adultery as a central issue. Even a limited review of our recognized literary masterpieces will provide a fruitful analysis of cultural history. The ever-popular *Le Morte d' Arthur* of Sir Thomas Malory provides an interesting view of the often romanticized age of chivalry when, it was believed, hearts were pure and the Church was supreme. In his introduction to Malory's book, Robert Graves comments that,

> The Round Table is Christian in name only. Extramarital unions abound, nor does any slur attach to the offspring unless born in incest like Sir Mordred. Sir Galahad and Sir Torre, for instance, are both blameless bastards, and at the end of long adventures we find Sir Tristram and Iseult living in adulterous ease at Sir Lancelot's castle, Joyous Gard, with Arthur and Gwynevere's full assent. It

would dishonor a knight to repudiate an extramarital union and Malory is sympathetic towards women who suffer from illicit love pangs. Thus Gwynevere comforts Iseult when she complains that Sir Tristram has married the King of Brittany's daughter, remarking that noble knights are often tricked into marriage but after a while weary of their wives and come back to their first loves (1962: xv).

The spirit of the times, as perceived by Malory, is probably best summed up by Lady Iseult. The wife of King Mark, but lover of Sir Tristram, reproaches a young knight who disdains love and passion with these words: "For shame! Are you a knight and no lover? The very purpose of a knight is to fight on behalf of a lady" (1962: 302).

A beautiful synthesis of theology and literature is found in the work of the 13th century Italian Dante Alighieri. His famous trilogy *Inferno, Purgatorio* and *Paradiso* reveals a knowledge of the theology of his fellow countryman Thomas Aquinas as well as the mythology and literature of earlier writers previously mentioned. In the *Inferno,* Dante portrayed Hell as consisting of nine levels. In the second level of Hell, which was reserved for those guilty of lust, he assigned many famous adulterers including Paris and Helen, Tristram, and Paolo and Francesca. This last pair of lovers seem to have been historical figures who lived and died in the 13th century. Francesca, wife of Gianciotto de Rimini, fell in love with her handsome, married brother-in-law Paolo. Gianciotto became aware of the adulterous affair between his wife and his brother, and subsequently plotted to catch them in the act. When he found them together locked in her bedroom during his supposed absence he became outraged and killed them (Singleton, 1970: 84-94). According to Dante, their souls are doomed to be tossed about by the winds for all eternity—a fitting punishment according to the Biblical principle, "by what thing a man sinneth by the same he is tormented" (Wisd. of Sol., 11:17). Since in life they were seen as having been pushed and pulled by the winds of passion, in death they are driven by "a hellish storm which never rests; whirling and smiting it vexes them" (*Inferno*: V, 31).

It is interesting to note that adulterers are assigned to the upper reaches of Hell, which is imagined as having nine levels. According to this vision of Dante, the deeper the level the more serious the sin, and hence, the more severe the punishment. Thus, level 1 is limbo; 2 the circle of Lust; 3, Gluttony; 4, Avarice and Prodigality; 5, Anger, Rage and Fury; 6, Unbelief and Heresy; 7, Violence; 8, Fraud; and 9, Treason. Discussing this placement of fornicators and adulterers, Slattery (1920: 131-132), explains that Dante

> assigns a lighter punishment to the unchaste than to the unjust. Back of his plan is a sound theological doctrine. Guilt is to be estimated not simply from the gravity of the matter prohibited to conscience and the knowledge that one has of the evil, but more especially from the malice displayed by the will in its voluntary choosing and embracing the evil. How impurity, it is held, is often a sin of impulses. It springs from concupiscence, a common human inclination, wrong only when there is inordinateness. Then though a man freely consents to the temptation and thereby commits a grievous sin, his will generally is not overcast with perversion or affected with malice. That being so, Dante in assigning punishment for sins against the virtue of purity is moved by the thought that such sins deserve a milder punishment in Hell, because they may be oftener surprises than infidelities.

Dante, like Malory, was influenced by the spirit of romance and courtly love. On his visit into hell, Dante cited Francesca as saying "Love kindles quickly in the gentle heart," so that her lover Paolo could not escape feeling the fire of love in his own heart. She also said that "Love absolves no loved one from loving in return" so that she, Francesca, must love him who loves her. These two laws of love are reflective of the sentiments and framed in the language of courtly love which will be discussed below (Singleton, 1970: 89).

The *Canterbury Tales* was a product of 14th century England in which Geoffrey Chaucer presented a collection of fictional narratives treating a wide range of subjects.

Included was a narrative of love and adultery as related by the wife of Bath, who was described in the following way:

> She had been an excellent woman all her life
> Five men in turn had taken her to wife,
> Omitting other youthful company—
> But let that pass for now. . .
> She was a good fellow; a ready tongue was hers.

all remedies of love she knew by name,
For she had all the tricks of that old game.

(Prologue, 447-450, 462-464)

The wife of Bath discussed the relative merits of virginity and marriage, noting that although the former may be a more perfect way of life, she personally found marriage much more pleasurable. She opined that God must not only allow but also approve ". . . the flower of life, the honey, upon the acts and fruit of matrimony." She continued:

Tell me to what conclusion or in aid
Of what were generative organs made?
And for what profit were those creatures wrought?
Trust me, they cannot have been made for naught.
Glose as you will and plead the explanation
That they were only made for the purgation
of urine, little things of no avail
Except to know a female from a male,
And nothing else. Did somebody say no?
Experience knows well it isn't so.
The learned may rebuke me, or be loth
To think it so, but they were made for both,
That is to say both use and pleasure in
Engendering, except in case of sin.

(trans., Coghill, 1977: 279-280)

Thus, while she praised marital love and love-making throughout her tales, and later made reference to Ovid, she did not praise adultery.

Two of Shakespeare's best-known tragedies, *Othello* and *Hamlet,* deal with adultery. A recurring motif in *Hamlet* is the hidden corruption which exists in man and society. Among the many charges of malevolent deeds attributed to Hamlet's mother Gertrude and his uncle Claudius, there is at least a suspicion, even though unstated, of an adultery that may have occasioned the murder of Hamlet's father. The plot is one of a progressive corruption, which may be stated as the proposition that "evil begets evil." Hamlet warns his mother that the mere pretense of virtues "will but skin and film the ulcerous

place, / Whiles rank corruption, mining all within, / Infects unseen"
(III, iv, 147-149). Hamlet's warning is prophetic—bodies litter the
stage by play's end.

In a subsequent play, *Othello,* Shakespeare deals directly and
specifically with adultery. *Othello* tells a story of jealousy, lies and
remorse. The villainous Iago causes the black Othello to believe his
young white wife Desdemona has been unfaithful. Othello's reflections recall Ovid's and demonstrate that knowledge of, or even a
mistaken belief in, a spouse's unfaithfulness can result in consequences worse than the act itself. Othello wonders:

> What sense had I of her stol'n hours of lust?
> I saw't not, thought it not, it harm'd not me:
> I slept the next night well, was free and merry;
> I found not Cassio's kisses on her lips:
> He that is robb'd not wanting what is stol'n,
> Let him not know't, and he's not robb'd at all. . . .
> I had been happy, if the general camp,
> Pioneers and all, had tasted her sweet body,
> So I had nothing known. O, now, for ever
> Farewell the tranquil mind! farewell content!
>
> (III, iii, 340-350)

Upon believing Iago's lie, Othello confronts his wife. Desdemona
denies any wrongdoing, which only serves to increase her husband's
anger and to precipitate his accusations:

> Was this fair paper, this most goodly book,
> Made to write 'whore' upon? What committed!
> I should make very forges of my cheeks,
> That would to cinders burn modesty,
> Did I but speak thy deeds. What committed!
> Heaven stops the nose at it, and the moon winks.
> The bawdy wind, that kisses all it meets,
> Is hus'd within the hollow mine of earth
> And will not hear it. What committed!
> Impudent strumpet!
>
> (IV, ii, 71-80)

Othello kills his wife, even though he still loves her, justifying the action on the basis of Desdemona's supposed misconduct. When he subsequently learns of Iago's treachery and Desdemona's innocence, Othello, in an action motivated by love and grief, commits suicide.

The tradition of courtly love incorporated elements of the works of Plato and Ovid, and addressed both love's spiritual and sensual sides. The clearest and most complete expression of this tradition is found in *Art of Courtly Love*. This work is attributed to Andreus Capellanus, the chaplain of the countess Marie of Champagne, stepsister of Richard the Lion-Hearted. Also known as "Andrew the Chaplain," Andreas was requested by the countess to record the twelfth-century conception of love that prevailed in the courts of France. The resulting manuscript was written in the form of advice to a young man named Walter.

At that time, the concept of courtly or romantic love commonly referred to a relationship between a married woman and a married or single knight. These relationships were not uncommon because marriages among the nobility at this time were typically motivated not by love but by practical concerns such as economic benefit or treaties. Therefore, the romantic or nonpractical concerns of a relationship, such as love, were more commonly extramarital. The influence of Ovid may be seen in the definition of love presented in the *Art of Courtly Love:* "Love is a certain inborn suffering derived from the sight of and excessive meditation upon the beauty of the opposite sex, which causes each one to wish above all things the embraces of the other and by common desire to carry out all of love's precepts in the other's embrace" (1959: 28).

As did Plato, Andreas delineated two types of love: pure and mixed. However, what Plato considered to be the higher, more spiritual type of love, i.e., homosexual, is rejected completely by Andreas: "Now, in love you should note first of all that love cannot exist except between persons of opposite sexes. Between two men or two women love can find no place, for we see that two persons of the same sex are not at all fitted for giving each other the exchanges of love or for practicing the acts natural to it. Whatever nature forbids, love is ashamed to accept" (1959: 30). For Andreas, pure love was heterosexual, was more spiritual than physical, and did not involve sexual intercourse. This type of love is seen in the famous 16th century Spanish novel *Don Quixote de la Mancha,* by Miguel de Cervantes, in which the somewhat crazy hero, Alonzo Quijano, alias Don Quixote, performs every manner of deed, or misdeed, in honor of his beloved-at-a-distance, Dulcinea del Toboso. It appears that this type of relationship was modeled on actual practices. Castiglione points out, in his *Book of the Courtier,* that a husband often approved of a nonsexual love relationship between his wife and another man. Such relationships consisted of discussing intellectual matters, such as the nature of love (Castiglione, 1959). One recent commentator on romantic love wrote that:

> It was Plato, through his dramatic mouthpiece Socrates, who proclaimed in *The Symposium* that eros was something more than mere relationships, something divine. Following Plato, Plotinus turned love into an infinite principle, St. Paul turned love into God, and the 12th century inventors of "Platonic love" completed the process that Plato started, turning love as an ordinary emotion of mutual desire and companionship, into the Love and Grace of God. (Solomon, 1981: 5)

Actually, pure love was not necessarily *non*sexual, but only nonconsummated. Kissing, petting and even nude embracing may be acceptable within a relationship dominated by pure love. In any case, pure love was said to change after a short time into "mixed love."

The type of love identified by Andreas Capellanus as "mixed" involved sexual intercourse. Both types of love were considered "real" love, notwithstanding their essential impermanence. For its part, mixed love does not last long either, according to Andreas, after it has been consummated.

Andrews saw passion as something which must be moderated, for too much passion can be a barrier to love. The love relationship proceeded through four stages: 1) the giving of hope; 2) the granting of a kiss; 3) the enjoyment of an embrace; and 4) the yielding of the whole person. The speed with which these stages are traversed depends upon the woman. She not only can delay the progress of the relationship, but can terminate it at any point before the final stage. A woman must be careful that her lover is not just using her in a selfish manner to satisfy his own passion or to provide him with the opportunity to boast of his conquest to others. In general, premarital love affairs were viewed as more damaging than extramarital affairs. A woman who lost her virginity to one man and then married another could be discovered and despised for her nonvirginity. A married woman, however, was already nonvirginal, and could more easily conceal her affair.

The following is a list of rules or statements (Capellanus, 1959: 184-186) which theoretically governed such relationships. Although they may appear somewhat foolish or naive, especially numbers 15 and 16, an honest appraisal of them will lead to the conclusion that most of them have been incorporated into our Western heritage and are found in much of our popular entertainment.

1. Marriage is no real excuse for not loving.
2. He who is not jealous cannot love.
3. No one can be bound by a double love.
4. It is well known that love is always increasing or decreasing.
5. That which a lover takes against the will of his beloved has no relish.
6. Boys do not love until they arrive at the age of maturity.
7. When one lover dies, a widowhood of two years is required by the survivor.
8. No one should be deprived of love without the very best of reasons.
9. No one can love unless he is impelled by the persuasion of love.
10. Love is always a stranger in the home of avarice.
11. It is not proper to love any woman whom one would be ashamed to seek to marry.
12. A true lover does not desire to embrace in love anyone except his beloved.
13. When made public, love rarely endures.
14. The easy attainment of love makes it of little value, difficulty of attainment makes it prized.
15. Every lover regularly turns pale in the presence of his beloved.
16. When a lover suddenly catches sight of his beloved, his heart palpitates.

17. A new love puts to flight an old one.
18. Good character alone makes any man worthy of love.
19. If love diminishes, it quickly fails and rarely revives.
20. A man in love is always apprehensive.
21. Real jealousy always increases the feeling of love.
22. Jealousy, and therefore love, are increased when one suspects his beloved.
23. He whom the thought of love vexes eats and sleeps very little.
24. Every act of a lover ends in the thought of his beloved.
25. A true lover considers nothing good except what he thinks will please his beloved.
26. Love can deny nothing to love.
27. A lover can never have enough of the solaces of his beloved.
28. A slight presumption causes a lover to suspect his beloved.
29. A man who is vexed by too much passion usually does not love.
30. A true lover is constantly and without intermission possessed by the thought of his beloved.
31. Nothing forbids one woman being loved by two men or one man by two women.

As Reiss has observed, "One can detect clearly in these thirty-one rules the Platonic stress on spiritual qualities and just as clearly the Ovidian stress on the outward signs of love and the physical gratifications of love" (1980: 129). In the final analysis, Romantic love represented a break from the Christian tradition. Whereas Christianity emphasized spiritual love and was suspicious of emotion that was not directed toward God, Romantic love glorified passion that was directed toward someone of the opposite sex. Christianity has also put the woman in a subservient position and had endorsed only procreational sex, while Romantic love put the man in the service of the woman and endorsed pleasurable sex. In sum, Christian tradition limited all sexual behavior to marriage, but Romantic love, especially as expressed in the Courtly Love tradition, separated sex from marriage.

PHILOSOPHY

In the realm of philosophy the most influential thinkers who had
something to say about adultery were generally church-related. Although their conclusions were not very different from their fellow
churchmen who addressed the issue of adultery from a theological
point of view, the philosophers attempted to arrive at their conclusions on the basis of reason rather than faith. One of the leading
scholastic philosophers from this general time period was the 13th
century Italian Dominican monk named Thomas Aquinas. His *Summa Theologica,* which was influenced by Aristotle, has had a monu-
mental impact on subsequent Catholic philosophical and theological
development. As often happens, he and his ideas were generally not
well accepted during his lifetime. However, he has since been officially canonized by the Catholic Church. St. Thomas Aquinas spoke
of adultery as a serious moral offense against the good of the conjugal community. It entails the breaking of the mutual trust on
which the matrimonial bond is based. Thus, adultery adds to the evil
of simple fornication an act of injustice against the aggrieved spouse.
Finally, he stated that it is also an act of irreligion where the marriage has been solemnized by the sacrament of matrimony (see Question 154). This evaluation of adultery as morally wrong is a continuation of the Judeo-Christian tradition. Rather than merely condemn adultery on the basis of God's law, however, Aquinas chose to
show the evil of the act by focusing on the aspects of justice and
socioreligious obligations which are violated.

The French political philosopher Jean-Jacques Rousseau believed the family was a source of strength for ancient Greece and
Rome. However, he viewed the French family of his time, and particularly the affluent Parisian family, more as a national weakness.
In his novel *Nouvelle Heloise* he appears to be concerned with the
relationship of the family unit to the problems of national power.
Marriages which lack a strong moral and emotional commitment, he
feels, lead to personal and social difficulties. Rousseau believes that
in such marriages natural sentiments find their expression mainly
through adultery. Shallow marriages and transient loves can be
traced to the same basic cause: men and women cease to be indi-

viduals. Men become effeminate and women become artificial. The value of individualism is lost. As a result, all suffer because the individual members, the family and society are interrelated (see Perkins, 1974).

The preceding illustrations point up some of the myriad influences which have been part of the heritage of the United States. Not only have men, women and children but also beliefs, values and traditions arrived on its shores from all over the world. As a result, this country exhibited a heterogeneity of both population and culture. The New World was developed by immigrants with Old World heritages. The widely promoted "melting pot" thesis of America is probably much more tenable when applied to culture than to people. Some of the old ways which immigrants brought with them found a home in this country, but many more had to be discarded or modified in relation to the new and different physical and social environment encountered in America. The resulting culture, commonly identified as American, while largely Anglo-Saxon, contains elements of each of the cultures which were brought here by the immigrants as well as some which were already present among the native Americans. As can be seen in the foregoing material, many of these traditions are dissimilar or even contradictory. Thus, a wide range of behavior, together with the reactions which such behavior evokes, is to be expected—including adultery.

NOTES

1. Included in this number are references to adultery, adulterer, adulteress and adulterous.
2. Included in this number are references to adultery, adulterer, adulteress and adulterous.
3. This incident was described in the documentary "I Claudius," Part 11, produced by BBC Films, Inc., 1977.

REFERENCES

Albright, William. 1953. *Archaeology and the Religion of Israel.* Baltimore: Johns Hopkins Press.
Aligieri, Dante. 1970. *The Divine Comedy: Inferno.* Trans. C. Singleton. Princeton, N.J.: Princeton University Press.

Althaus, Paul. 1972. *The Ethics of Martin Luther*. Philadelphia: Fortress Press.

Aquinas, Thomas. 1947-48. *Summa Theologica*. Trans. Fathers of English Dominican Province. New York: Benziger Brothers.

Bardis, Panos. 1963. "Main Features of the Ancient Roman Family" *Social Science*. 38 (October): 225-240.

Brundage, James. 1982a. "Sex and Canon Law: A Statistical Analysis of Samples of Canon and Civil Law." In *Sexual Practices and the Medieval Church,* edited by Vern Bullough and James Brundage, 89-101. Buffalo, N.Y.: Prometheus.

Brundage, James. 1982b. "Adultery and Fornication: A Study in Legal Theology." In *Sexual Practices and the Medieval Church,* edited by Vern Bullough and James Brundage, 129-134. Buffalo, N.Y.: Prometheus.

Bullough, Vern. 1976. *Sexual Variance in Society and History*. New York: John Wiley.

Calisse, Carlo. 1928. *History of Italian Law,* vol. 8. Boston: Little, Brown.

Capellanus, Andreas. 1959. *The Art of Courtly Love*. Trans. J. Parry. New York: Ungar.

Castiglione, Baldesar. 1959. *The Book of the Courtier*. C. Singleton. New York: Doubleday.

Cervantes, Miguel de. 1964. *Don Quixote of La Mancha*. Trans. W. Starkie. New York: New American Library.

Chaucer, Geoffrey. 1977. *The Canterbury Tales*. Trans. N. Coghill. New York: Penguin.

Dante, Aligieri. 1970. *The Divine Comedy: Inferno*. Trans. C. Singleton. Princeton, N.J.: Princeton University Press.

Davitt, Thomas. 1951. *The Nature of Law*. St. Louis: B. Herder.

de Foras, A. 1886. *Le Droit du Seigneur au Moyen-Age. Estude Critique et Historique*. Chambery: Andre Perrin.

Firth, Francis. 1981. "Catholic Sexual Morality in the Patristic and Medieval Periods." In *Human Sexuality and Personhood,* pp. 36-52. St. Louis: Pope John Center.

Grant, Michael. 1975. *The Twelve Caesars*. New York: Charles Scribner's.

Guinagh, Kevin. 1965. *Dictionary of Foreign Phrases and Abbreviations*. New York: W. Wilson.

Hartdegen, Stephen. 1977. *Nelson's Complete Concordance of the New American Bible*. New York: Nelson.

Harvey, Sir Paul. 1955. *The Oxford Companion to Classical Literature*. London: Oxford University Press.

Hitchcock, James. 1981. "The Development of Catholic Doctrine Concerning Sexual Morality 1301-1918." In *Human Sexuality and Personhood,* pp. 53-56. St. Louis: Pope John Center.

Holdsworth, Sir William. 1952. *A History of English law*. London: Methuen.

Homer. 1951. *The Iliad*. Trans. R. Lattimore. Chicago: University of Chicago Press.

Huebner, Rudolf. 1918. *Continental Legal History Series,* vol. 4. Boston: Little, Brown and Co.

Hunt, Morton. 1950. *The Natural History of Love.* New York: Knopf.

Lehmann, Helmut. 1962. *Luther's Works,* vol. 45. Philadelphia: Muhlenberg Press.

Malory, Thomas. 1962. *Le Morte d'Arthur.* Intro. R. Graves. New York: Bramhall House.

MacKechnie, Hector. 1930. "Ius Primal Noctis." *Judicial Review,* 303-311.

Martos, Joseph. 1981. *Doors to the Sacred.* New York: Doubleday.

Naso, Publius Ovidius. 1957. *The Art of Love and The Loves.* Trans. R. Humphries. Bloomington, Ind.: Indiana University Press.

Perkins, Merle. 1974. *Jean-Jacques Rousseau: On the Individual and Society.* Lexington: University Press of Kentucky.

Quasten, Johannes. 1953. *Patrology,* vol. 2. Westminster, Md.: Newman Press.

Reiss, Ira. 1980. *Family Systems in America.* New York: Holt, Rinehart and Winston.

Rousseau, Jean-Jacques. 1968. *La Nouvelle Heloise.* Trans. J. McDowell. University Park: Pennsylvania State University Press.

Schmidt, Karl. 1881. *Jus Prima Noctis, Eine Geschichtliche Unterschung.* Freibrug in Breisgau: Herdes.

Slattery, John. 1920. *Dante: The Central Man of All the World.* New Jersey: P. H. Kenedy.

Soloman, Robert. 1981. "Should We Dump Romantic Love? Not Yet." *The Texas Observer,* 73 (February 13): 5-7, 23.

Stone, Merlin. 1972. *When God Was a Woman.* New York: Dial Press.

Tavuchis, N., and W. Goode. 1975. *The Family Through Literature.* New York: McGraw-Hill.

Toumbouros, George. 1959. *Parallel Legislation of England, USA, France, Germany, Italy, and Comparative Law: The Laws of Ancient Greece,* vol. 1. Munch: Suddeutscher Verlag Press.

Westermarck, Edvard. 1922. *The History of Human Marriage,* vol. 1. New York: Allerton Books.

2 THE MANY DIMENSIONS OF ADULTERY

In order that the reader and the author could share a common definition of the word "adultery," chapter 1 began with a brief definition. In this case it was felt the most appropriate definition would be that which was also the most commonly employed, as found in the dictionary. However, for the more detailed objective study of the phenomenon, such as is desired in the remaining chapters, it is appropriate to examine the concept of adultery in much greater depth and thus both expand and sharpen its meaning. Many dimensions of adultery as a type of social behavior will be explored in this chapter and, where possible, alternative terminology in current usage referring to specific types of adultery will be identified.

First, recognition must be given to something which is not *per se* a dimension of adultery, but which, nonetheless, is an important consideration in any understanding and treatment of it—namely, perception. Perception refers to the way something is viewed or the meaning and value applied to it. It is a person's perception, or judgment, which places a thing or action in a category with other like things or actions. This sets the stage for different responses. Therefore, if two or more people perceive a thing to be different their respective responses or reactions to it will be different. Perceptions are learned and shared. A common perception may be referred to as a perspective. History reveals that there has been no one single perspective regarding sex shared by all people.

There have been three major perspectives regarding sexual behavior, including adultery. What appears to be the oldest and most widespread (at least within our Western heritage) is what may be termed the *moralizing* perspective. This entails viewing and interpreting sexual behavior as falling within the scope of religion, and, therefore, subject to the designation of moral and immoral behavior. From this perspective, specific sexual behavior such as adultery may be perceived as evil and sinful, as it is from the perspective of the

Judeo-Christian tradition. On the other hand, it may be viewed as moral in another religious tradition when, as mentioned in the previous chapter, it is part of a religious ritual. A subtype of this perspective which goes beyond the imputation of moral judgments is what may be identified as the apotheosizing perspective wherein sexual behavior is exalted and glorified, and may even be elevated to a level or status of the divine. Thus, sex may be perceived as either good or bad, and hence to be either sought or avoided. In the United States sex outside of marriage has generally been judged to be immoral, while sex within marriage (at least certain types of sexual behavior) has been judged to be good and moral. Often motives for the behavior, i.e. procreation, pleasure, obligation, are as important, or even more so, than the behavior itself for deciding morality. The moralizing perspective is commonly utilized by theologians.

A second and related perspective is what may be termed *medicalizing*. Both perspectives are concerned with judgments, the one of morals and the other of health; sickness is substituted for sin. The medicalizing perspective also views sexual behavior in terms of positive and negative consequences. Sexual behavior is seen as possibly dangerous to a person's health, at least if engaged in promiscuously. All manner of physical and/or emotional maladies have been attributed to frequent sexual activity, such as impotence, pulmonary consumption, vertigo, epilepsy, loss of memory and death (Bullough, 1976: 543-548). The medicalizing perspective is potentially more influential than the moralizing perspective in a sense because it is given an aura of objective and scientific respectability that the moralizing perspective does not have, since it is *supposedly* based on the judgments and knowledge of medicine (or science). It is concerned with immediate (natural) rather than remote (supernatural) concerns. Furthermore, it transcends theological and denominational lines. This perspective has often been found among doctors and psychiatrists. The results of the moralizing and medicalizing perspectives are similar in their promotion of possibly negative attitudes and inhibited behavior.

The third major perspective may be termed the *normalizing* perspective. Historically, this is the most recent of the three and represents a break from the other two in that it neither involves negative attitudes or terminology, nor is it promotional or prescriptive. The normalizing perspective views sexual behavior, including adultery, as a type of social behavior or interaction. As such, this perspective attempts to understand and explain behavior rather than judge it. The normalizing perspective is the one which is currently most often identified with science, and is promoted among behavioral scientists.

Next, adultery itself may be examined within the context of two broad areas: normative and behavioral. The normative area refers to expectations or patterns, with the idea of being directive. The term norm is used in two ways: statistical norm as a measure of what actually is, and cultural norm as a concept of what should be. Thus, the normative area incorporates aspects of both meanings, but with emphasis on direction or evaluation. It analyzes what is done from the perspective of what is expected. The behavioral area refers to the activity itself, without introduction of the idea of judgment or preference. Emphasis is on analysis of the action into its various components.

NORMATIVE DIMENSION

The first dimension we will explore is that which can be termed *legitimacy*. By this is meant the acceptability or unacceptability by society of the behavior in question (i.e. adultery). Society, for many reasons, proscribes some behavior, prescribes other behavior and completely ignores much of the rest. That behavior which is not proscribed, prescribed or ignored is usually judged on the basis of the situation or circumstances under which it occurs. Social evaluations, whether general or situational, are not static but ongoing and, hence, often change over time. Members of society are taught these cultural judgments and the resulting expectations, referred to respectively as values and norms, during the socialization process. Behavior which is deemed acceptable is socially legitimate behavior and will be encouraged, supported and rewarded, while behavior which is unacceptable is socially illegitimate and, consequently, will be discouraged, repudiated and punished. Legitimacy may be relative in certain cases and depend on the circumstances in which the action occurs.

For example, one man patting another man on his behind is generally regarded as unacceptable especially if it occurs in a public place unless, of course, the action is between athletes as a form of congratulations for a good play. Some behavior is socially neutral and, as such, is completely optional. In addition, every society contains what behavioral scientists sometimes refer to as universals, specialties and alternatives. Universals are those things which are expected of everyone (i.e., obey the law), while specialties are things which are limited to a certain group or category of individuals (i.e., only a priest can celebrate Mass). Most common are alternatives, which allow for individual choice (i.e., get married or remain single). In the United States adultery is, and has been, considered socially unacceptable behavior for everyone and as such violators have been subject to both formal and informal negative sanctions.

A second and closely related dimension is *legality*. While legitimacy deals with the social acceptability of an action, legality deals with whether or not the action is permitted or required by existing laws. So, depending upon where it takes place, behavior may be classified as either legal or illegal. Of course, what is socially acceptable is usually also legal—but there are exceptions. One of the most famous exceptions was the attitude toward drinking alcoholic beverages during the Prohibition Era. Such disparities are sometimes described by the phrase "norm of evasion." Meanwhile, socially unacceptable behavior is just as likely to be legal as illegal—eating a meal with your hands in a restaurant, for example, may violate social custom but not the law. Incongruities between legitimacy and legality are often consequences of social change; norms change at a different rate than laws. This situation is indicative of what sociologists refer to as cultural lag. Furthermore, behavior which is unacceptable but legal is more likely to occur in relation to folkways, which are relatively unimportant traditions, than to mores, which are important traditions. In the United States, for example, a young man is more likely to dress in a manner inappropriate to his age (folkway) than to his sex (more). Adultery, which is a violation of a more, is illegal in most of the United States (see chapter 3).

A third relevant dimension is *morality*. Morality, which is related to but separate from legitimacy and legality, may be distinguished into subjective (or individual), and objective (or communal). Subjective morality refers to the personal beliefs of the individual concerning the moral goodness or evil of the behavior. Objective morality refers to morality which transcends and is independent of the individual beliefs of the members. This standard of morality is based on something outside the individual such as sacred writings, traditions or natural law. In this sense we can speak of Catholic morality as opposed to Moslem morality. Of course even among members of these moral communities there may be individual differences. Behavior which violates one's personal or communal morality may be termed immoral, and is usually accompanied by feelings of guilt. Behavior which is according to or in compliance with personal or communal morality may be termed moral and is usually accompanied by feelings of pride and/or self-satisfaction. That behavior which is considered to be morally neutral is termed amoral. Ideas of personal morality are learned and usually shared but may differ from those espoused by society in general. Within most large modern societies there are numerous competing systems of morality which may influence individuals differently. It should be noted that behavior which is considered legitimate by society may not be considered moral by individual members of that society, or vice versa. The United States, as a society with a Judeo-Christian religious heritage, has considered adultery to be immoral behavior.

The fourth dimension can be termed *consensuality*. With respect to adultery, the reference here would be to the consent or lack of consent of one's spouse(s) to the extramarital sex. And consent, or lack of it, depends upon the marital partners' interpretation of the nature of the marriage bond. Of particular importance is whether the marriage is considered to be sexually inclusive or exclusive of other persons. An interpretation of inclusiveness on the part of a spouse is related to consent while exclusiveness is related to lack of consent. Behavior which has the consent of one's spouse may be called consensual and may be of three types: that which is actively encouraged, passively approved, and mutually supported. A union incorporating the latter subtype wherein both spouses agree upon and engage in the activity, but not with each other, is sometimes called a sexually "open marriage."

Behavior which does not have the consent of the spouse may be called nonconsensual. This includes both lack of consent of an unknown situation (which if known may or may not be consented to), as well as lack of consent to a known situation. The former situation wherein the spouse is generally favorably disposed of adultery but is not, in fact, aware of the adulterous behavior of his/her marital partner is potentially consensual but actually nonconsensual (unless a sexual *carte blanche* along with instructions to keep the specific relationships private had been agreed upon). See the diagram below.

Spouse's Knowledge of the Adultery	Spouse's Attitude Toward the Adultery	
	Accepted	Unaccepted
Known	consensual adultery	nonconsensual adultery
Unknown	potentially consensual (actually nonconsensual)	nonconsensual (conventional adultery)

While consensual behavior more often leads to approval and harmonious relations with the affected party, nonconsensual behavior, if known or later discovered, leads to disapproval and often conflict. The consent of the spouse may, of course, change at any time and may even be ambivalent. "Wife hospitality" or a husband who encourages his wife to have sexual intercourse with someone for economic gain, i.e., pimping for a wife or urging her to be sexually intimate with his boss in order to obtain a promotion or raise, provide examples of spouse-encouraged adultery.

When a spouse has little or no sexual desire and feels relieved of the burden of providing sex for his or her partner by the knowledge that he or she has an outside "outlet" for sexual satisfaction, we have an example of passively approved adultery. Mutually supportive adultery occurs when husband and wife go to a bar or party to meet another couple so that the partners may be temporarily exchanged for sexual reasons. Such adulterous behavior is commonly called "swapping" or "swinging." It may also be referred to as "co-marital sex," particularly if it meets two important criteria: 1) an agreement between spouses that they will both have sexual realtionships with specified others at the same time and place, and 2) these sexual experiences will take place in an organized framework rather than be allowed to occur spontaneously (Walshok, 1971). Another type of mutually supported consensual adultery is identified by the Ziskins (1973), who speak of the existence of extramarital sex contracts that some married couples have built into their marriages. These include such things as a "swinging contract," a "partial living apart contract," and a "one-way contract which allows one spouse (usually the husband) to have at least some sexual freedom. Thus some sexual relationships outside of the marriage are an agreed-upon dimension of the marriage.

BEHAVIORAL DIMENSION

Here the first dimension to be considered is *sexuality*. This refers to the nature of the sexual behavior in terms of the sex of the partners. As such, the behavior may be termed homosexual when the sex of the partners is the same, heterosexual when the sex of the partners is different, or bisexual when the behavior may include both homosexual and heterosexual activity. Bisexual adultery is reportedly common among female swingers, with the husbands actually encouraging homosexual activity during breaks in heterosexual activity (Bartell, 1970). The traditional or commonly recognized type of adultery has been heterosexual. Homosexual adultery has not been commonly recognized. This does not mean, however, that it has been unknown or uncommon. The lack of recognition is undoubtedly due, in large part, to the fact that all forms of homosexuality were severely sanctioned in the United States. Consequently homosexuals stayed "in the closet." Not only was homosexual behavior considered immoral, but was also defined as a form of mental illness (see Bullough and Bullough, 1977). This situation persisted until 1974 when the American Psychiatry Association removed homosexuality from the list of pathological disorders. During this time an increase in gay rights and gay pride resulted in many homosexuals coming out of the closet. However, to be gay and single was one thing but to be gay and married was another.

In May 1981 homosexual adultery received widespread news coverage in the case of the well-known tennis star Billie Jean King who has publicly admitted to having had a homosexual affair with a female friend. Mrs. King's husband acknowledged that he had been aware of the affair even before the ex-lover publicly threatened to sue Mrs. King for "galimony," and unsuccessfully attempted to gain possession of the waterfront lodge which she had shared with Mrs. King (see *Newsweek,* 1981).

A related but separate dimension is coital *consummation.* Sexual behavior may be consummated or it may be nonconsummated. While both heterosexual and homosexual adultery may be nonconsummated, only heterosexual adultery can be consummated. Nonconsummated adultery may include all forms of sexual activity, and may even result in orgasm, but it does not include the actual penetration of coitus. A practice of looking at or evaluating sexual behavior from a practical as well as technical perspective is found in the treatment of virginity, where a distinction is often made between virginity and "technical virginity" (see Reiss, 1960; Bell, 1966). A similar approach may be taken with regard to adultery. Stress on avoiding extramarital sexual intercourse after marriage when coupled with temptation and opportunity may lead to a situation where married people engage in such things as breast and genital manipulation with others, but still view themselves as "faithful" and not "adulterous" (Reiss, 1980: 290). But this nonconsummated sexual behavior can, from a practical standpoint, still be considered a type of adultery.

A third dimension can be termed *consciousness.* Consciousness generally refers to an awareness or knowledge, and in this sense adultery may be either conscious or nonconscious. The former applies to a sexual relationship in which the participant(s) know(s) that one or both are married to someone else. The latter applies to a sexual relationship wherein the participant(s) do(es) not know a marriage is involved. A person's religious beliefs may enter here, since some people believe that a marriage is ended by divorce while others do not (e.g., the Catholic teaching that marriage is ended only by death). Thus while a sexual relationship may be either consciously or nonconsciously adulterous for both partners, it is also possible that either because of lack of knowledge that one's own sexual partner is married or because of a difference in personal religious beliefs concerning divorce, a relationship may be consciously adulterous for one partner but nonconsciously adulterous for the other.

A fourth dimension can be referred to as *affective*. Adultery may be engaged in with or without affection for the sexual partner. The distinction incorporates, but is different from that made regarding love-oriented and pleasure-oriented behavior. It is broader than this, however. Adultery with affection includes the love-oriented behavior which occurs with someone towards whom there is some romantic feelings. But it may also include what is basically pleasure-oriented behavior with someone who is merely known and liked, such as a sexual relationship. Adultery without affection includes pleasure-oriented behavior with someone for whom there is no actual liking. This may include the casual "one-night stand" with someone picked up in a bar or the impersonal act with a paid prostitute. Lack of affection is usually a requirement for participation in spouse swapping because it is more impersonal, less threatening to their marriages. However, adultery without affection may also include the more negative feelings and attitudes which may be involved in rape.

A fifth dimension is called *volitional*. Here the distinction is between voluntary, involuntary, and nonvoluntary sexual behavior. In voluntary behavior a rational, mentally competent participant is willingly engaged in the activity, whereas in involuntary behavior he or she is being used or coerced, such as occurs in rape and may also occur, when the perpetrator is a married person, in the case of some sexual child abuse or incest. Nonvoluntary behavior may occur when a nonrational or mentally incompetent person, such as an infant or severely retarded individual, is engaged in the activity. As is evident, adultery may be voluntary for both partners or for only one. In some rare cases it is even possible that the activity is involuntary or nonvoluntary for both of the participants, if both are coerced by some third party. It is not common to refer to an action as adulterous, however, if it entails coercion and is obviously involuntary or nonvoluntary on the part of at least one of the participants. Such actions are usually illegal and, thus, have their own specific nomenclature.

The sixth dimension to be considered is that of *visibility*. An action may be overt behavior, highly visible to outsiders, or it may be secretive, covert behavior, unknown to outsiders. These two opposing types should not be viewed as mutually exclusive; they should be seen as forming opposite ends of a visibility continuum. In reality, most cases of adultery are probably neither completely secret, where no one knows or "suspects a thing," nor completely visible where everyone is aware of the relationship. Thus, most cases would fall somewhere between these two extremes, but could be classified as being nearer to the overt or covert type. Lynn and James Smith (1973) refer to the covert type of adultery which involves concealment and deception as "conventional adultery." Visibility is one of the more important considerations which affect the consequences of the relationship.

The final dimension is that of *frequency*. An individual may engage in adulterous behavior on only one occasion or very infrequently. In this case the action is sometimes spoken of as being periodic and may be nothing more than an isolated experience which is out of keeping with the individual's usual behavior and general personality. On the other hand, an individual may live in an adulterous relationship or otherwise frequently engage in adultery. In such a case the action is sometimes referred to as chronic and is very much a part of the individual's life style and is probably an accepted and integrated part of his or her personality. Thus, the frequency dimension must also be viewed as forming a continuum. A prolonged adulterous relationship between two individuals is generally referred to as an "affair." It is possible to identify at least three types of affairs: the sexual liaison, the "other wife," and spouse swapping or group sex (see Bell and Gordon, 1972). The sexual liaison refers to what is usually a clandestine sexual relationship that is carried on over a period of time at a special or prearranged time and place. This is commonly what is meant by the expression "having an affair." The "other wife" is a much less common relationship wherein a married person, usually a man, is actually participating in two domestic units, or households, at the same time. Each household has a "wife" (one legal, one not) and may or may not have children. Although the nonlegal "wife" generally knows of the legal wife, the latter may not be aware of the former. In Latin America this second household is often referred to as "la casa chica." Spouse swapping, as a long-term form of extramarital sex, is primarily a middle-class phenomenon wherein two or more couples exchange spouses for sexual purposes. The 1969 Hollywood movie entitled "Bob and Carol and Ted and Alice" presented a humorous example of an attempt at this type of adulterous arrangement. Like its real life counterpart, the movie revealed some of the social and emotional difficulties which must be confronted by the individuals involved.

POSSIBILITIES AND CONSEQUENCES

The legitimacy of an action is determined by society and the resulting determination of acceptability or unacceptability is accompanied by the imposition of sanctions. Performing a socially acceptable or expected action brings positive sanctions (rewards) while engaging in unacceptable action results in negative sanctions (punishments). There is, however, a continuum of acceptability-unacceptability rather than a simple dichotomy. Hence, degrees of each are accompanied by the appropriate kinds and degree of sanction. Social reaction to adultery will generally be positive and supportive where it is legitimate. There is, of course, a difference between social sanctions and personal reactions. On a personal level, jealousy appears to be one of the more common consequences of adultery. Stephens has commented that even in those relatively few societies which accept adultery, "the jealousy problem still exists; some people are still hurt when their spouses engage in perfectly proper and virtuous adultery" (1963: 252).

In the United States adultery has been deemed unacceptable behavior and as such has been proscribed (although, like most forms of sexual behavior, it is probably somewhat less unacceptable today than in the past). It violates the more important norms of society, called mores, in relation to morals and common good, and as such is subject to societal criticism and rejection. Participants in such behavior may be labeled and ostracized. Adultery is also recognized as grounds for divorce and has even been considered to be a crime, punishable by fine and/or imprisonment. During the 20th century social norms regarding sexual behavior have been changing. These changes have reached such proportions in the last two decades that the term sexual revolution has become common. Three important and relevant results may be noted. First, the traditional double standard has greatly lessened. People have come to realize that females also enjoy sex and have sexual desires. Second, sex is more openly discussed and much of it is now subject to folkways rather than mores. Third, and directly related to the first two changes, laws regulating most sexual behavior between consenting adults are now no longer enforced.

In the United States sexual intercourse has been completely acceptable to all segments of society only in relation to marriage. It has been viewed as appropriate between spouses or, possibly, if done discreetly, between spouses-to-be. Even in today's more sexually liberal society, sexual intercourse is most acceptable when it is non-promiscuous and based on an emotional attachment. Thus, sexual intercourse continues to be thought of as related to an intimate and emotional relationship. From this perspective adultery is considered to be a serious threat to the marital relationship in a monogamous society. The resulting lack of social acceptance is evident in the reported findings of the National Opinion Research Center (1977) and those of the Levitt and Klassen (1974) national study which found that over 70 percent of the adults sampled in the United States feel that adultery is "always wrong," and an additional 15 percent believed it is "almost always wrong."

Although adultery is socially unacceptable, the degree of unacceptability appears to vary in relation to the marriageability of the participants. Adultery with an imminently marriageable partner, such as an unmarried adult of the opposite sex, is generally viewed less negatively than that with a partner who is not presently marriageable, such as a married person or a legal minor. Most unacceptable is an adulterous relationship with someone permanently unmarriageable, such as a person of the same sex or a close family member. This can be seen as a judgment of the relationship which is considered appropriate between sex and marriage.

There is probably no area in which the consequences of adultery are as diverse and problematical as that of legality, and this is due to three factors. First, many laws often slide into disfavor and disuse but are kept on the books. These remain as a basis for possible action at any time, but are typically unenforced and, consequently, ignored. In recent years it is virtually unheard of, for example, to prosecute someone for adulterous behavior, even when it is highly publicized in newspapers and magazines, such as happens in gossip columns dealing with well-known people. Second, laws concerning adulterous behavior vary from state to state. Even in those states which have laws against adultery there may be significant differences in meaning and intent. Thus, a married man, as opposed to a married woman, or a single man or woman who has sexual relations with someone else's spouse may be guilty of adultery in some states but not others. Also, differences exist in who can bring charges against the alleged guilty parties, i.e., only the affected spouse(s) or any indignant citizen. Furthermore, the legal consequences of a conviction may differ greatly. In some states adultery is a misdemeanor whereas in others it is a felony. Therefore punishment may range from fines to imprisonment (Norton, 1981). Third, the form the adulterous behavior takes as well as the partner selected may affect the legal nature of the criminal violation. Adulterous homosexual activity may be legally distinct from the same heterosexual activity. In addition, certain specific forms of sexual activity may be distinguished, and punished, apart from the general crime of adultery. Thus, a person may be prosecuted for anal and/or oral intercourse, and legal differentiation may be made between fellatio and cunnilingus. Also of legal relevance is the volition of the partners (an unwilling partner may make the action a crime of rape), the age of the partner (even a willing minor may make the action a crime of statutory rape), and the closeness of the affinal or consanguineal relationship of the partners (a family member may make the action a crime of incest).

The dimensions of morality and consensuality are both, as presently defined, predominantly subjective. This is not to be interpreted as a denial of the existence or importance of an objective morality. It is instead a recognition of the realistic limitations of the present approach to deal with adultery objectively since, ironically, objective morality necessarily entails appeals to faith. Personal morality, with which we can deal, has an effect on adultery. An individual makes moral judgments of the actions of others, as well as his or her own, based on a personal code of morals. Condemnation of those who violate one's morals is common, while guilt is the usual consequence of one's own violations. Guilt has been cited as one of the reasons for terminating adulterous behavior (Denfield, 1974). A stressful, change-producing situation arises when an individual's behavior is not consistent with his or her beliefs. This situation is known as cognitive dissonance (see Festinger, 1957). Such dissonance impels the individual to change either the behavior or the beliefs that are at odds. Thus, while many individuals cease their adulterous behavior, many others continue adultery but alter their beliefs and attitudes regarding it. What was once considered immoral becomes for them moral or amoral, at least under certain circumstances.

Whether adultery is consensual or nonconsensual depends upon many factors, including how society evaluates the actions, i.e., legitimacy and legality, and whether the spouse perceives the behavior to be moral or immoral. Yet another important consideration upon which the final decision depends is the personal symbolism accorded to the sexual activity. Giele (1977: 272) explains this consideration:

> On the one hand, the body may be viewed as the most important thing the person has to give, and sexual intercourse therefore becomes the symbol of the deepest and most far-reaching commitment, which is to be strictly limited to one pair-bond. On the other hand, participants may define sexual activity as merely a physical expression that, since it does not importantly envelope the whole personality nor commit the pair beyond the pleasures of the moment, may be regulated more permissively.

Those who engage in consensual adultery often deny the charges of others that they have been "unfaithful" in their marriage. They point out that marriage is an agreement between two people, and if those two agree that sexual relations with a third person are acceptable such behavior is in accordance with or faithful to their particular marriage agreement.

The interrelationship between the normative and behavioral dimensions of adultery is illustrated by a finding that extramarital sex is reportedly less pleasurable or satisfactory than marital sex (see

Hunt, 1974). Commenting on this finding Bob and Margaret Blood write, "we assume that only when extramarital partners have the consent of their primary partners, the support of their peer group and subculture, and the time and energy to work out their secondary relationship is their experience likely to become as sexually satisfying as marital sex generally is" (Blood, 1978: 247).

As previously mentioned, there are degrees of unacceptability. In the United States heterosexual behavior, regardless of the form it takes, is more socially acceptable than the corresponding form of homosexual behavior. The latter has often been viewed as *per se* immoral, unnatural and, until relatively recently, as a form of mental illness which requires treatment. Therefore while adultery in any form is illegitimate and negatively sanctioned, its unacceptability is compounded when between partners of the same sex. As a result, the corresponding consequences will also necessarily increase.

Social consequences of adultery in a heterosexual relationshp will probably be basically the same whether it is coital or noncoital since, as was earlier explained, it would generally necessitate taking the word of the participants themselves to be able to distinguish between the two possibilities. Many people would be reluctant to do this because it would, from their point of view, require them to trust the word of individuals who are *prima facie* untrustworthy. There is, of course, one important and obvious biological consequential difference between consummated and nonconsummated adultery. The latter cannot result in pregnancy, which could further complicate the possible overall legal and social consequences.

Differences in the affective dimension can have important consequences for the future of the marital relationship. Adultery based on affection is generally seen as being more threatening to the marital relationship. Co-marital sex, for example, is based on the understanding that the agreed upon adulterous relationships will be strictly physical. They are to be nothing more than recreation, a game in which players, ground rules and "playing field" are all known and agreed upon in advance. Even in the case of nonconsensual adultery it is probably easier for the nonadulterous spouse to control or limit his or her reactions if there is the knowledge and certainty that the action of the spouse was impersonal and without affection. Under these circumstances the other person would not be seen as a rival and the incident could be more easily attributed to temptation and human weakness.

From the perspective of society, however, adultery without affection is probably less acceptable than that which is based on affection. Since the person engaging in adultery has a spouse, society seems to feel that there is no good reason, except possibly for the prolonged absence or illness of the spouse, why that person should go outside of the marriage for sexual satisfaction unless it is for reasons of love. That is something which members of society can understand, and while it is not completely condoned, it does fit into the accepted value system of love, sex, and marriage. This sort of thinking is prevalent in the extremely popular reflections of American culture as represented in the so-called daytime soap operas. One of the main themes of soap operas is adultery. An analysis by the anthropologist Bean (1981) in this regard is of interest. She states:

> Triangles demonstrate the ingredients, and the connections between the ingredients in the ideal relationship between a man and a woman: the co-occurrence of love, marriage and sex. Love is the basic ingredient on which the ideal relationship is built. Marriage (which temporally should come second) is the desired culmination of love; sex is its natural expression. Love can only really be felt for one person at a time. Therefore, sex (love's sign), and, of course, marriage (its culmination) should be engaged in only with one person at a time. Sex and marriage are matters of choice, but one cannot choose to love or not to love (1981: 66).

When one has sexual relations without choosing to do so, the man or woman is termed a victim rather than partner, and the sexual act becomes a legal offense. Minors and mentally retarded individuals are not generally considered capable of exercising their volition in this regard. Sexual relations are generally believed to be very personal decisions made by mature individuals. Ideally, each individual is always free to choose to abstain from sexual activity for whatever reason. Hence we often hear the phrase "between consenting adults" to describe and defend certain sexual activity. The theory of so-called "conjugal rights"—commonly understood to mean the "husband's right" and the corresponding "wife's duty" in matters of marital sexual intercourse—offers an important exception to the principle of mutual consent. Historically, a husband has not had to wait for his wife to be a willing sexual partner. However, there are some signs, both social and legal, that this is now changing. In some states a wife can now charge her husband with rape. Some traditional Christian denominations may argue that married people no longer have the right to choose not to have sexual relations with their spouse or to have sexual relations with someone other than their spouse since they have already freely entered into a permanent, exclusive sexual commitment and have become "two in one flesh." Whatever the person's status, sexual activity—including adultery—against one's will may have legal consequences.

In considering the possible consequences of visibility it is helpful to turn to a distinction made by Merton (1966) between a nonconformist and an aberrant. The former is someone who violates a norm openly, rejects the validity of the norm and tries to convince others to do likewise. The latter, on the other hand, is someone who violates a norm secretly, does not question the validity of the norm and does not attempt to influence others in this regard. Thus, both may be adulterers but their characteristics are different and so too, one might suspect, are the responses they elicit. Generally speaking, the nonconformist may be viewed as a greater threat to the existing social order, which is openly challenged, and may, therefore, be more harshly treated. At the same time, however, some people may be more critical of the apparent hypocritical nature of the aberrant.

It should be remembered that in the United States adultery is still generally considered to be socially, legally and morally wrong. Therefore, the more frequently an individual engages in adultery, the greater the possibility and probability of being discovered and in some way punished. Thus, greater frequency of adultery would appear to bring greater—or more certain—social repercussions. Paradoxically, however, the chronic adulterer or adulteress probably suffers less psychologically than the periodic adulterer or adulteress. This is because the former is more likely to have overcome whatever dissonance that may have existed and to have made whatever changes or adjustments which were necessary to arrive at a state of consonance.

Intuitively it would appear that for a marriage the most harmful form of adultery would be that which was nonconsensual, bisexual, affectionate, overt and chronic; while the least harmful would be consensual, heterosexual, nonaffectionate, covert and periodic. However, such is not necessarily true. There are spouses, some of whom have themselves engaged in adultery, who are unwilling or unable to forgive or forget the adulterous behavior of their marriage partner. Moreover, some adulterous individuals are unable to forgive themselves or to accept the forgiveness of others. Thus even one act of adultery may be too many.

It is impossible to predict the specific consequences, either immediate or long-range, in any case of adultery. That is one of the weaknesses of situation ethics which holds that the morality of adultery depends on its consequences (see chapter 4). Each of the dimensions discussed above has some effect and must be considered by anyone who desires to predict the consequences of their actions.

REFERENCES

Bartell, Gilbert. 1970. "Group Sex Among the Mid-Americans." *Journal of Sex Research,* 6 (May): 113-130.

Bean, Susan S. 1981. "Soap Operas: Saga of American Kinship." In *The American Dimension: Cultural Myths and Social Realities,* edited by S. Montague and W. Arens, pp., 61-75. Sherman Oaks, Calif.: Alfred Publishing.

Bell, Robert. 1966. *Premarital Sex in a Changing Society.* Englewood Cliffs, N.J.: Prentice-Hall.

Bell, Robert, and Michael Gordon, eds. 1972. *The Social Dimension of Human Sexuality.* Boston: Little, Brown.

Blood, Robert, and Margaret Blood, 1978. *Marriage,* 3rd ed. New York: Free Press.

Bullough, Vern. 1976. *Sexual Variance in Society and History.* New York: John Wiley.

Bullough, Vern, and Bonnie Bullough. 1977. *Sin, Sickness and Sanity.* New York: Garland.

Denfield, D. 1974. "Dropouts from Swinging." *Family Coordinator,* 23 (January): 45-49.

Festinger, Leon. 1957. *A Theory of Cognitive Dissonance.* New York: Harper and Row.

Giele, Janet Z. 1976. "Changing Sex Roles and the Future of Marriage." In *Contemporary Marriage: Structure, Dynamics and Therapy,* edited by H. Grunebaum and J. Christ. Boston: Little, Brown.

Hunt, Morton. 1974. *Sexual Behavior in the 1970's.* Chicago: Playboy Press.

Levitt, Eugene, and Albert Klassen. 1974. "Public Attitudes Toward Homosexuality: Part of the 1970 National Survey by the Institute for Sex Research." *Journal of Homosexuality,* 1: 29-43.

Merton, Robert. 1966. "Social Problems and Sociological Theory." In *Contemporary Social Problems,* 2nd ed. New York: Harcourt Brace and World.

Newsweek. 1981. "Billie Jean's Odd Match." May 11: 36-37.

Norton, Clark. 1981. "Sex in America: An Outlaw's Guide." *Inquiry,* October: 11-18.

Reiss, Ira. 1960. *Premarital Sexual Standards in America.* New York: Free Press.

————. 1980. *Family Systems in America,* 3rd ed. New York: Holt, Rinehart and Winston.

Smith, Lynn, and James Smith. 1973. "Co-marital Sex: The Incorporation of Extramarital Sex into the Marriage Relationship." In *Critical Issues in Contemporary Sexual Behavior,* edited by J. Zubin and J. Nioney. Baltimore: Johns Hopkins.

Stephens, William. 1963. *The Family in Cross-Cultural Perspective.* New York: Holt, Rinehart and Winston.

Walshok, Mary L. 1971. "The Emergence of Middle-Class Deviant Sub-cultures: The Case of Swingers." *Social Problems,* 18 (Spring): 488-495.

Ziskin, Jay, and Mae Ziskin. 1973. *The Extra-Marital Sex Contract.* Los Angeles: Nash.

3

Sue M. Hall and Philip A. Hall
LAW AND ADULTERY

INTRODUCTION

During most of Western recorded history both civil and religious authorities have reinforced the social institutions of marriage and the family as the basic structural units of society. Interrelated family members, clans, and communities constituted largely self-reliant and self-contained socio-economic units. Within this context adultery represented a serious perceived threat to social stability.

Contemporary norms and behaviors regarding marriage or matters related to marriage vary to such an extent that some people suggest traditional, monogamous, enduring marital relationships have now been relegated to a lesser position. For proof they point out the growing number of female-headed households, marriage contracts which preserve the property interests of the individual partners and commit them only to specific joint activities in the marriage, the gay rights movement, the high divorce rate, and the number of persons who remain single by choice in our society.

This chapter will discuss the current legal status of adultery in the United States and further detail a relationship outlined in the last chapter—the one between legality and legitimacy. While adultery has, in essence, been decriminalized in the United States, some civil law remedies remain when one partner in a marriage is injured by the adulterous behavior of the other partner. These civil actions reflect several of the behavioral aspects of adultery also outlined in the preceding chapter.

This chapter will analyze the distinction between civil (or tort) law and criminal law, and how these laws apply in the case of adultery, focusing especially on the concepts of consortium, abduction and alienation of affection. The development of American attitudes and laws resulting in three different models utilized by states in addressing adultery will also be presented, to be followed by a discussion of divorce and child custody cases. Finally, we will examine both artificial reproduction and the Equal Rights Amendment (E.R.A.) as they relate to adultery.

ADULTERY AS INTERFERENCE WITH THE MARITAL RELATIONSHIP

Under the law, adultery historically could occur only with respect to the activities of married people. Fornication is the term applied to sexual intercourse between unmarried persons. Adultery or sexual activity by a married person with a person other than her or his marital partner has usually received greater social attention, concern and condemnation than has fornication, and this more serious evaluation of adultery has been reflected in the law. For example, some states have had adultery laws without corresponding fornication legislation. (It's not surprising that adultery causes greater concern: it represents a threat to the marital relationship, a relationship civilly recognized as a legal bond.)

CIVIL VERSUS CRIMINAL PROCEEDINGS

In Britain during the Anglo-Saxon period—which saw development of the "common law," i.e., a body of rules based on judicial decisions rather than legislation—there was no distinction between civil and criminal law. A single prearranged penalty served both to punish the accused (defendent) when found guilty of the crime committed and to compensate the injured party (plaintiff) for the wrong suffered. Gradually there developed separate bodies of civil and criminal laws (Kenny, 1936), so today a distinction must be made between the tort and the criminal status concerning adultery.

A crime refers to a transgression against the interests of the public. Therefore, the state conducts criminal prosecutions with the intent of protecting the concerns of the public at large (e.g., the "common good"). This is accomplished by incarcerating and/or fining the criminal, attempting to reform the behavior of the convicted person, and discouraging other persons from behaving in a similar manner (Prosser, 1971).

By contrast, a tort represents a wrong committed against a particular individual. The injured individual, therefore, must initiate and carry through a lawsuit under civil law. This lawsuit has the purpose of preserving the individual's personal interests by recovering monetary damages from the wrongdoer. However, tort actions may also involve an increased award, above and beyond restitution for harmed personal assets, for the supposed injury against the feelings of the victim by a wanton or reckless act which is felt to deserve punishment and needs to be discouraged in others; these are called "exemplary" or "punitive" damages.

To complicate matters, the terms tort and crime are not mutually exclusive. The same conduct may constitute both a tort and a crime (Statsky, 1984). In these instances both a tort proceeding and a criminal action may usually be pursued either in succession or concurrently because of the separate purposes of each type of action (Clark, 1968). Since the burden of proof is different in civil and criminal actions and since they are independent causes, the outcome of one type of action normally does not dictate the outcome of the other action. Furthermore, a tort and a crime may both be referred to by the same name, e.g., "assault," "battery" or "adultery"; but the similar name may not carry the same meaning in both contexts.

Varying numbers of states have considered adultery a criminal act, but the definition of the crime of adultery has differed from one jurisdiction to another. Such differences suggest that local influences, usually at the state level, have reflected local public attitudes and that these attitudes have varied with time.

TORTS OF ADULTERY

The current trend in the United States is to abolish the crime of adultery by repealing these criminal statutes. However, the civil tort of adultery persists in several states, and is but one of three types of civil actions which evolved to remedy interference with the unique and highly valued bond of marriage. The other two tort actions are "abduction" and "alienation of affections".

The concept of "consortium" underlines these three types of civil torts. Consortium is defined as the "conjugal fellowship of husband

and wife, and the right of each to the company, cooperation, affection and aid of the other in every conjugal relation" (Black, 1968: 382). Despite some ambiguity in practice, consortium generally includes four elements: services of the partner, sexual intercourse, conjugal affection, and society (Prosser, 1971). The notion of consortium includes miscellaneous intangible relationships between spouses who enjoy an ongoing marital relationship. The meaning of consortium has changed over time, and it still remains a somewhat ambiguous legal term. Initially, consortium referred to the exclusive right of the husband to the wife's services and included the exclusive right to sexual intercourse. This was based on the concept that the wife was a servant to her husband. As the master-servant concept changed gradually to the present idea that husband and wife are legal and social partners, it became more common to define consortium as the mutual right of each spouse to the other. The current notion of consortism is multifaceted. While it encompasses the usual norms of ideal love, this concept does so only at a relatively high level of abstraction which makes it difficult to apply in concrete cases.

ABDUCTION

Historically abduction developed as the earliest cause of action. When a wife was forcibly taken by, or went voluntarily with a man other than her spouse, her husband could then act against the other man. Society considered wives and minor children as the virtual property of the husband and father (Statsky, 1984). As such, they did not have the right to give themselves to someone else. Therefore husbands and fathers could recover their wives and children with the assistance of a common law which allowed masters to regain the services of a stolen servant. The right to services of the wife evolved slowly into the present day right to consortium, which reflects the social ideal of the monogamous marriage.

ADULTERY

Adultery, also called "criminal conversation," combines terms used in criminal and civil law. Criminal conversation, which is defined as "sexual intercourse of an outsider with husband or wife, or a breakdown of the covenant of fidelity" (Black, 1968: 448) represents a civil tort and not a crime, despite the word "criminal." Though specific laws vary among the states, it now generally holds that a complaining spouse need only prove that the other spouse engaged in sexual intercourse with someone else while legally married to the complaining spouse. The essence of this cause of action is the idea that the exclusive right to engage in sexual relations lies with one's spouse. The actual basis of the civil lawsuit, however, has been described in such potent emotional terms as "defilement of the marriage bed," "blow to family honor," and "suspicion cast upon the legitimacy of offspring" due to the adultery. The civil suit seeks to compensate the complaining spouse for violation of marital rights and to preserve the social institution of monogamous marriage by discouraging adultery. Although technically distinct, "fornication" is encompassed within this course of action. In some states sexual relations between one person who is married and an unmarried partner result in a charge of adultery against the first person and a charge of fornication against the second. Other jurisdictions hold that despite the unmarried partner's status, both partners are charged with adultery.

ALIENATION OF AFFECTIONS

The concept of "alienation of affections" is more complex and confusing than those of abduction or adultery. Intent to "interfere" with the marriage relationship must be proved in such a lawsuit, whereas this intent is presumed in a suit for adultery if proof of sex with someone other than the spouse exists. An alienation of affections lawsuit must show that the offending spouse was influenced to leave the couple's home by a third person. The key issue is not sexual, but the loss of affection.

LIMITED DEFENSE ALLOWED

Perhaps the most helpful way to distinguish between adultery and alienation of affection suits is to examine the defenses which are permitted by statutes and rules of procedure. The accused person's ignorance of the marriage is a defense in a suit for alienation of affections, but it is not a defense in a case of adultery, even if the unfaithful spouse deliberately misrepresents his or her marital status. The only "complete" defense to the charge of adultery—one which will decide the suit by itself—is proof that the complaining spouse consented to the adulterous act. This involves the consensual dimension of behavior mentioned in chapter 2. The complaining spouse's actions must imply consent or connivance, i.e. knowledge of and tacit consent of the adulterous relationship. Neither previous adulterous behavior of the complaining spouse or the unfaithful spouse nor the complaining spouse's abandonment or neglect of the unfaithful spouse may be used as defenses.

Similarly, a third person who is being sued cannot claim as a defense that the other person's spouse with whom he or she was sexually involved consented or was even the seducer because the complaining spouse has been harmed regardless of the offending spouse's consent or lack of consent. An alienation of affections suit also excludes consideration either of the quality of the marriage or the living arrangements of the couple before the other person appeared.

DEVELOPMENT OF AMERICAN ATTITUDES AND LAWS

An understanding of the evolution of the concept of adultery in early American law would not be complete without a brief discussion of ancient accounts and English history. The earliest inhabitants of Babylonia saw a need to punish adultery. It appears that wounded pride and a sense of justice were what prompted sanctions. A dual standard of punishment existed, however, under which adulterous wives were executed while unfaithful husbands were required only to pay damages in money or property to the offended spouse (Murray, 1961).

Attitudes toward adultery vacillated. During the period 356 to 330 before the Christian era, adultery by husbands was not controlled insofar as husbands might engage freely in sexual relations with their servants, and children of such unions were desired. Although it was common for every woman to visit the Temple of Venus to engage in sex with a stranger once in her lifetime, an adultress was executed unless spared by her husband, whereupon she was expelled from his home to become an offering to any males who might pass by.

During the years 330 to 323 before the Christian era, however, marriage contracts which expressly forbade adultery became common. An offending spouse was liable to punishment, although the punishments were not the same for both husband and wife. Breach of the agreement by the wife resulted in the mutilation of her face, while a conviction of the husband resulted in the loss of property.

Similarly, during Caesar's time there were no laws pertaining to adultery. When the Emperor Constantine adopted Christianity in 313 of the Christian era, however, the importance of the family received renewed emphasis. As the clergy became influential and began to legislate behavior, as in the Canons of the Council of Illiberis, for example, milder penalities for adultery became the norm as church fathers sought to keep the people interested in Christianity. Furthermore, concubinage was tolerated and was never subjected to the penalties of adultery.

By the twelfth century the Catholic Church's influence in Europe was such that marriage came to be treated as a sacrament rather than a civil contract. This belief remained dominant for several centuries and eventually was interwoven securely into English common law.

In English common law, from which we derive many legal principles still employed today, a complaint of adultery could be brought only by a husband and the crime could only be committed with another man's wife. The wife had no legal standing. Sexual affairs by her husband with unmarried women, in contrast, were excluded from the classification of adultery. Furthermore, upon marriage the husband and wife became one in the eyes of the law, and that one was the husband. The wife could not enter a contract herself nor sue or be sued without the consent and participation of her husband as either accuser or accused. In effect, a wife could not sue her husband. Following this logic, the wife's right to sue her husband's paramour belonged to her husband, and as he must consent and participate in the lawsuit, it made little sense to assess monetary damages against the husband's lover when the money would then be paid to the husband.

This was the legal heritage which English settlers brought to America. Despite the pursuit of certain freedoms by colonial New England settlers, a decidedly puritanical approach was brought to questions of marriage and adultery. Punishment tended to be harsh, whether it was physical or involved public display and ridicule. When one spouse caught the other in the act of adultery (*flagrante delicto*), the offending couple could be killed. This "self-help" remedy persisted due to the belief that the provocation and heat of the moment excused the outraged spouse.

In 1639, Mary Mendane, a married woman, was convicted of adultery and was sentenced to be whipped. She also was required to wear an insignia on her left sleeve to publicize her conviction. The punishment for failing to wear the badge while she remained in Plymouth consisted of holding a hot iron to her face until she was burned. In 1641, a single man and a married woman were convicted of adultery. In addition to public whippings, they were directed to wear badges (the letters "AD") for the duration of their stay in the colony. The wearing of this badge, however, does not appear to have been a universal punishment throughout the colonies (Dobbs, 1973).

An alternative punishment of the era required expulsion from the particular colony (Feinsinger, 1935). Individuals convicted of a lesser charge than adultery (e.g., "Very filthy carriage" or "lascivious gross and foul actions tending to adultery") were whipped and fined. If they were unable to pay immediately they were often imprisoned until their fines were paid. Because expelled persons had difficulty locating a settlement which would accept them, and imprisoned persons had no means of earning the money to pay their fines, these sanctions tended to isolate and leave helpless their recipients.

Despite the unification of America after the Revolutionary War and the adoption of the Constitution, each state retained the right to make and enforce its own laws regarding adultery and, indeed, most family matters. To this day different states have different adultery statutes.

When states addressed adultery which involved a person who

was married with one who was not they tended to follow one of three models, each of which made adultery a crime. The most popular model held that although only one party to the affair was married, public policy demanded that both of the parties to the affair be held guilty of adultery, rather than to find the unmarried person guilty of fornication. The second model held that unmarried parties could only be charged with fornication and not adultery. However, the spouse involved was charged with adultery, whether that spouse be husband or wife. The third model, rooted in the common law notion that adultery involves injury to the husband, held that adultery could only be committed by or with a married woman. A married man engaging in sexual relations with an unmarried woman was not committing adultery. This logic held sway in the case of *State vs. Hood*. Nelson Hood was indicted for fornication with Jane Chancy, whom he had married in 1876. The problem arose because in 1869 he had married Maggie Horton and had never obtained a valid divorce from her. Thus, the court found Hood guilty of fornication only, since Chancy was a single woman.

There remains a question whether conviction of adultery or of fornication had, in practice, different consequences for the convicted person. Certainly, in socio-behavioral terms, conviction of either could result in different informal sanctions according to the local norms prevalent in a particular community. However, the sanctions for fornication were often less severe than for adultery.

By the 1930s, every state except Louisiana had adopted some form of civil law against adultery. The perceived abuse of these remedies, which were referred to derisively as "heart balm" torts, which allowed an individual to take legal action against an adulterous spouse and/or the lover, soon brought on reform efforts which met with varied success (Feinsinger, 1935). Pennsylvania's 1935 General Assembly abolished the suit for alienation of affections. (The House of Representatives had included the abolition of the suit of adultery, but the Senate deleted that provision without comment.) In the same year, Nebraska's House of Representatives passed an anti-heart balm bill, but the Senate postponed it indefinitely. Although the bill appeared to have had popular support, and passed the House by a two-to-one margin, it was in effect killed by some individuals in the

Senate who were opposed to the change.

By 1935, three states had abolished the cause of action for adultery. By 1972, nine states had abolished all heart balm torts and five others had repealed alienation of affections and abduction. In that same year, the Pennsylvania General Assembly abolished the crime of adultery. However, the tort of adultery was not to be erased until four years later, then by the Courts, not the Legislature, in *Fadgen vs. Lenkner*. The Court determined that society and the law had changed so much since the cause of action first arose that the tort of adultery no longer could be justified.

Fadgen is suggestive of the current trend to do away with the tort of adultery because it perpetuates the archaic fiction that spouses have a property right over each other. Women, who in the past have often been treated as property, claimed that adultery torts reeked of sex discrimination and they called for equal treatment. What many jurisdictions did, instead of opening it to married women, was shut down the cause of action to *all* potential parties. (Lippman, 1930). Currently at least 20 states and the District of Columbia have abolished the civil cause of action for adultery.

ADULTERY AS IT RELATES TO DIVORCE

Religious courts greatly influenced marriage and divorce in England and, as a consequence, America. Many unacceptable sexual acts were considered sinful rather than criminal and were dealt with by church rather than by state, with the goal of both promoting and protecting the institution of marriage. Consequently, for many years England remained virtually a divorceless society. Due to the fact that divorce was unavailable even to a spouse whose partner was unfaithful, the tort of adultery was the primary relief sought under common law. In this country, the New England states first made judicial divorce available around the year 1800.

As we have seen, society has always regulated marriage by custom, religion, and/or statute, but the degree of regulation has changed. The institution of marriage itself shifts to accommodate a never-static society. Therefore, as the demand for divorce increased, it became easier to obtain one. (Freed and Foster, 1983). Our current "no-fault" divorce laws are typical of this trend. Whereas for most of our history a person wanting a divorce was required to show that the other spouse was guilty of some act which had caused the demise of the marriage—adultery, abandonment, conviction of a serious crime, as examples—"no-fault" means what it implies, that a divorce can be granted even though neither spouse is alleged to have "caused" the marriage to fail. Most states now have no-fault divorce, but have also retained statutes allowing for divorce on the grounds that one of the spouses was at fault for the breakdown of the marital relationship.

Just as it was once necessary to prove the other spouse guilty of some fault in order to be eligible to divorce that spouse, it was likewise possible to defeat the divorce by showing that the petitioning spouse was also at fault or that the petitioning spouse had condoned the complained-of behavior. For instance, one could defend a divorce suit alleging adultery by showing that the complaining spouse was likewise guilty of adultery.

As of late 1973, at least seventeen states had abolished all defenses against divorce and almost every state had done away with at least some defenses (Public Health Service, 1973). Some states officially abolished the defenses of adultery and of countercharging the accusing spouse with the same charge as the accused (recrimination). However, they maintain voluntary forgiveness of the accused spouse by the accusing spouse (condonation) as a defense if the court finds that there is a reasonable expectation of their reconciliation (Texas Family Code, 1983).

While fault is still important in those states which, upon divorce, divide community property, the trend is to minimize its importance regarding alimony and property division in non-community property jurisdictions. Currently, at least nineteen states exclude fault considerations, while only about fifteen states allow evidence of fault regarding such matters.

ADULTERY AS IT AFFECTS CHILD CUSTODY

Under common law, the father—as the natural guardian—maintained a superior right to the custody of his children over the mother, and even over the best interest of the child (Peck, 1930). During the

1800s, however, various laws required that equity courts grant custody of very young children to their mothers. Currently, the standard of "best interest of the child" is the controlling consideration, although some states still allow preference to be given to the mother. To be sure, custody disputes demonstrate that the best interest of the child is not a clearly and commonly understood standard. There are currently four subgroups of this the child's best interest model in use in the United States.

The first subgroup flatly denies custody to an adulterous parent as a matter of law. Jurisdictions following this interpretation hold that adultery is a sufficient disqualification in questions of custody. An adulterous person is labeled "unfit" due to the supposed inherent inconsistency between adultery and any child's best interest.

The second subgroup presumes that the adulterous acts of a parent directly and adversely affect the child. Though this presumption can be challenged theoretically, in practice it is very difficult to overcome. This being the case, there is very little difference between the results of these first two subgroups.

The third subgroup in this model employs a presumption of unfitness. The courts that adhere to this idea usually reason that an award of custody to an adulterous parent is "probably" inconsistent with the child's best interest. This is not as absolute a stand as taken in the two subgroups discussed above. The presumption of unfitness may be overcome by an adulterous parent who shows repentance, terminates the relationship, and changes his or her behavior so that there is little or no likelihood of a recurrence of the objectionable behavior.

The fourth subgroup reflects the current trend to ignore the adulterous conduct unless it clearly causes a direct and adverse effect on the child (Lauerman, 1977). Initially the court must therefore find whether the parent's adulterous actions directly affect and harm the child.

To aid courts in custody decisions, a number of states delineate specific criteria regarding custody. One typical criterion, such as found in Illinois Revised Statutes, states that the "interaction and interrelationship of (a) child and (his or her) parent or parents, siblings, and *any other person who may significantly affect the child's best interests* (emphasis added) should be considered when awarding custody."[1] As the other person may prove to be the adulterous spouse's lover, who may or may not have direct contact with the child, this acknowledges the fact that a parent's adultery is not necessarily detrimental to a child. Within the framework of the fourth subgroup this means that, as it relates to custody, adultery is a "relevant consideration" only when it can be shown to have a significant adverse affect on the child. (Weyrauch and Katz, 1983).[2]

ARTIFICIAL REPRODUCTION

Could artificial insemination ever constitute adultery? While such a question may seem absurd at first glance, some courts have indeed held that artificial insemination constitutes adultery.

There are three basic types of artificial insemination. The first, AIH (artificial insemination homologous) involves only the husband's semen. For instance, when the husband has a consistent and persistent low sperm count, the husband's sperm is often collected over time until there are sufficient numbers of sperm to have a reasonable chance to produce a pregnancy. The collected semen is then injected into the wife's womb with a syringe or other medical instrument at a time believed to be ideal for conception.

The second form, AIC (artificial insemination confused), combines the husband's semen with that of an unknown donor. This process compensates for the husband's low sperm count while allowing for the possibility, albeit slight, that he is the natural father. This in turn justifies listing the husband on the birth certificate and allows the court some rationale upon which paternity may be established.

Finally, the AID (artificial insemination heterologous) process uses only the semen of a third party donor. This method is advantageous when the husband is sterile or may transmit genetic disorders to his child. It is this form of artificial insemination which poses the most questions in the area of adultery (Green and Long, 1984).

In a 1921 divorce action the Ontario Supreme Court held that a woman who had undergone AID without her husband's consent had in effect committed adultery. The justices argued that "the essence of the offense of adultery consists, not in the moral turpitude of the act of sexual intercourse, but in the voluntary surrender to another person of the reproduction powers or faculties." In 1954 an American court citing the Ontario Court reached the same conclusion in *Doornbos vs. Doornbos.*

In a 1963 divorce action brought by the wife, the New York Supreme Court in *Gursky vs. Gursky* held that even with her husband's consent Mrs. Gersky was functionally guilty of adultery and had borne an illegitimate child. Despite the contention that adultery by its very nature involves sexual intercourse, some courts have avoided this issue by concentrating on the intent of the process, which is to impregnate, while disregarding the fact that artificial insemination is a sexless act according to medical and legal definitions. While "sexless adultery" may seem impossible, this reasoning deserves some analysis. As at least one team of legal writers has suggested:

> Adultery, as conventionally understood, implies sexual intercourse, but its essence as an offense lies not in the act itself but its symbolic significance. Between spouses, sexual intercourse usually represents consortium, or the exclusion bond of intimacy that holds the relationship together. Accordingly, third party sex often will constitute a major affront to consortium and thereby impair the bond of exclusive spousal intimacy. An unconsented-to AID child may have the same effect on a husband who would regard procreation as a matter of spousal intimacy and exclusivity. (O'Donnell and Jones, 1982).

Sexual activity short of intercourse, however, does not amount to adultery unless the relevant statute expressly includes the specific acts complained of. Following this logic it has been held that "sexless adultery" is not adultery at all. In a 1968 criminal case, the California Supreme Court in *People vs. Sorenson* held that is was "patently absurd" to link artificial insemination with adultery. To hold otherwise would create an unlikely list of "adulterers" including the inseminators (female as well as male), the husband and anonymous sperm donors, living or dead.

The *Sorenson* logic is clearly the law at this time in the United

States. Artificial insemination has become a widely accepted and almost routine alternative for many infertile couples. Current legislation and court decisions reflect society's general acceptance of artificial insemination as a legitimate means of achieving parenthood.

ADULTERY AND THE E.R.A.

In America at one time or another a woman could not own her own property, engage in a contract in her own name, bring suit or be sued, vote, participate as a juror, execute a deed, or even make her own will (Statsky, 1984). All of this has changed as women have freed themselves from some of their domestic "duties" and become more of a part of the world around them. While it is not the purpose of this chapter to debate what prompted this change, it is interesting to note that the equality of women continues to be slow in coming. In a United States Supreme Court decision the justices declared, "no longer is the female destined solely for the home and the rearing of the family, and only the male for the market place and the world of ideas" (*Stanton vs. Stanton,* 1975). While this is an accurate, if not laudable statement, it is surprising that such revelations were being made as late as 1975, and are still needed today.

Since the bulk of ERA litigation is made up of family law matters, it is logical that adultery laws have long been affected by such amendments and other similar enactments. Among the early forms of women's rights legislation were the Emancipation Acts and Married Women's Acts. Eventually, such acts were passed in every American jurisdiction. Basically this legislation restored to married women the rights they had previously enjoyed as single women, i.e., separate ownership and control of their property, and the capacity to sue and be sued without consent and participation of any male. This, of course, is not to say that women enjoyed the same rights as men. They were merely reinstated to their former status—less than men in many respects but more than being their husband's property.

These emancipation acts were generally understood to allow women the right to bring an action for adultery against their husbands, but the gist of the action was never uniformly enunciated by the courts or the legislatures. While it was never explicitly stated that a husband could institute an action against his wife because she was his property, this appears to have been the underlying rationale. So when the right was extended to a married woman, the basis of this extension was not addressed.

While some American jursidictions allowed women the right to sue in cases of adultery prior to state equal rights amendments, as late as 1959 this right was not available in all jurisdictions. The Fourteenth Amendment, which was passed in 1868 and mandates equal protection to United States citizens by states, was considered to be the basis of this right. Until recently, however, it was not commonly applied to the rights of women.

With the latest and most powerful insurgence of "ERA fever" in the 1970s, fourteen states amended their constitutions to include anti-sex classification provisions. As a result of Maryland's Equal Rights Amendment, the Court of Appeals, that state's court of final jurisdiction, in the case of *Kline vs. Angell,* held the cause of action for adultery unconstitutional. Instead of expanding the action to permit a wife to file suit, adultery as a tort action was closed to both men and women. The *Kline* court is the only court known to repeal an adultery action via an equal rights amendment argument.

DISCUSSION AND COMMENT

The presumption that adultery leads to divorce and that divorce in turn harms both the individual and society has kept the state involved in regulating the institution of marriage. This rationale has, for many years, lent credence to the notion that society must combat adultery if it is to preserve marriage (Frank, Berman and Mazur-Hart, 1978). But the crime of adultery has virtually disappeared. And many legal writers have argued that state statutes have failed to preserve marriage and, therefore, the tort of adultery should also be abolished. They argue that the many inherent inconsistencies in the underlying theory of the law make it ripe for judicial or legislative repeal, and that the very purpose of the civil statutes (i.e., to preserve or restore the marital relationship) is circumvented by a myriad of factors (O'Donnell and Jones, 1982). The argument continues that common sense and experience tell us that by the time a spouse brings such a suit, the marriage has usually decayed far beyond any hope of restoration.

Throughout the past the idea that adultery undermines the interests of the "innocent" spouse as well as society has existed under varying degrees of popularity. In relatively recent times, since the availability of divorce, it has been suspected that adultery leads to divorce. But there is evidence that adultery is not a major factor in current divorce statistics. Adultery is more often a symptom than a cause of marital problems. This view is also mirrored by corresponding shifts in legal responses to adultery and "no fault" divorce laws. For example, in 1977 Nebraska's legislature enacted a statute whereby *only* married persons could be convicted of the crime of adultery which is a Class 1 misdemeanor punishable by one year in prison or a $1,000 fine. While the Nebraska judiciary refuses to abolish the tort, the decriminalization of adultery as to single individuals evidences a relaxation of sexual attitudes. The idea that consenting adults should be able to conduct themselves without government or social interference has been advanced for decades and is now gaining legal momentum. Inherent in this philosophy is the belief that society will, and, in fact, does, withstand adultery. Therefore, it should not meddle in the private affairs of individuals.

In short, many proponents of the trend to abolish the tort of adultery argue that not every human wrong can be judicially corrected or compensated for. In response, the opposition is quick to point out that the majority of states still recognize the tort of adultery and many states have recently upheld the cause of action when they could have easily done away with it. They argue that *all* civil actions are subject to abuse but this provides no rationale for abolishing them. Further, courts can instruct juries to consider the complaining spouse's vindictive motives when assessing damages, thereby lessening the incentive to bring suit in which the wronged sponse is only out to "get even."

Some commentators feel that statutes attempting to prohibit adulterous behavior have little or no deterrent effect and are of little use. Inherent in this view is the idea that human emotions are rarely planned. An adulterer has no time to weigh the consequences of his or her reactions and thus be deterred.

Those who support abolition of these tort laws also argue that monetary awards cannot undo the spouse's suffering nor recapture the couple's lost relationship. They point out that psychic damages are difficult to measure and show how excessive damages are often awarded when the jury has to decide on emotional matters—even when no harm has been proved. Proponents of tort abolition argue further that only after a divorce is obtained should nominal damages be recovered by the spouse when there is no proof that undesirable consequences resulted from such wrongdoing. If there is such proof greater compensation is in order (special damages). And in any event, only compensation for real, substantial loss or injury should be awarded (actual damages).

The reverse side of this argument is that damages are assessed in all sorts of difficult cases and can be limited fairly in the instance of adultery by specific instructions to the jury from the judge. This is especially true regarding the complaining spouse's motives, and the court's power to require the reduction in the amount of damages in exchange for the upholding of the jury's verdict (remittitur). It must also be remembered that damages, in every award, serve as an approximate compensation in lieu of preventing an injury that has already occurred. While damages are never a perfect solution in any suit, they are a viable substitute. Tort damages were not designed to fully and completely compensate for injuries.

The authors believe that where these tort actions are maintained, defenses should be allowed that will permit the person being sued to fairly explain the circumstances at the time of the infraction and the actual role the complaining spouse played in the breakup of the marital relationship. The opportunity to present defenses, plus other safeguards built into the legal system for overturning judgments not proven by the facts presented, should be sufficient protection against abuse of these laws.

Throughout history the legal consequences of adultery have swung back and forth from one extreme to the other, from execution to "no fault." Within the American judicial and legislative systems the pendulum will no doubt continue to swing, but the arc across which it moves will probably not be so wide.

On the whole, the harshest penalties for adultery have been

directed against women. This was so because women were considered to be either the property of or an adjunct to their husbands and because women did not occupy positions of power either in society or the legal system. Until recently they rarely held positions in legislative bodies or in the courts. As more women begin to occupy such positions, laws and practices which discriminate by reason of sex will no longer be tolerated.

As a society we will, no doubt, continue to fluctuate in our tolerance of sexual behavior outside the marital relationship. These authors do not believe that we will ever again reach the point where we imprison individuals for adulterous behavior. We will, however, continue to recognize the effect that this behavior may have on spouse, children and other members of society. Therefore, as societal moods change, we will allow for differing civil remedies for the injuries that may result from adultery.

NOTES

1. *Illinois Revised Statutes*, 1977: Chap. 40, para. 602(a)(3).
2. But see *Jarrett vs. Jarrett*, 400 NE 2d 421 (1980), where the mother's live-in boyfriend was a factor causing the court to change custody to the father despite no finding of adverse effects upon the children.

REFERENCES

Black, Henry C. 1968. *Black's Law Dictionary*. St. Paul, Minn.: West.

Clark, H. 1968. *The Law of Domestic Relations in the United States*. St. Paul, Minn.: West.

Dobbs, D. B. 1973. *Handbook on the Law Remedies*. St. Paul, Minn.: West.

Doornbos vs. Doornbos. Nos. 54 S. 14981, 23 U.S.L.W. 2308 (Superior Ct., Cook Co., Ill., December 13, 1954).

Fadgen vs. Lenker. 365 A. 2d 147 (Pa., 1976).

Feinsinger, N. P. 1935. "Legislative Attack on 'Heart Balm.' " *Michigan Law Review*, 33: 979-1009.

Frank, A. H., J. Berman, and S. Mazur-Hart. 1979. "No Fault Divorce and the Divorce Rate: The Nebraska Experience." *Nebraska Law Review*, 58: 1-99.

Freed, D. J., and H. H. Foster. 1983. "Family Law in the Fifty States: An Overview." *Family Law Quarterly*, 16: 289-383.

Green, S., and J. Long. 1984. *Marriage and Family Law Agreements*. New York: McGraw-Hill.

Gursky vs. Gursky. 39 Misc. 2d 1083, 242, N.Y.S. 2nd 406 (1963).

Kenney, C. S. 1936. *Outlines of Criminal Law,* 25th ed. London: Cambridge University Press.

Kline vs. Angell. 414 A. 2d 929 (md. 1180).

Lauerman, N. 1977. "Nonmarital Sexual Conduct and Child Custody." *University of Cincinnati Law Review,* 46: 647-724.

Lippman, J. 1930. "The Breakdown of Consortium." *Columbia Law Review,* 30: 651-673.

Murray, D. E. 1961. "Ancient Laws on Adultery—A Synopsis." *Journal of Family Law,* 1: 89-104.

O'Donnell, W. and D. Jones. 1982. *The Law of Marriage and Marital Alternatives.* Lexington, Mass.: Lexington Books.

Peck, E. 1920. *The Law of Persons and of Domestic Relations, 2nd ed.* Chicago, Ill.: Callaghan.

People vs. Sorenson. 437 P. 2d 495 (1968).

Prosser, W. 1971. *Handbook of the Law of Torts,* 4th ed. Mineola, N.Y.: Foundation Press.

Public Health Service. 1973. *100 Years of Marriage and Divorce Statistics,* Series 21, No. 24. Washington, D.C.: Department of Health and Human Services.

Stanton vs. Stanton. 95 S. Ct. 1373 (1975).

State vs. Hood. 56 Ind. 85 (1879).

Statsky, W. 1984. *Family Law,* 2nd ed. St. Paul, Minn.: West.

Texas Family Code, 1983.

Weyrauch, W., and S. Katz. 1983. *American Family Law in Transition.* Washington, D.C.: Bureau of National Affairs.

4

Tarcisio Beal
RELIGION AND ADULTERY

RELIGION AND SEXUALITY

The sexual revolution that has swept American society in the last thirty years has left few prohibitions standing. But the larger religious institutions, notably the Roman Catholic Church, have not only been slow to react to this new cultural atmosphere, they have generally rigidified their traditional views of sex. The Catholic church's ban on all artificial means of birth control and premarital sex are cases in point. This stance has not, however, impeded the emergence of conflicting points of view on the part of moralists and theologians.

The traditional Judeo-Christian stance on adultery has been perhaps less challenged than its stances on other sexual matters. Yet, as we shall see in the following pages, there are many who no longer view adultery as a moral monstrosity. Some moralists even claim that a three-party relationship within marriage can sometimes offer a better alternative to divorce.

Those Christian theologians and moralists who challenge traditional doctrine have constantly pointed out that American society has undergone vast and revolutionary changes as the result of major advances in technology and the social sciences; most churches, however, still insist on approaches to man and morality that carry the world views of past centuries—approaches, these critics note, which include pagan teachings. The end result, they say, is that while American society faces the increasing complexity of human relations in an age of technology, the churches often speak to its fold in the language of bygone eras. Nowhere is this more true than in the realm of sexuality. Yet, as Rustum and Della Roy observe: "it surely takes no great humility to acknowledge that since Augustine the attitude of the church on sex had been colored by a fundamental error in understanding the place of sex in life" (1968: 48).

Most Christian churches either adhere to a literal interpretation of the biblical injunctions regarding sexual activity or follow the rationalizations of St. Augustine or St. Thomas Aquinas. When Augustine converted to Christianity, after spending his youth in both sexual dissolution and Manichaean practice, he retained the Manichaeans' harsh and pessimistic view that sex was degrading, the consequence of man's Fall. Augustine, who was often caught up in gross anti-female prejudice, developed what has been called the "theology of the two planes," which posited a dichotomy between matter and spirit, body and soul, the spiritual and the temporal. He accepted, for instance, that female subordination to the male harmonizes with nature because it parallels the subordination of the flesh to the spirit. He wrote that in the resurrection the female body would lose its sexuality and become more fitted to glory than shame. The male, he thought, must love in the woman the creature of God, but he must also despise her sexual characteristics (Augustine, 1900: 778-779).

Augustine represented the common understanding of the church fathers, who viewed sexual intercourse as inherently evil and advised married men to stay away from the house of God and the sacraments if they had engaged in it recently. The Medieval scholasticism of Thomas Aquinas followed essentially the teaching of the church fathers in the area of sexuality. Aquinas contended that sexual intercourse had been tainted with concupiscence and irrationality as a result of the Fall. He believed it to be a woman's duty to assume a passive role during sexual intercourse, an act he insisted must always carry the intent of procreation. The evil of the sexual act resides not in desiring it, or in the pleasure that accompanies it, but rather in the way it numbs reason, a faculty already weakened by original sin (*Summa Theologica* i, ii, XXXIX, Art. 1).

What religious institutions have been increasingly confronted with is the necessity to provide moral guidelines which are consistent with the teachings of the Gospels and yet responsive to the needs of individual Christians and today's American society. As a whole, American society even if professing to base itself on Judeo-Christian morality, pursues a hedonistic philosophy of life. It advertises the moral goodness of comfort and wealth and the right of the individual to pursue as many material riches as he possibly can. In this philosophy, which pervades the advertising media, sex plays an overwhelming role. Almost everything that needs to be peddled is advertised within a sexual atmosphere of acquisition. The rise in the standard of living for millions of Americans has meant more time for leisure and for the temptations of the flesh.

The churches usually react sharply and negatively to what they consider explicit sex, but at the same time they themselves make use of essentially the same advertising techniques that they criticize. Campaigns against pornography in the media, especially against hard-core magazines such as *Penthouse* and the *Playboy* television channel, are carried out by fundamentalist groups who themselves propagate throughout the media the individualistic ethics of consumerism and material comfort.

Yet, the Roys remark, "American culture is a living lie in its attitude toward sex: it preaches one set of values; it lives another" (1968: 32). We are flooded by sexual stimulants—magazines, books, movies—which constantly insinuate the desirability and thrill of illicit and adulterous love affairs. But at the same time our culture severely punishes anyone who dares to contradict in practice the traditional puritanical concepts of fidelity and monagamous love. This contradiction between theory and practice, plus the overwhelming impact of modernity, have contributed to a rethinking of the moral guidelines on the part of many Christian churches. Consequently, the emphasis on the moral duty of following one's conscience and of taking responsibility for one's actions is being balanced by a catechism that insists on one's duty to love his neighbor and his faith community. As usual, we find that some individual Christian theologians and moralists are going beyond the position of the institutional churches and are searching for and offering solutions to these dilemmas. Nevertheless, some churches have dared to blaze new paths in the area of sexual morality. Prominent among them are the Quakers, the British Council of Churches, and the Presbyterian Church.

THE CHURCHES AND ADULTERY

The 1966 Quaker pronouncement on sexual morality set some bold new standards for Christian conduct in sexual matters. Taking its cue from the Gospels' central command to "love thy neighbor," the pronouncement defines sin as "the exploitation of another human being." It states that, "the Christian standard of chastity should not be measured by a physical act, but should be a standard of human relationship, applicable within marriage as well as outside of it." Confronting the specific reality of American sexual habits, it says "it is right and proper that many boys and girls and young men and women should fall in and out of love a number of times before they marry." Furthermore, "whenever the most transient relationship has, as it may have, an element of true tenderness of mutual giving and receiving, it has in it something of good" (1972: 74). The Quaker statement tackles the issue of adultery directly by recommending that triangular sexual relationships be resolved on the basis of human relationships, not on "the nature of the act" (1972: 121). The statement is deliberately vague so as to allow individuals to make decisions on these matters on the basis of concrete human situations rather than on the presumption that triangular sexual relationships are *per se* sinful.

In matters of sexuality, the Protestant Churches of the British Isles (the Church of England, the Church of Scotland, the Free Churches, the Church of Wales and Ireland, the Salvation Army, the Quaker Church, the Unitarian and Free Christian Churches, plus five interdenominational groups) have incorporated into their guidelines a far-reaching report prepared by their advisory committee on "Sex, Marriage and the Family." The report says that simply following the rules of the church dogma is not what makes an act morally good and that rules admit of exceptions. Then the report makes the precedent-setting statement, "sexual intercourse should not be confined within the married state" (1966: 62-63).

The United Presbyterian Church's position is not too different. A report prepared by a committee to its General Assembly entitled "Sexuality and the Human Community" affirms that "interpersonal relations should enhance rather than limit the spiritual freedom of the individuals involved." Sexual fidelity in marriage is seen as not necessarily broken by a triangular relationship: "We recognize that there may be exceptional circumstances where extramarital sexual activity may not be contrary to the interests of a faithful concern for the well-being of the marriage partner, as it might be in the case when one partner suffers permanent mental and physical incapacity" (Francoeur, 1972: 96). As Robert Francoeur remarks, the United Presbyterian Church no longer thinks that fidelity in marriage and coital exclusivity are synonymous (1972: 97).

PROTESTANT MORALISTS AND ADULTERY

These new official attitudes on the part of some Protestant churches have had a clear impact on the thinking and praxis of Protestant theologians and moralists and reflects as well the thought of Protestant theologians who follow the lead of the Lutheran Dietrich Bonhoeffer. Whenever the Christian, says Bonhoeffer, conceives of his obligations in terms of the legalistic application of ready-made rules and principles (even the Sermon on the Mount), he evades his responsibility. To base Christian decision on a universally accepted set of moral laws is to provide a "way from man to God," and to make our relationship with God something that we can control. Acting according to principle inevitably becomes a form of self-justification. Furthermore, adds Bonhoeffer, dependence upon principles and laws imperils freedom. Only "acting from freedom is creative." The responsible man acts in the freedom of his own self, although he must consider his fellow beings as well as questions of principle. It is he himself who must observe, judge, weigh up, decide, and then act (1965a: 46, 217; 1956: 43-44). Thus the morality of an act is not simply decided by the individual as he pleases, as if he could create his own morality for each situation. Bonhoeffer is as far from situational ethics as he is from "going by the book."

SITUATION ETHICS

Prominent among Protestant theologians and moralists who follow in the footsteps of Bonhoeffer and other Lutheran divines such as Reinhold Niebuhr and Paul Tillich, but that have gone far beyond them in the area of human sexuality, are Rustum and Della Roy and Joseph Fletcher. The Roys, who have taught physical sciences at

Pennsylvania State University, are fully involved in church affairs, especially counseling, and have led the debate on sexuality from the perspective of Christian morality since the late 1960s. Noting that many Christian churches have abandoned the Manichaean view that sex is dirty *per se,* they defend the position that not all extramarital sexual relations are automatically sinful: "Rightness or wrongness has nothing, absolutely nothing, to do with whether or not physical juxtaposition of sex organs has occurred" (1968: 87).

The Roys have tried to formulate guidelines for sexual morality that they consider realistic as well as truly Christian, even when their concept of what being a Christian is runs counter to the interpretations of the churches. They confront the thorny issue of adultery by acknowledging that the traditional monogamous marriage is in deep trouble in the United States. Not only has the divorce rate reached fifty percent but, worse still, the actual divorce rate, which does not show up in statistics, is estimated to be around seventy-five percent because seventy-five percent of American marriages today are a bust (Francoeur, 1972: 87). They note that in a society where there is a disproportionately larger number of women, where boredom and routine are compounded by a dramatic increase in life expectancy, and where millions of middle-class housewives have returned to work after their children are grown, even the most ideal of marriages faces an uphill battle. It is, therefore, unrealistic to insist on an all-out ban on extramarital sex.

Actually, the Roys don't believe that access to regular sexual satisfaction is a basic human right on a plane with the right to food and shelter or the right to worship (1970: 19-26). But they also believe that taboos have turned sexuality into an esoteric activity when, in fact, it should be viewed like many other human activities, such as art and music (1968: 96). They point out that traditional monogamy has exacerbated the problem of divorce in the United States; we should find a less hurtful way to terminate marriage (1970: 19-26). But the Roys are far from advocating free love. They make the distinction between *extra*-marital and *co*-marital; extra-marital affairs are seen as usually wrong and harmful, while co-marital affairs are noncompetitive and have the consent of the three parties involved. This means that if an affair harms an already existing relationship between husband and wife, it is morally wrong; if it does not, it may be morally proper (1968: 98-99).

The Roys see in bigamy a possible solution for a troubled marriage: "The flat assertion that no man can have a good, deep relationship, including sexual intercourse, with more than one woman at at time is patent idiocy. . . . To sum up: We find that sexual relations with persons other than a spouse are becoming more common. When other criteria of appropriateness are fulfilled, such relations do not necessarily destroy or hurt a marriage, nor do they inflict an unbearable hurt on the partner not involved. Indeed, when human need is paramount, such relationships can serve as the vehicle of faithfulness to God. . . . We are claiming then that no black-and-white case can be made against sexual intimacies (including coitus) between persons not married to each other" (1968: 99-107). They consequently suggest that bigamy be legitimized—in order to strengthen monogamy.

The Roys believe that monogamy might even be harmful to the fundamental aims of society. They argue that the traditional American family often breeds egotism at the expense of educating and developing concerned, loving, sharing citizens. The nuclear family monopolizes one's time, affections, and concern: "It is just damned difficult to be any kind of a committed Christian with a family in the suburbs." Their advice is that the erotic family community be expanded into a network of relationships that takes into account the millions of single women who are sexually active yet unable to marry, by legalizing bigamy, and by making marital difficulties and divorce less destructive of the personality (1970: 153-157).

Joseph Fletcher, a Congregationalist and moral theologian who has caused quite a stir in the last fifteen years, is recognized as the main proponent of Situation Ethics in the United States. With Anglican Bishop John Robinson, he is an important defender of what has been called "situational morality" (see Robinson, 1963; 1968). The cornerstone of Fletcher's ethics is *agape,* or Christian love, and his methodology for moral decision-making encompasses the following steps: (1) Begin always from the one supreme law of love; (2) take into consideration the *sophia* (wisdom) of the church and of the given culture with their principles and laws; and (3) reach a decision as to whether or not *sophia* can help the responsible self fulfill the commands of love (1966: 27-28). These premises lay the foundation for Fletcher's six maxims of morality: (1) Only one "thing" is intrinsically good; namely, love. Nothing else at all; (2) The ruling norm of Christian decision is love and nothing else; (3) Love and justice are the same, for love is justice distributed and nothing else; (4) Love wills the neighbor's good whether we like him or not; (5) Only the end justifies the means and nothing else; (6) Love's decisions are made situationally, not prescriptively (1966: 33).

Fletcher's main target is Legalism, or the enslavement to absolute principles or laws: "It is more moral to go to bed with the woman next door whom you really love, than to have coital exercise with your wife whom you hate." Since no act can be considered evil or immoral *per se,* sexual intercourse may or may not be an act of love; it is neutral *per se,* and acquires moral value from the minds and wills who make it: "Even a transient sex liaison, if it has the elements of caring, of tenderness and selfless concern, is better than a mechanical exercise of 'conjugal rights' between two uncaring and antagonistic marriage partners" (1966: 431). And he specifies: "Adultery, for instance, is ordinarily wrong, not in itself but because the emotional, legal, and spiritual entailments are such that the overall effects are evil and hurtful rather than helpful—at least in our present-day Western society. But there is always the outside case, the unusual situation, what Karl Barth calls the 'ultima ratio,' in which adultery could be the right and good thing. This writer knows of such a case . . ." (1966: 431).

CRITIQUE OF SITUATION ETHICS

If a number of Protestant divines and moralists agree with Fletcher, his Protestant critics are many and quite thorough. Most would initially disagree that moral laws are not part of divine Revelation (Fletcher, 1967: 133). John C. Bennett of the Union Theological Seminary of New York, James M. Gustafson of the Yale Divinity School, E. Clinton Gardner of the School of Theology at Emory University, Gabriel Fackre of the Lancaster Theological Seminary in Pennsylvania, Harmon L. Smith of the Duke Divinity School, and

Gerald Kennedy, Methodist Bishop of the Los Angeles area, are all major critics of Fletcher's *Situation Ethics* (1967, *passim*). Bishop Kennedy contends that Fletcher absolutizes *agape* and eliminates the place of law in morality. Good intentions and good motives, says the bishop, are not enough for sound moral judgement; too much is left to choice and to individual decision. Even in a society of Christian saints, the law would be a necessity. In commenting on Fletcher's stand on adultery, Bishop Kennedy adds: "There might be extenuating circumstances for adultery and one should not sit in judgment of the individuals involved, but it is objectively against the law of God (1967: 140-141, 144-145). The bishop concludes by remarking that Fletcher's *Situation Ethics* is filled with moral arrogance (1967: 148).

In analyzing Fletcher's situational morality concerning adultery, Evelyn Millis Duval (a Methodist) and Wayne Anderson (a Congregationalist, like Fletcher) point out that sexual intercourse outside its proper context of monogamic marriage can wreck the value system of the human personality and can destroy the whole meaning of loyalty, service, sharing, caring, and genuine love; this is so, they add, because sexual intercourse entails the totality of sharing, of persons, of value systems, and of all that is most intimate and personal in man (cf. E. M. Duval, 1965). William F. May, another Protestant moral theologian, also sees major flaws in situation ethics, especially in its apparent failure to take into account the biblical concept of sin, with all its implications: "My sin is not the name of a perfume that supplements my personality in its allure. It stands for whatever mars, anuls, inflates, depresses, disrupts, distorts, or abandons humanity" (1965: 7). "This"—says the Jesuit theologian Thomas Wassmer—"is a striking example of what sin does to others; what it does to the personality of the sinner is contained in the term *stain* (macula), i.e., uncleanness, dirt, filth, guilt" (1969: 34).

CATHOLICISM AND SEXUALITY

The Roman Catholic Church has, since Vatican II, made a gigantic effort to bring itself into closer contact with contemporary man and society. This "aggiornamento" was necessitated by the fact that a widening gulf had been opened both between the language of the church and that of the modern world and between the church's teachings and their acceptance by the faithful at large. Vatican II (especially its Constitution, *Gaudium et Spes*) views human sexuality, and especially marriage, as an expression of love which is also associated with procreation. Although it does not see the function of marriage as essentially procreative and it defines marriage as a community of love, it does not attribute a value of its own to sexual love *per se*. Not surprisingly, Pope Paul VI's encyclical *Humanae vitae,* which reiterated the Catholic Church's ban on artificial means of birth control, led many Catholic theologians to be critical of its argumentation and of its conclusions. Their main opposition stemmed from the fact that the encyclical essentially espouses a theory of natural law (that of Scholasticism, notably Thomism) that they say is pagan. Thomas Aquinas defines natural law very much as does Ulpian (d. 228 A.D.), the Roman jurist of the late empire: "that which nature teaches all animals." Man's rationality and freedom of choice are not given primary consideration. This they see as unrealistic and in conflict with the findings of contemporary philosophy and science (Wassmer, 1969: xii).

Pronouncements issued by Rome after Vatican II, including the latest *Instruction of the Congregation for the Doctrine of the Faith* (CDF) *on the Pastoral Care of Homosexual Persons,* have substantially reflected the thrust of that Council and of *Humanae vitae.* On December 29, 1975 the CDF issued its *Declaration of Sexual Ethics* where one reads: "The use of the sexual function has its true meaning and moral rectitude only in true marriage." After stating that such truth comes from Revelation and from the Church's authentic interpretation of natural law, the Declaration continues: "Every genital act must be within the framework of marriage," because premarital sex "cannot ensure, in sincerity and fidelity, the interpersonal relationship between a man and a woman, nor especially can they protect this relationship from whims and caprices" (1975: nos. 5 and 7). It is quite obvious that if the CDF condemns premarital sex, adultery is absolutely out of the question. In fact, the 1983 guidelines issued by the Sacred Congregation for Catholic Education confirm CDF's 1975 *Declaration:* Intimate relations are licit only within marriage. It specifically states that "manifestations of the merely genital are a moral disorder because they are outside the matrimonial context of authentic love" (1975: 30).

The main thrust of every official declaration of the Catholic Church has been the primacy and absoluteness of moral standards and an obvious hesitation to allow for exceptions in the areas of premarital and extramarital sex. Still, Catholic teaching greatly emphasizes the role of the individual conscience in all decision-making. Passing judgment on the objective morality of human actions, even of specific actions, does not warrant sitting in judgment of the individual.

CATHOLIC MORALISTS AND NATURAL LAW

Catholic moral theologians in the United States have taken seriously Vatican II's proclamation of freedom of expression and of debate within the Church and, consequently, have dared to engage in such controversial issues as birth control, premarital sex, abortion, sterilization, adultery, and even homosexuality. Many of these theologians are unhappy with the guidelines emanating from Rome and have, as a result, taken what they consider a more realistic and more correct approach to human sexuality. Prominent among them are Charles Curran, Daniel Maguire, Michael Valente, Robert Francoeur, and Thomas A. Wassmer.

Father Charles Curran, Professor of Moral Theology at the Catholic University of America, has been recently involved in a dispute with the Vatican over issues such as abortion and birth control. He argues that a Catholic theologian has the right to freely discuss doctrinal matters not defined as dogmas by the magisterium. The crux of the controversy seems to be how much freedom of inquiry the magisterium allows to an individual Catholic. According to the thinking of the Church, the magisterium may be extraordinary, namely, the teaching authority exercised by the pope or the ecumenical council when defining matters of morals or of doctrine for the whole Church. Otherwise all magisteria are ordinary. Curran contends that teachings of the ordinary magisterium are not set in stone and do not compel the individual theologian to give his unquestioned assent until they are proclaimed as dogmas. The church's approach to sexuality, says Curran, has been conditioned for many centuries by its acceptance of a definition of natural law that comes from Aquinas's and Ulpian's definition of natural law as "that which nature teaches all animals"; as a result, traditional theology has been using the words "nature" and "natural" to mean animal or biological processes. Man's rational nature, in contrast, is not necessarily "natural" (1970: 108). The consequence of this understanding of natural law was that most manuals of moral theology neglected the personal aspects of the sexual unions. A dichotomy was created between man's rationality and his animality: the animal layer of man was seen as retaining its tendencies independently of the demands of his rationality. Man, therefore, was not to intervene in animal processes such as procreation. To do so—to use contraceptives, for example—would be to violate the Creator's designs regarding sexual intercourse (1970: 109).

But true anthropology, says Curran, must start with what is proper to man, namely, his rationality, his ability to bring order and intelligence into the world and to orient the animal and the biological world toward a truly human purpose. No human moral act should be viewed in terms of its physical structure. Nature must not be the norm but rather the servant of man (1970: 109). According to Curran, Thomistic ethics do not do justice to Aquinas himself, who distinguishes between natural law *(lex naturalis)* and natural right *(ius naturale)*. Natural right comprises the basic human tendencies and inclinations which need to be studied empirically and then regulated and directed by reason; natural law is human reason seeking to regulate the total human reality, man's body as well as his soul. Natural law, then, is not a source of obligation and restraint for man, but a rational guide for the development of human existence.

Curran contends that "there is no one Roman Catholic position on a particular moral issue, barring all other possibilities, because of the complexity of moral issues and the need for relational and empirical considerations which can lead to different ethical judgments" (1974: 27). He also believes that there has never been an authoritative, infallible, *ex-cathedra* teaching of the magisterium on any specifically moral matter (1974: 22).

Michael Valente, who has taught religious studies at Seton Hall University, and has been involved in the controversial issue of homosexual rights and pastoral care of homosexuals, claims that the church has often not drawn the proper conclusions from its own principles. He notes that when, in 1951, Pope Pius XII authorized the rhythm method of birth control, he already implied that intercourse and procreation were not indissolubly bound together and that, consequently, the enjoyment of the sexual act did not have to carry the intention of the propagation of the species. The pope, by allowing human intervention in what was called "natural law," recognized the role of reason in directing human nature. This means, says Valente (1980: 150), that "if sexual activity can be guaranteed non-procreative, it is no longer hemmed in by the rules and guidelines previously established out of reverence for the life of the potential child."

Valente agrees with Curran that a different interpretation of natural law makes traditional Church rules on sexuality obsolete: "Christian morality is almost entirely the morality of the Old Testament, especially as it concerns Christian attitudes toward sexuality." He points out that contemporary biblical scholarship has made clear that moral pronouncements found in the Scriptures are simply the expressions of the author's convictions and, as isolated pronouncements, do not have the absolute value of inerrancy (1980: 153). If the central objective of matrimony is to create a community of love, and if all sexuality must be directed to contributing to the growth of the total person, then every "sexual act must be judged on its own merits, by what it contributes in a particular situation to the growth and mutual . . . creativeness of the two persons involved" (Valente, 1970: 75). He even seems to echo Fletcher's situation ethics when he says that in procreational sex, morality is determined according to "the extent to which love or concern is present or absent and on the basis of whether the presence or absence of this love or concern causes injury to oneself or one's neighbor or is essentially non-injurious" (1970: 135).

Robert T. Francoeur, an embryologist and educator, has probably gone further than any other Catholic moralist in the area of sexuality. Beginning from a position quite similar to that of the

Roys and Joseph Fletcher, he argues that traditional monogamy is in trouble in this country for two reasons: it withholds from a widening portion of the American citizenry both a voice and a role in society, and it also denies millions of Americans a socially acceptable way of obtaining sexual satisfaction. Furthermore, traditional monogamy has failed to adjust to the possibility that marriages originally based on parental arrangement and economic advantages may years later become unlivable from the standpoint of the husband and wife's private desires (1972: 88).

Francoeur contends that insistence on the rule that there should be no sex outside marriage, either before or after the ceremony, actually militates against today's monogamous marriage. If, as it is the case, premarital sex is often tolerated, fidelity is reduced to a very simplistic black-and-white prohibition of sexual intercourse with anyone other than one's spouse (1972: 90). Most married persons, continues Francoeur, define infidelity as adultery and nothing more, and take no account of emotional and psychological infidelity. A more accurate definition would be to see adultery as taking place whenever a married person repeatedly has to look outside marriage for a need not fulfilled by the person's spouse. Thus, marriage experts who estimate that sixty percent of the married men and one-third of the married women engage in adultery sometime in their married lives may be understating their case simply because what they define as adultery may not necessarily be so. In fact, says Francoeur, "our classical definition of fidelity is clearly inadequate and has become even more so with the debates over artificial insemination, embryo transplants, etc. as violators of marital exclusivity" (1972: 93).

If traditional monogamy is finding itself increasingly under siege, what can be done about it? Francoeur suggests that we accept a more flexible definition of fidelity, one which allows for occasional sexual relations with persons other than one's spouse within the context of a lifelong marriage. This, he comments, will become more popular than the institutionalized American practice of serial polygamy—i.e., one marriage after the other—because it adapts better to the present pressures of life and society within a more stable framework (1972: 93). He does not specifically say that "more popular" is the equivalent of "morally right," but he cites the case of Sweden, where some couples are allowed to save or strengthen their marriages through extramarital experiences; the wrong or right of those experiences is then decided in terms of the whole context, and not of the sex act itself. "If extramarital sex harms the already existing human relationship, then it is morally wrong. If the extramarital sex enhances the human dimension, then it may be morally proper" (1972: 99).

Francoeur agrees with the observation of the British philosopher and theologian John Macmurray, who calls for an ethics based on emotional integrity, and not just on external intellectual morality. Therein lies "the essence of Christ's teachings because the individual, contrary to what Descartes believed, cannot be abstracted from his social context and this same person is not reducible to his intellect. Since the individual is inseparably intellect/emotion and his dynamic personality exists only in a unique situation in relation to other persons, it is just as immoral to act in violation of one's emotions, or to pretend to feel otherwise than one in fact does, as it is to speak contrary to what one's intellect knows to be true. Emotional lies are just as immoral as intellectual lies" (1972: 114-115). Francoeur then cites William Graham Cole: "Sexual intercourse based on genuine love, on sincere mutuality, requires no other justification to validate it, not even marriage" (1972: 115).

Finally, Francoeur echoes the observations of Rustum and Della Roy regarding what they consider the destructive tendencies of monogamic marriage in the United States: the institution of marriage American-style, as practiced by the majority, encourages selfishness, possessiveness, and exclusivity instead of sharing and openness. As a consequence, "the marital contract, which actually only aims at restricting exclusivity to sexuality, does a great deal of damage symbolically" (1972: 91).

CATHOLIC CRITIQUE OF SITUATIONAL MORALITY

The Jesuit priest, Thomas A. Wassmer, has undertaken a major critique of Joseph Fletcher's *Situation Ethics,* so he can hardly be classified as a situational moralist. He is, however, also critical of the rigidity of the Vatican's position on sexual morality, especially of its claim that in union with the world's Catholic bishops, it is the sole teaching authority in the Church. There is, contends Wassmer, more than one magisterium. Other than papal/episcopal magisterium, there is also the magisterium of the laity and that of the theologians (1969: 96). He concurs with Father Daniel Maguire that "episcopal consecration does not convey theological expertise."

In analyzing situation ethics, Wassmer notes what other critics have remarked, namely that Fletcher's system revolves around a single concept that he never properly defines or qualifies. If situational morality, says Wassmer, wants to be a true Christian morality, it must be absolutely serious about *all* the values found in a situation: "The action must correspond to a love which strives to help men to the fullest possible development of their personality in responsible freedom" (1969: 160). And he adds: "Situationalism faces the difficulty of trivializing morality. By making all morality subjective and situational, by denying that there are any acts, however definable, which are intrinsically evil, the situation should have become the real ethical computer room for situational analysis" (1969: 144).

Properly understood, observes Wassmer, all morality is situational—it takes into account the paramount importance of circumstances, motives, historical evolution, and the subjectivity of the moral agent (1969: 133). Wassmer implies that the New Morality, or Situation Ethics, is not truly Christian morality because its frame of reference is not Christian; its concept of love reflects clearly humanistic, secular characteristics. The one question that a situationalist should ask himself, notes Wassmer, is not what love demands but what the Person who is Love Incarnate demands. "Jesus never denies the existence or the need of the law nor of wrongdoing. He never denies that man can transgress the law of God" (1969: 143).

Wassmer also disagrees with Fletcher's belief that no act is *per se* moral or immoral, that it is always dependent on the person who commits it. Certain acts, such as rape and genocide, are in themselves acts of hatred and without any redeeming value, and no good intention can turn them into morally good acts. And he also seems to challenge Herbert McCabe's assertion that sexual intercourse is *per se* a loving act (1966: 432-434). To deny that goodness can only come from man's mind and will and never from man's body is to fall into a dualistic morality of fateful consequences: "Sexual intercourse has intrinsic value as an act of love, is *per se an act of love,* and this meaning and significance can be abused by the circumstances and motivation in and for which it is performed (1969: 147).

According to Francoeur, Wassmer believes that having sexual intercourse with someone other than one's spouse is not necessarily adultery (1972: 95-96). There is nothing in Wassmer's *Christian Ethics for Today,* however, that confirms such a conclusion. What Wassmer said in a book he co-authored with Fletcher (1970) is that he "would not call an act adultery if it is an act done with loving concern" (1972: 95). What remains to be shown is whether there is true and authentic Christian love in any extramarital or comarital act of sexual intercourse. Wassmer makes his position clear by quoting another Jesuit, W. Molinski, professor of the Free University of Berlin: "The Christian position is definitely this: it is only in the stable security of indissoluble marriage that the self-surrender of the sexual act can fully correspond to the dignity of the human person . . . Our attitude to sexual matters is ultimately determined by a conception of man which derives from revelation" (1969: 161-162). What Wassmer actually says is that "it cannot be shown categorically that premarital sexual relations are always wrong, either subjectively or objectively" (1969: 162).

Wassmer believes that situation ethics does not take full account of the consequences of acts which, though made with loving concern and all the good intentions, can undermine and even wreck the personality. He quotes James T. Burtchaell's sharp criticism of the New Morality: "The New Moralists are saying that the moral value of an act is what you put into it. They neglect, it seems to me, that it also involves what you get out of the act." Morality should be concerned with more than just guilt and innocence: "A morality that is concerned with guilt or innocence thinks of acts only as responsible expressions of the self, and neglects that they are also shapers of the self. Now the fact that repetitive evil actions incur guilt is extrinsic; the intrinsic, and to my mind more important, fact is that they make the doer less loving" (Burtchael, 1966: 11-13).

More than one critic has accused situation ethics of being the ethics of a secular or humanistic religion and little more than a sophisticated form of relativism. For the humanistic or existentialist ethics of the secular religion, "God is a myth," "sin is like any other form of human emotion," "a sociological view of guilt points to nothing beyond man," and one's moral conduct must be determined solely by an "insight into particular people's needs and expectations at particular times" (Hannay, 1978: 179-192; Barnes, 1978: 71-72). Fletcher imagines his New Morality as playing the role of mediator between ethical absolutism and "the unprincipled ethics of existentialism" (1967: 168). He seems to associate himself with humanistic ethics: "We have to validate happiness and moral concern humanly, not theistically. . . . The ancient maxim was true, *conscientia semper sequenda est* [one must always follow his or her own conscience], but it is our conscience, not God's" (1978: 254).

Both Fletcher and Francoeur often appear to justify the morality or advisability of human actions in terms of a secular religion: "everyone is doing it," "science (or nature, or philosophy) point in this or that direction," "it is all right if nobody gets hurt," etc. Furthermore, situational morality, just like secular religion, seems to ignore or play down the biblical and Christian concept of sin. Fletcher's well-coined phrases hide serious flaws in the understanding of the Christian virtues of faith, hope, and love. Some examples: "By faith we live in the past; by hope we live in the future; but by love we live in the present." "Legalism is wrong because it tries to push love back into the past, into old decisions already made" (1966: 142). Bishop Gerald Kennedy remarked, in his critique of the New Morality, that good intentions and motives are not enough for sound judgments, that too much (in *Situation Ethics*) is left to choice and to individual decision, and that, again, even in a society of saints the laws would be indispensable (1967: 144-145). It appears that the kind of ethics advocated by Fletcher, Francoeur, and the Roys will always be the ethics of an elite, of a well-educated minority of people who can make well-rounded judgments by weighing all the implications of their acts in terms of their Christian commitment; it cannot be the ethics of the majority who must rely on rules, maxims, and guidelines to go along with their desire to do the loving thing.

FINAL OBSERVATIONS

It is my conviction that the churches will not significantly relax their guidelines on such issues of sexual morality as homosexuality and adultery. The nature of institutions is to deal with rules and absolutes, and they normally trail the thinking of their intellectual elites or, in this case, their theologians. But, will they allow their educators and pastors increasingly more freedom to move in the direction of a sexual morality which integrates not only the thrust of the "Good News of Christ" but also is in line with the advancements of the social and physical sciences? What happened to Father Curran seems to indicate that the Catholic Church might not do so.

Within Protestantism, one will see a continuation and even a widening of the gulf that separates the extremes of fundamentalist rigidity in the areas of sexual morality on the one hand and the relativism and flexibility of situational morality on the other. The majority of Protestants at large would, at least in questions of sexual morality, perhaps be closer to the fundamentalist position even if in socio-political and economic questions their allegiance will remain with an individualistic ethics of limited Christian content.

As for Catholics, official positions on sexual morality will greatly depend on the kind of leadership they get from the pope and the bishops. If present attempts to recentralize doctrinal decision-making and to turn back the clock by repudiating Vatican II fail, one may expect a much greater flexibility in the guidelines for sexual morality emanating from Episcopal conferences and local Ordinaries, especially in regard to birth control. It is most unlikely, however, that the Roman Catholic Church's position on adultery will change measurably. From a sociological point of view, it is highly unrealistic to expect that a sexual morality elaborated by unmarried males will satisfy a large portion of Catholic couples. It is no surprise that those views seen as more extreme among Catholic moral theologians are espoused by laymen and married people like Francoeur and Valente. What one can expect is that church authorities will show greater understanding and compassion with specific cases in which adultery is involved without changing their theoretical stance.

On the other hand, I believe that Andrew Greeley's observation that most Catholics in the United States do not follow the moral injunctions of their Church must be properly qualified. It might be so in the area of contraception, an area where their thinking is usually shaped by a brand of literature and of media advertising which purports to reflect the findings of science and medicine. It is here that a secular, humanistic ethics plays a significant role in the praxis of the sexual morality of Protestants, Catholics and Jews. This will continue to be so as long as Christians see their spiritual lives in terms of separate and hardly related compartments, as if what they do during the week had little relation with what they do in church on Sunday.

One can expect that the majority of the Christian churches will continue to see adultery as an abomination, even while increasing numbers of individual Christians see it as morally justifiable and, in exceptional cases, even as an act of Christian love. Most Christians, however, will continue to believe that adultery is always wrong, no matter what the circumstances and the motives. Only a major shift in the perception of the role of sexuality in human life would force a significant rethinking of the Judeo-Christian ethics of sexuality. The German Catholic theologian C. Jaime Snoek sketches the following picture: "How will the man of tomorrow live his sexuality? Will he have destroyed the tyranny of genitality and replaced it by a more discreet form of eroticism, more widespread, more communicative, permeating all human relationships?" (1970: 121). If socio-political and economic morality undergoes a drastic change and if all Snoek's questions are then answered in the affirmative, adultery will still remain a controversial and divisive issue for years to come.

REFERENCES

Abbott, W. 1966. *The Documents of Vatican II.* New York: Herder & Herder.
Aurelius, Augustus. 1900. *De Civitate Dei.* Paris: Garnier.
Barnes, Hazel. 1978. *An Existentialist Ethics.* Chicago: University of Chicago Press.
Batchelor, Edward, Jr. 1980. *Homosexuality and Ethics.* New York: Pilgrim.
Boeckle, Franz. 1970. *The Future of Marriage as Institution.* Concilium 55.
Bonhoeffer, Dietrich. 1965a. *Ethics.* New York: Macmillan.
———. 1965b. *No Rusty Swords.* New York: Harper & Row.

Burtchael, James. 1966. "The Conservation of Situation Ethics." *New Black-friars* (October).

Curran, Charles. 1970. *Contemporary Problems in Moral Theology.* Notre Dame, Ind.: Fides.

──── . 1974. *New Perspectives in Moral Theology.* Notre Dame, Ind.: Fides.

Doherty, Dennis. 1979. *Dimensions of Human Sexuality.* Garden City, N.Y.: Doubleday.

Duval, Evelyn. 1965. *Why Wait Until Marriage.* New York: Association Press.

Fletcher, Joseph. 1967. *Moral Responsibility.* Philadelphia, Pa.: Westminster.

──── . 1966. "Love is the Only Measure." *Commonweal,* 83.

──── . 1966. *Situation Ethics: The New Morality.* Philadelphia, Pa.: Westminster.

──── . 1980. "Situation Ethics: The Groundwork." In *Humanistic Ethics,* edited by Morris B. Storer, 253-261. Buffalo, N.Y.: Prometheus.

Fletcher, Joseph, and Thomas Wassmer. 1970. *Hello Lovers: An Invitation to Situation Ethics.* Washington, D.C.: Corpus Books.

Francoeur, Robert. 1972. *Eve's New Rib.* New York: Harcourt, Brace, Jovanovich.

Greeley, Andrew. 1977. *The American Catholic.* New York: Basic Books.

Hannay, Alastair. 1980. "Propositions Towards a Humanist Consensus in Ethics." In *Humanistic Ethics,* edited by Morris B. Storer, 179-192. Buffalo, N.Y.: Prometheus.

Heron, A. 1964. *Toward a Quaker View of Sex: Friends Home Service Committee.* London.

Kennedy, Gerald. 1967. "The Nature of Heresy." In *Storm Over Ethics.* Philadelphia, Pa.: United Church Press.

Lewis, C. S. 1951. *The Allegory of Love.* London: Oxford University Press.

May, William. 1966. *A Catalogue of Sins.* New York: Holt, Rinehart, and Winston.

McCabe, Herbert. 1966. "The Validity of Absolutes." *Commonweal* 83.

Morrison, Eleanor, and Vera Borosage. 1973. *Human Sexuality: Contemporary Perspectives.* Palo Alto, Calif.: Mayfield.

Robinson, John. 1964. *Christian Morals Today.* Philadelphia, Pa.: Westminster.

──── . 1963. *Honest to God.* Philadelphia, Pa.: Westminster.

Roy, Rustum, and Della Roy. 1968. *Honest Sex.* New York: New American Library.

──── . 1970. "Is Monogamy Outdated?" *The Humanist,* 30: 19-26.

Sacred Congregation for Catholic Education. 1983. *Educational Guidance in Human Love: Outline for Sex Education.* Rome.

Sacred Congregation for the Doctrine of the Faith. 1975. *Declaration of Sexual Ethics.* Washington, D.C.: National Conference of Catholic Bishops.

Sex and Morality: A Report Presented to the British Council of Churches. 1966. Philadelphia.

Sexuality and the Human Community: Report to the General Assembly of the United Presbyterian Church in the United States. 1967.

Snoek, Jaime. 1970. "Marriage and the Institutionalization of Sexual Relations. *Concilium,* 55.

Valente, Michael. 1970. *Sex: The Radical View of a Catholic Theologian.* New York: Bruce Books.

Various authors. 1967. *Storm Over Ethics.* Philadelphia, Pa.: United Church Press.

Wassmer, Thomas A. 1969. *Christian Ethics for Today.* Milwaukee, Wis.: Bruce.

5

Rose Marie Cutting
ADULTERY IN AMERICAN LITERATURE

THE EUROPEAN TRADITION

"To go by literature, adultery would seem to be the most notable occupation of both Europe and America. Few are the novels that fail to allude to it," says Denis de Rougement in his pioneering study, *Love in the Western World* (1940: 4). In the masterpieces of the great nineteenth-century European writers—such as Stendal, Flaubert, Balzac, Zola—adultery is indeed a chief theme. De Rougement traces the origin of this theme to the courtly love tradition which flourished to such an extent during the Middle Ages that it became a kind of religion. While virtually all writers professed to be Christian, the lovers whom they glorified in their work often engaged in the unchristian practice of adultery—see, for example, Tristram and Iseult, Lancelot and Guinevere.

In the courtly love tradition, "love and marriage were incompatible" (1940: 25). Too easy a consummation of love was not likely to lead to the intense passions of the great love stories. This intensity of passion was generated only when love was forbidden and had to overcome apparently insurmountable obstacles. According to Leslie Fiedler, the woman in the courtly love tradition must be married to someone else and be thus "attainable only with the sense of breaking the deepest taboo" (1966: 52).

Long before the Middle Ages, Homer's epics and the plays of Aeschylus dramatized the destructive effects of adultery on society and family. And after the Middle Ages, adultery formed the basis of tragic or comic plots for Elizabethan and Restoration drama. The novel, a new type of literature developed in the late-eighteenth and early-nineteenth century, likewise focused on adultery as its central subject matter. Written for the middle class, the novel reflected bourgeois values. In this society, marriage was the central contract, the way in which humans harmonized passion and sexuality with

God's laws and society's need for stability. Hence a threat to marriage was considered a major threat to society (Tanner, 1979: 2-3, 13). Because the infidelity of the wife was more likely to destroy the marriage than the husband's infidelity, such novels almost always centered on adulterous women (Tanner, 1979: 13).

THE AMERICAN TRADITION:
THE NINETEENTH CENTURY

Readers of American literature would find it difficult to name American novels written before the twentieth century that treat the theme of adultery. The most notable exception is Nathaniel Hawthorne's *The Scarlet Letter* (1850). Otherwise, only a few extraordinary American writers joined contemporary European writers in focusing on adultery as a literary theme.

In the classic literature of the nineteenth-century America, men explore the freedom offered by the American frontier, a freedom inconsistent with family responsibilities (D. H. Lawrence, 1923; R. W. B. Lewis, 1955). On the frontier, heterosexual relationships gave way to male bonding. Thus the heroes of James Fenimore Cooper's Leatherstocking series (1821-1840) stalk the forest or the prairie with a male Indian companion. As whalers who sail far away from women, Melville's Ishmael and Queequeg forge a strong tie (1851). Huckleberry Finn and Jim similarly leave the women on shore to travel the Mississippi seeking freedom (Twain: 1884).

TEMPTATION AND RENUNCIATION:
NINETEENTH-CENTURY AMERICAN FEMALE AUTHORS

One form of nineteenth-century literature—verse written by and largely for women—often treats the theme of adultery head-on. The dissatisfaction they felt for their husbands and marriages at times tempted these writers to focus on illicit love. After all, women could not raft down the Mississippi like Huck, or sail around the world like Ishmael. Marriage still determined the course of women's lives and limited their adventures.

The very popular female poet Francis Sargent Osgood flirted

with the attractions of adultery. In "Oh! Hasten to My Side" (Watts, 1977: 112-113), for instance, a wife asks her husband to return to her because she is more and more tempted to yield to her love for another man:

> Alas! my peril hourly grows,
>   In every thought and dream;
> Not—not to thee, my spirit goes,
>   But still—yes, to him!
>
> Return with those cold eyes to me,
>   And chill my soul once more,
> Back to the loveless apathy
>   It learn'd so well before!

No respectable nineteenth-century writer could openly advocate adultery. So Osgood avoids the charge of immorality by having the speaker resist her dangerous love. But a marriage of "loveless apathy" with a "cold" husband hardly compensates for renouncing a passionate attachment.

In Osgood's poem "Had We But Met," a woman singularly struggles to overcome an adulterous yearning. "Honor" and "Faith" forbid the love because she is bound by "ties that make my lightest sigh/My faintest flush, at thought of thee, a crime" (Griswold, 1856: 273). Typically, Osgood's readers could enjoy the titillating situation but were not required to give conscious approval. After all, the speaker of the poem was struggling and had not given in to temptation—at least not yet.

Osgood was considered "bold" for her day. In her pioneering study of America's early female poets, Emily Watts concludes that Osgood "said things in verse that would not be said again in America by a woman until the 1890s" (Watts, 1977: 106). Watts is referring to Osgood's frank sensuality and even open sexuality, but the comment applies equally well to Osgood's recurrent theme about the attractions of adultery.

Osgood's life helps explain her poetry. Her husband left her when her marriage failed. He was gone by 1843 when she wrote "Oh! Hasten to My Side." In 1845-1846, Osgood had an affair of some sort with Edgar Allen Poe; this relationship produced poems such as "Song," in which the speaker complains because poetic creation is difficult after a love affair has ended (Watts, 1977: 110).

Osgood's boldness did not prevent her from becoming popular; on the contrary, it probably helps account for the fact that she is one of the poets given the greatest amount of space in the classic nineteenth-century collections of women's verse: Caroline May's *The American Female Poets* (1848: 381-401) and Griswold's *Female Poets of America* (1856: 272-287).

One famous nineteenth-century poet wrote about the temptation to adultery in verse that was not published until the twentieth century. Biographers and critics attribute some of Emily Dickinson's best poetry to her love for the Reverend Charles Wadsworth, a respectably and apparently happily married minister. Wadsworth and Dickinson saw each other only three or four times, and their intimacy was probably emotional rather than physical (Chase, 1951: 74). But they exchanged letters, and Dickinson transformed their separation into a tale of passionate "renunciation" reminiscent of other stories of forbidden love.

Thomas H. Johnson, editor of Dickinson's verse, believes that she channeled her pain into a substantial number of poems when Wadsworth left for San Francisco in 1861. The first lines of these poems clearly indicate the poet's intensity of involvement:

> I got so I could hear his name
> What would I give to see his face
> Wild nights! Wild nights!
> Although I put away his life
> How sick to wait
> I live with him,
> I see his face
> Mine by the right of the white election
> I cannot live with you—that would be life

> Johnson, 1955: 82

If we examine some lines of "I cannot live with you—that would be life," we can see that the prohibition is religious:

> I cannot live with you—
> It would be life—

And life is over there—
Behind the shelf

The Sexton keeps the key to—
Putting up Our life—
His porcelain—
Like a cup—

(Dickinson, 1960: 317)

None of the poems that show Dickinson's relationship with Wadsworth were published in her life, nor were they sent to a correspondent. All remained private expressions of love and renunciation (Johnson, 1955: 82).

NINETEENTH-CENTURY AMERICAN NOVELISTS: THE EXCEPTIONS

Nathaniel Hawthorne

It is not surprising that Nathaniel Hawthorne wrote the most significant treatment of adultery in American literature in the nineteenth century. The frontier myth of freedom from marriage and family was not attractive to Hawthorne. His work continually demonstrates the perils of isolation. In Hawthorne's work, when a husband such as Young Goodman Brown leaves his wife to go to the forest, he encounters the devil rather than the transcendental good discovered by Emerson and Thoreau.

Three basic interpretations have dominated readings of *The Scarlet Letter* since its first publication in 1850. The traditional critic declares that Hawthorne views adultery as a clear violation of the laws of God and of society. Hester Prynne was guilty of breaking one of the commandments by her act of adultery. Nevertheless, Hester's sin is less serious than that of her hypocritical lover Arthur Dimmesdale. Hester sins through passion, but her lover sins through passion and the refusal to publicly share the blame for the consequences of his act. Hester's revenge-hungry husband, Roger Chillingworth, sins in even worse ways by torturing Dimmesdale in secret (Carpenter, 1944: 308-310).

Even those who consider Hester guilty of sin see that there are mitigating circumstances—chiefly the fact that she truly loves Dimmesdale. However, the "romantic" interpretation of the novel says that Hester is not guilty of sin; she "merely acted according to the deepest human instincts" (1944: 309). The guilt in the novel resides *in society* for setting up laws that restrain natural instincts. This interpretation of Hawthorne's classic was suggested by D. H. Lawrence and was popular with the French critics (1944: 311). These critics see the novel as a version of the "religion of love," especially in its adulterous form, created by the tradition of courtly love.

Why, then, did Hawthorne conclude his novel in a moralistic way? Hester and Arthur do not live happily ever after; he dies and she lives only for her daughter and to serve others, without the personal reward of sexual love. Nevertheless, Hawthorne never shows any true repentance in Hester herself, and he does not have her admit that she has sinned: She tells Dimmesdale that "What we did had a consecration of its own" (Hawthorne, 1978: 140) and boldly urges him to go off with her to start a new life.

Hester becomes one of the first great American heroines. Because the Puritan community cast her out, Hester's mind is no longer bound by the traditional morality that judges her actions as sinful. In a famous passage, Hawthorne describes Hester's emancipation from allegiance to traditional beliefs:

> Standing alone in the world . . . alone hopeless of retrieving her position . . . she cast away the fragments of a broken chain. The world's law was no law for her mind . . . She assumed a freedom of speculation, then common enough on the other side of the Atlantic, but which our forefathers, had they known of it, would have held to be a deadlier crime than that stigmatized by the scarlet letter. (1978: 119)

These lines supply evidence for the third major interpretation of Hawthorne's novel: Hester is a heroine because she stands for the lesson of American individualism. She is an example of the philosophy of self-reliance that Ralph Waldo Emerson preached to Americans in the nineteenth century.

The exceptional American writers who treat adultery in the nineteenth century novel tend to follow Hawthorne's example. They focus on a strong independent woman whose claims for freedom make her a new type of heroine in literature. She may resist the pull to adultery or she may claim the right to give herself to whom she wishes. But she does not waver in her faith that she has the right to shape her own destiny on the basis of a personal search for freedom.

Henry James

The theme of adultery is prevalent in the fiction of Henry James, for he is the most European of American novelists. Brought up in Europe as well as in America, he lived much of his adult life in Europe, and was acquainted with Flaubert and other French realists and naturalists who wrote the bourgeois novel centering on marriage and infidelity. Yet James introduces a unique element into this classic plot—the clash between European and American morals.

In the first period of James's writing (approximately 1870 to 1885), the characters are chiefly American and the setting is either America or Europe. Isabel Archer, the protagonist of *The Portrait of a Lady* (1881), is an American heroine who demands the right to control her own destiny in a way that would be impossible for a European woman. Isabel, who has inherited a fortune, turns down two very eligible suitors in order to marry the expatriate Gilbert Osmond. She is tricked into this marriage by Osmond and Madame Merle, who had been adulterous lovers in the past and are chiefly interested in Isabel's money. Osmond is a dilettante and monstrous egoist who attempts to rob Isabel of any personal independence. Isabel gradually comes to understand Osmond's character and Madame Merle's treachery; for the latter promotes the marriage to provide for her daughter Pansy, who has been raised as Osmond's legitimate daughter.

The final scene of the novel shows Isabel resisting her American suitor, Caspar Goodwood, who wants her to leave her husband and live with him. Although Isabel is physically attracted to Goodwood, she returns to her husband in a conclusion that disturbs many readers, but which is in keeping with James's depiction of Isabel as a heroine. Her arrogance in demanding the freedom to control her own life has caused her to reject better suitors, including Goodwood, for a despicable husband. Yet accepting Goodwood would be equivalent to substituting one form of servitude for another—she would be letting physical passion control her life and submitting her destiny to yet another man. So she returns to Rome to the grim fate she has chosen—her determination to accept the consequences of her actions is her first real act of freedom.

James's middle period (1885-1900) focuses mostly on English characters in English settings. In these books, the sex is likely to be fairly degenerate. *What Maisie Knew* (1897) provides a good example of how complex adultery could become in British society. When Ida and Beale Farange are divorced, their six-year-old daughter, Maisie, must spend six months with each parent. Maisie observes much sexual, often adulterous behavior when she visits each parent. The governess employed by Ida eventually marries Beale Farange. This second Mrs. Farange becomes involved in an adulterous affair with Ida's second husband, Sir Claude. By the end of the novel, the thirteen-year-old Maisie is offering herself to Sir Claude on the condition that he will leave his mistress. Maisie has learned the lessons of her elders only too effectively.

James's last period of writing comes in the twentieth century. In these novels, he once again writes about American characters in English and European settings. In *The Ambassadors* (1903), for instance, Madame de Vionnet is an adulteress, but she is treated sympathetically. A French woman who was married by a calculating mother to a depraved husband, Madame de Vionnet is a Catholic and cannot seek a divorce, so she is having an affair with the American Chad Newsome. Several "ambassadors" are sent to detach Chad from this supposedly corrupt product of the Old World. Actually, Madame de Vionnet is a refined and highly respectable woman who has transformed Chad into a more cultured person. When he deserts her, it is not because of the puritanical morality of his New England heritage, but apparently to have an affair with another woman.

James's last completed novel tells a story of adultery that is twofold. In *The Golden Bowl* (1904), the American Adam Verver uses his wealth to "purchase" the Italian Prince Amerigo as a husband for his daughter Maggie Verver. The Prince has had a love affair with Charlotte Stant, an expatriate American friend of Maggie's, but the two were worldly and practical enough to know they were too poor to marry each other; they had to both find *wealthy* spouses. When the Prince marries Maggie, he intends to be faithful. Charlotte likewise wishes to give the Prince up, although she is not able to do so emotionally.

Adam Verver is pursued by fortune-hunting women, so Maggie arranges a match between him and Charlotte, thus providing Charlotte with the fortune she needs. Even after their marriages, the father and daughter are tied more intimately to each other than to their spouses, so the Prince and Charlotte are thrown together, and they resume their affair. When Maggie discovers her husband and stepmother's affair, she realizes she must sacrifice her passionate tie to her father in order to preserve her marriage. So Adam and Charlotte return to America, leaving Maggie and the Prince in Rome.

The Golden Bowl has several "morals." Charlotte has sold herself to an older man and must "pay the price" by giving up the emotional and physical satisfactions she finds with her lover. Both she and the Prince deceive themselves by believing that no one is harmed as long as Maggie and Adam do not know about their affair. But the novel also teaches that there are other forms of "infidelity" besides adultery. The American father and daughter must give up their intense and intimate tie in order to accept the new loyalties of marriage.

Kate Chopin

By the end of the nineteenth century, one American woman novelist wrote about adultery with a boldness that led to many protests. Kate Chopin's *The Awakening* (1899) was reviewed with hostility by contemporary critics, and the book was even removed from the public library in St. Louis. Chopin herself was ostracized from the St. Louis Fine Arts Club because of her book's subversive nature. After the book was reprinted in 1906, it was not reprinted again until half a century later (Chopin, 1976: VIII).

Chopin's Edna Pontellier is a heroine in the manner of Hester

Prynne and Isabel Archer; she is ruthless in her demand that she have the right to live her life as she wishes. Edna is an American woman married to a Creole businessman of New Orleans. Central to Edna's "awakening" is her realization that she does not love her husband. She is attracted to a younger man, Robert Lebrun, but he runs off to Mexico when he realizes that the flirtation between him and Edna has developed into a passionate attachment.

Edna reads Emerson (Chopin, 1976: 73), an appropriate author for a woman who claims a form of self-reliance that seemed outrageous and immoral to nineteenth century readers. With no feelings of guilt, Edna refuses to go on playing the role of a "good" wife or mother. Instead of acting as her husband's housekeeper and hostess, she devotes her time to developing her artistic talent as a painter. She sends her children to live with their grandmother for the summer, and refuses to accompany her husband on a lengthy trip. When he is gone, she boldly writes to her husband that she is moving out of his house into a small dwelling she has purchased with her own money.

Edna has an affair with Alcee Arobin, a playboy who skillfully takes advantage of the fact that Edna's latent sensuality (untouched by her husband) has been awakened by Robert and left unfulfilled. The following passage depicts Edna's reaction to her first sexual experiences with Arobin. Significantly, she is more concerned about her disloyalty to Robert than to her husband:

> Edna cried a little that night after Arobin left her. . . . There was her husband's reproach looking at her from the external things around her which he had provided for her external existence. There was Robert's reproach, making itself felt by a quicker, fiercer, more overpowering love, which had awakened within her toward him. . . . But among the conflicting sensations which assailed her, there was neither shame nor remorse. There was a dull pang of regret because it was not love which held this cup of life to her lips. (1976: 83)

Robert finally returns, declaring that he has been "dreaming of wild, impossible things, recalling men who had set their wives free" (1976: 106). Edna's reply shows that she has transformed herself into the American heroine who demands that external rules, even the tie of marriage, not inhibit her freedom: "You have been a very,

very foolish boy, wasting your time dreaming of impossible things when you speak of Mr. Pontellier setting me free! I am no longer one of Mr. Pontellier's possessions to be disposed of or not. I give myself where I choose" (1976: 107).

Edna tells Robert that they "shall be everything to each other." Nothing else in the world matters except their love (1976: 107). At this crucial moment, Edna is called away to help a friend who is having a baby. Robert begs her not to leave, but Edna keeps the promise she has made. When Edna returns, Robert is gone. He has left a note saying, "Good-bye—because I love you," demonstrating his own inability to free himself from conventional moral judgments.

In the last chapter of the book, Edna deliberately drowns herself in the waters of the Gulf of Mexico. She does so partially because of the loss of Robert, but she is not really acting in the tradition of thwarted lovers who die for passion. Even as she goes to her death, Edna knows that her love for Robert is just one of many infatuations she has had throughout her life: "There was no human being whom she wanted near her except Robert; and she even realized that the day would come when he, too, and the thought of him would melt out of her existence, leaving her alone" (1976: 113). Edna will never be able to find a man who can understand and agree with her radical claim for freedom: "Robert would never understand" (1976: 114).

Edna drowns herself primarily because she will not let her life be determined by others. She will not live her life for husband and children as society demands: "She thought of Leonce and the children. They were a part of her life. But they need not have thought that they could possess her, body and soul" (1976: 114).

Hester Prynne lives a life of self-denial and renunciation. Isabel Archer proudly goes back to face life with a husband she despises. Edna Pontellier is the most uncompromising of these heroines. As Edna herself says: "I don't want anything but my own way. That is wanting a good deal, of course, when you have to trample upon the lives, the heart, the prejudices of others. . ." (1976: 110). Living when she does, Edna cannot have the freedom she wants. Rather than live without that freedom, she chooses to die.

THE TWENTIETH CENTURY

Adultery is more prevalent in American fiction written in this century than the last. At the same time, however, adultery became less important as a theme of literature. This paradox grows out of the fact that marriage as the central contract of society became less and less stable. Offenses against monogamous marriage could hardly be viewed as a great moral problem when society no longer had faith in marriage as something that could endure. The great conflict between passion and the laws of God and society, a conflict which intensified the bond between adulterous lovers such as Lancelot and Guinevere—and Hester and Dimmesdale—no longer existed.

THE THEME OF THE ARTIST

In 1900, a classic American novel was published which shows clearly that novelists of the new century would not necessarily play by the rules of the previous one. Hawthorne carefully shows us how Hester is punished. And Chopin kills off Edna Pontellier because *The Awakening* would have caused even more outrage if a woman who believes she has the right to violate her marriage vows had survived. But Theodore Dreiser's Carrie Meeber receives no punishment for becoming a "fallen woman."

When it was published in 1900, *Sister Carrie* shocked even sophisticated readers. Carrie Meeber is the archetypal simple country girl who goes to the big city and drifts into a fate that the moralists would condemn. First, she is seduced by a traveling salesman, Drouet, and lives with him as his wife. When a prosperous member of the middle class, Hurstwood, falls passionately in love with Carrie, she is attracted because he has more culture (and money) than Drouet. But when Carrie finds out Hurstwood is married, she says they can no longer see each other.

Hurstwood steals some money from his employer and tricks Carrie into running off to New York with him. It is typical of Carrie's passivity that she stays with Hurstwood after discovering his duplicity. It was not the multiple seductions that disturbed Dreiser's readers but rather the fact that Carrie is not punished for them. At the conclusion of the novel Carrie is a successful actress. Dreiser carefully emphasizes the fact that she is not yet happy: "Though often disillusioned, she was still waiting for that halcyon day, when she would be led forth among dreams become real" (Dreiser, 1970: 369).

Carrie's lovers have represented steps in her development (Pizer, 1976:63-67). At the conclusion of the novel, she is being tutored by a third man, the engineer Ames, who teaches her about the artistic nature of her role as an actress. Hence there is hope for Carrie's future development.

Tony Tanner, author of *Adultery in the Novel,* has pointed out that writers who focus on the theme of the artist are not likely to condemn adultery (Tanner, 1979: 99). Carrie becomes Dreiser's symbol of the artist through her development as an actress. This theme exists in incipient form in *The Scarlet Letter,* for Hester Prynne's gorgeous needlework—which she uses to embellish not only her daughter Pearl but the scarlet letter itself—is the means by which she expresses her artistic creativity. *The Awakening* shows stronger development of this theme: Edna Pontellier is a successful painter. Yet Edna fails in terms of the message about art given by Chopin. The one successful artist in the book tells Edna that "the artist must possess the courageous soul that dares and defies" (Chopin, 1976: 114). As Edna goes to her death, the image of a bird with a broken wing shows that she cannot be this triumphant artist, capable of defying the world and its conventions (1976: 113).

Carrie Meeber has far less fire and strength than Hawthorne's or Chopin's heroines. Yet Dreiser admires Carrie's capacity for survival and development. Because Carrie is an evolving artist, her sexual sins and disgrace as a "fallen woman" no longer matter. The religion of love has given way to the religion of art: "Man has not yet comprehended the dreamer any more than he has the ideal. For him the laws and morals of the world are unduly severe. Ever harkening to the sound of beauty, straining to the flash of its distant wings, he watches to follow, wearying his feet in travelling. So watched, Carrie, so followed. . . ." (Dreiser, 368).

SYMPATHY VERSUS PUNISHMENT

In writing about the European novel of adultery, Tanner says that the Old and New Testaments provide two different approaches to adultery. The Old Testament emphasizes the violation of the law and demands punishment. In the New Testament, Christ makes others aware of the woman taken in adultery and the fact that those who would punish her are sinners also (Tanner, 1979: 14).

Most of the novels written by twentieth-century Americans emphasize sympathy and understanding rather than punishment. Edith Wharton's *The Age of Innocence* (1920) proves how easy it is to form an unsatisfactory marriage and consequently yearn for a better relationship. Newland Archer's affection for the Countess Ellen Olenska shows the better side of his personality. The Countess had married disastrously, and she shocks her relatives by allowing the attentions of Archer and of less respectable men. Archer believes that he can protect himself from his infatuation with the Countess by marrying the conventional and correct May. After his marriage, however, he realizes he has made a mistake.

Archer remains technically faithful to May, but only because the Countess refuses to go away with him. She is the one who sets limits to their relationship, saying that they can love each other only as long as he does not demand that the love be consummated.

In *A Lost Lady* (1923), Willa Cather shows an even stronger understanding and sympathy for an adulteress, Marrian Forrester. Married to Captain Forrester, she has an affair with Frank Ellinger, a ruthless ladies' man who finally deserts her for a wealthy marriage. By the standards of her society, she is "lost."

The young Niel Herbert, who has idolized Marrian, is shocked and disillusioned when he learns of his idol's infidelity. But Captain Forrester himself knows and forgives his wife, and goes on loving her. By marrying the Captain, a man much older than she is, Marrian condemned herself to a life of social and, eventually, material poverty. Captain Forrester takes her to live in Sweet Water, Nebraska, a small prairie town lacking in social amenities. Marrian's relationship with Frank Ellinger is the one connection she has with her former life of gaiety and excitement as a society belle.

Marrian is "lost" only technically, for Cather makes her a survivor, a woman with enough energy and zest for life to triumph over the poverty that her husband's death brings her. She ends up married to a wealthy South American rancher, "well cared for, to the very end" (Cather, 1972: 174).

Ellen Glasgow tells a much grimmer tale of infidelity in *The Sheltered Life* (1934). Glasgow has no sympathy for anyone who lets the gospel of romantic love guide his or her life. Eva Birdsong is one such woman; she believes that giving up her chances for fame and distinction by marrying was justified by love. But her husband, George, drinks, keeps a black mistress, and has lost his inheritance.

At the conclusion of the novel, Eva shoots George dead when she sees him in the arms of their young neighbor Jenny Blair. Death comes as the delayed punishment to George and early punishment to Jenny Blair for disillusioning Eva about the religion of love.

A SECONDARY THEME

The protagonist of F. Scott Fitzgerald's *The Great Gatsby* (1925) suffers the same fate as George and ostensibly for the same reason: Gatsby wants to take Daisy Buchanan away from her husband Tom Buchanan. But Gatsby never actually commits adultery. Technically, Tom Buchanan, Daisy's husband, is the only adulterer in the novel. Tom's mistress, Myrtle Wilson, is killed accidentally by Daisy when she runs in front of a car Daisy is driving. Tom tricks Myrtle's husband into believing Gatsby killed Myrtle. So, the husband shoots Gatsby in revenge for Myrtle's death.

The real conflict in *The Great Gatsby* is not over adultery. Daisy is more symbol than woman to Gatsby. Thus he can forgive her for loving Tom at the beginning of their marriage because this love was "just personal" (Fitzgerald, 1953: 152). Gatsby wants Daisy because she is the symbol of the American dream fulfilled: She is the "golden girl" whose "voice is full of money" (1953: 120).

In the next decade, Fitzgerald produced another novel in which marital infidelity was a symptom of moral problems, but again Fitzgerald's chief concern was wealth and its effects on human character.

Dick and Nicole Diver of *Tender is the Night* (1934), wealthy expatriate Americans living in Europe, are more famous for their parties than for any more substantial achievements. Dick is a psychologist and writer, once a man of great promise, who never produces anything of much quality after marrying the wealthy Nicole.

Dick met Nicole when she was a patient in a clinic in Zurich, and she is still subject to occasional attacks of schizophrenia in which she accuses Dick of being unfaithful to her. During the course of the novel, Dick deteriorates: he has an affair with a young actress who has long been attracted to him, he begins to drink heavily, and he loses his job in the clinic. Dick's decline serves to make Nicole more independent; she too has an affair, with the war hero Tommy Barban, and finally divorces Dick for Tommy. Although Nicole's instability contributes to Dick's fall, Dick is himself responsible for his choice to abandon his work and live off his wife's wealth.

SOUTHERN MORALISTS

Many literary critics and historians consider William Faulkner, who was consistently engaged by moral issues, the greatest American novelist of the twentieth century. In the world of Faulkner's fiction, fornication and adultery are sins which grow out of innate human weakness. That none of us can escape sin is one of Faulkner's great themes; that we must consequently be able to forgive sin in others is another.

Although fornication is far more common in Faulkner's work, there are some celebrated adulterers. Will Varner, who appears in Faulkner's Snopes trilogy—*The Hamlet* (1940), *The Town* (1950), and *The Mansion* (1959)—is one of the most memorable. In *The Hamlet* he is a lusty old man who sleeps with the wives of the tenants who rent farms from him. While Will Varner's behavior is hardly admirable, his sins grow out of a positive zest for life. Moreover, he is in some ways an attractive rascal who can show his humanity in relating to other people. For example, he pays ten dollars to sleep with a woman who needs the money to help her husband run from the law (Faulkner, 244-245).

True evil for Faulkner is embodied in Flem Snopes, a man who rises from the poverty of the sharecropper class to achieve wealth and position. A man who is without feeling for other humans, Flem lives only for greed and power. He is not tempted by sexual sins because he does not have enough humanity to have a sexual appetite. Eula Varner, Will Varner's beautiful, voluptuous daughter, is married to the impotent and asexual Flem in order to save her "honor" when she becomes pregnant by a young man who runs off without marrying her.

The second novel of the series, *The Town,* shows some of the results of this marriage. Eula has an eighteen-year affair with Manfred de Spain, the mayor of Jefferson. Flem profits by this affair, for de Spain helps Flem secure several jobs that lead to his increased wealth and influence. Finally, after accepting his wife's infidelity for eighteen years, Flem gains enough wealth and position to aspire to de Spain's job as president of the bank. Flem uses his knowledge of his wife's affair to blackmail de Spain into resigning his position. Eula refuses to run away with de Spain, because she does not want her daughter to learn about her affair. She stays in Jefferson and commits suicide. For Faulkner, the adulterous lovers have far less guilt than the man who callously exploits their affair for his own profit.

Robert Penn Warren is another writer who belongs to the tradition of Southern moralists. In his *All the King's Men* (1946), adultery and other forms of moral transgression inevitably lead to suffering that the sinners do not foresee.

Warren has the Southern writer's obsession with history. The protagonist of *All the King's Men,* Jack Burden, cannot complete his dissertation in American history because the pre-Civil War papers he is working on tell a tale of sin and recompense for sin that frightens him.

The main part of the novel is set in the late 1920s and early 1930s in the South. After leaving graduate school, Jack goes to work for the governor of the state, Willie Stark. Willie begins as an idealist who wants to serve people. By the time he becomes governor, however, Willie uses any means available to achieve and hold power. Part of his compromise with his earlier purity of ethics is apparent in Willie's sexual life. He has a long-standing affair with Sadie Burke, a woman who is one of his most useful political aides. Willie's wife is separated from him but appears with him in public to help his political career.

In the process of the novel, Willie has an affair with Anne Stanton, the woman whom Jack Burden has loved since he and Anne were young. Jack has never consummated his love with Anne because of his fear that involvement with others can produce evil.

Willie is assassinated by Anne's brother Adam, who learns about the affair and believes that his position as head of the Willie Stark Hospital was given to him in payment for the loss of his sister's honor. Adam is killed in turn by Willie's bodyguard. History has apparently repeated itself—for adultery has led to more evil. Ironically, however, before his death Willie had left both Sadie and Anne and returned to his wife. And Anne's affair with Willie—which grew out of genuine love and admiration—was also the result of Jack's refusal to marry her.

Another adulterous relationship from the past that caused far-reaching results is revealed at the end of the novel. Jack discovers that his mother had had an adulterous affair with Judge Irwin and that he is the child of that relationship. Instead of leading to greater cynicism on his part, this revelation teaches Jack the meaning of love, sympathy, and forgiveness.

Jack had condemned his mother as a "woman without heart" (Warren, 1946: 433). But the knowledge that she loved someone— even though it was an adulterous love—transforms his view of the world: "She had given me a new picture of herself and that meant in the end, a new picture of the world. . . . I could accept the past now because I could accept her and be at peace with her and with myself" (1946: 432).

Accepting others and ourselves means accepting the fact that we are all sinners. *All the King's Men* teaches that humans have to pay for sins like adultery. But evil results from trying to refrain from involvement with human beings also. As in the literature of William Faulkner, sins of the flesh may grow out of love. Since no one is free from sin, no one has the right to cast the first stone.

STEREOTYPES

Some twentieth-century fiction shows relatively traditional stereo-types of male and female adulterers. Tom Buchanan of *The Great Gatsby,* for instance, is the stereotyped figure of the selfish, philan-dering husband who starts running around on his wife shortly after the honeymoon. Tom is true to the type when he responds with outrage to the idea that Gatsby is interested in his wife. Faced with this threat, Tom hypocritically spouts rhetoric about the sacredness of the family: "I suppose the latest thing is to sit back and let Mr. Nobody from Nowhere make love to your wife. Well, if that's the idea you can count me out. . . . Nowadays, people begin by sneering at family life and family institutions and next they'll throw everything overboard. . . ." (1953: 130).

Arthur Miller similarly presents a stereotype of the philandering male in his *Death of a Salesman* (1949). Willy Loman fits the jokes about traveling salesmen by having affairs with women while out selling his wares. In one key scene in the play, Willy's son Biff catches Willy with a woman in his hotel room (Miller, 1958: 38-39, 114-20). This revelation of Willy's infidelity intensifies Biff's disil-lusionment with his father and precipitates an estrangement between father and son.

Miller emphasizes Willy's pathetic efforts to achieve the Ameri-can dream of success and wealth. Willy becomes an adulterer because his is a lonely job, and because his ego is flattered when women desire him. Willy is a failure as a lover, and he pays for his disloyalty to his wife by earning the disgust and hostility of his son.

Ernest Hemingway crystallizes one of the stereotyped views of American womanhood in his famous short story "The Short Happy Life of Francis Macomber" (1936). Margot, wife of Francis Macom-ber, commits adultery with Robert Wilson, the hunter who has taken the Macombers on a safari in Africa. Margot is genuinely attracted to this strong, silent model of the great white hunter. But her infidelity is primarily her way of demonstrating contempt for her husband, who has proved himself a coward by running from a wounded lion.

Wilson accepts Margot into his bed because she's beautiful, but he is appalled by her personality. For him, she is the essence of the wealthy, beautiful American bitch. Although the international set of wealthy people who go on safaris often expect the white hunter to sleep with the women of the party, Margot's infidelity is not condoned by Francis. He correctly sees her actions as a punishing insult to him. But Francis, who at the tale's start is one of the "great American boy-men," overcomes his cowardice on a buffalo hunt. This courage, and his elation, mark his passage into manhood (Hemingway, 1966: 33).

Margo is afraid of this change in her husband. In Wilson's judgment, she knows that Francis now also has the courage to leave her. She has stayed with her husband for eleven years because of his wealth and is no longer young enough to attract another rich man. But the "new" Francis has only a short life; while supposedly aiming at the wounded buffalo charging her husband, Margot kills him (1966: 33). The conclusion is ambiguous. Was Margot aiming at the buffalo or at her husband?

The American bitch remains a character type in later literature of the twentieth century. Edward Albee created one of the best examples in his play *Who's Afraid of Virginia Woolf?* (1962). Martha is a large and boisterous woman who tries to satisfy her sexual appetites with men younger than her middle-aged husband, George.

The play is set during one evening when Martha and George are entertaining a younger couple, Nick and Honey, after a university party. Predictably, Martha takes Nick up to her bedroom, while Honey passes out from liquor and emotional exhaustion. George, who is aware of his wife's infidelity, also knows that her seduction of Nick is part of the power struggle of their marriage.

Martha is ultimately seen as a pathetic character. Her numerous acts of adultery are neither sexually nor emotionally satisfying. Typically, the usually virile young Nick is impotent in his exchange with Martha, a failure that causes her to yell, "You're all flops. I am the Earth Mother, and you're all flops. . . . I disgust me. I pass my life in crummy, totally pointless infidelities. . . ." (Albee, 1981: 189).

Who's Afraid of Virginia Woolf? presents a cynical view of modern marriage and the chances for fidelity. "Musical beds" is the "faculty sport" in this modern academic community (1981: 34). Yet

Albee's play shows us how this "sport" does not lead to happiness or even to much real sex. Moreover, by the end of the play there is some hope that George and Martha will mend their ways and their marriage. Martha realizes that George is the only man who has ever made her happy (1981: 189). And George promises that the future will be better (1981: 241).

THE FEMINIST NOVEL

Erica Jong's *Fear of Flying* (1972) is probably the best example of the crucial role that adultery can play in the literature influenced by the feminist movement of the second half of the twentieth century. Because of her graphic depiction of sex and raucous sex humor, Jong's novel seems very far from the reticent treatment of this topic by nineteenth-century writers. But an examination of the book also shows some relatively traditional attitudes toward marital infidelity.

Isadora Zelda White Wing (née Weiss) has been married for five years to the psychologist Bennet Wing. Their marriage has reached a critical juncture typical for modern couples: "time to decide whether to buy new sheets, have a baby perhaps, and live with each other's lunacy ever after—or else give up the ghost of the marriage (throw out the sheets) and start playing musical beds all over again" (Jong, 1979: 8).

The central conflict in the novel is the old one between the ties of marriage and the desire for other pleasures. Isadora is tempted to have an affair with a British psychologist—Adrian Goodlove—whom she meets while attending a conference of psychologists with her husband in Vienna. Her husband has come to symbolize "steadfastness and security" in her life, but she wants more intensity, and Adrian seems to promise the "exuberance" that Isadora has been suppressing during the years of her marriage (1979: 73).

Isadora believes that she is passionately in love with Adrian. The imagery of being "possessed" and a "goner" provides humorous links to the classic tales of forbidden love (1979: 121). But the reader is likely to see the attraction as primarily physical—for Isadora is a lover of the male body in the way that men have traditionally been lovers of the female body.

Adrian proposes that he and Isadora go off together on an "odyssey" of Europe, an unplanned existentialist adventure in which they will forget about the future and live as "free" beings (1979: 132). Adrian promises the opposite of what Isadora finds in her marriage: intense passion, adventure, excitement, and "freedom." The temptations appeal powerfully to part of Isadora's nature: "I had never been happy with the bourgeois virtues of marriage, stability, and work above pleasure. I was too curious and adventurous not to chafe under these restrictions (1979: 73).

Isadora has conflicting feelings because she also values marriage and realizes that it requires a commitment that is destroyed by extramarital affairs: "I really believed in pursuing a long-standing and deep relationship with one person. I could easily see the sterility of hopping from bed to bed and having shallow affairs with lots of shallow people" (1979: 74). But Isadora does not resist having adulterous sex with Adrian. That comes early and easily in their relationship, and in fact, stimulates Bennett's ardor for his wife (1979: 76-90). But she does struggle over the invitation to go off with Adrian because she fears the trip may produce a breach serious enough to end her marriage. When she gives in and spends two and one-half weeks touring Europe with Adrian, Isadora learns the moral lesson that the majority of twentieth-century writers seem to teach as consistently as earlier writers. The affair turns out to be less than satisfactory. Adrian, impotent in private, is virile only in public places; he is more obsessed by the need to break taboos than he is with Isadora (1979: 183). Isadora finds out that "freedom" is a hard concept to transform into reality. Adrian pretends that there are no rules to their trip, but he makes his own and changes them whimsically. Isadora concludes sadly: "The trouble with existentialism is . . . that you can't stop thinking about the future. Actions do have consequences" (1979: 250). Like other more traditional female fictional characters (Marrian Forrester, for instance), Isadora is betrayed by her lover. Adrian goes off to collect his family and abandons his frightened and angry mistress (1979: 269-71).

The history of the treatment of adultery in American literature is repeated to some extent in the novel. The conflict between the marriage's stability and commitment and freedom's intensity of feeling has not really been solved by human beings or by novelists. Leaving these problems unsolved, Jong shifts from the theme of marriage and adultery to the theme of the artist who stands as a special example of those who demand and achieve "freedom" and self-fulfillment.

At the end of the book, Isadora returns to her husband. But she does not go back until she has spent a period of time alone, proving her ability to be alone and survive. And she spends much of this time examining her notebook. Writing is an art that has helped Isadora grow into a more independent person. As she reviews her notebooks, Isadora comes to a positive sense of her own strength. She will write about her affair with Adrian—thus taking control of the experience and transforming it into art (Jong 1979: 300).

Erica Jong takes the themes of the artist and of freedom one step beyond the novelists of the nineteenth century. "I'm beginning to like me quite a lot," thinks Isadora, with a joyful sense of self-acceptance (1979: 304). And Jong is hopeful that Isadora will find others in her society—perhaps even a husband—who will respond with the same acceptance.

It seems highly unlikely that the literature of the future will avoid the topic of adultery. Contemporary literature usually treats the relationships between the sexes as the area where most problems are likely to occur. The great female characters created by Hawthorne, James, and Chopin—who demanded that love and freedom go together—have their modern descendants in heroines such as Isadora Wing. Literature becomes ever bolder in its treatment of adultery. Adulterous women are no longer punished or condemned to a life of unhappiness at the end of the novel. Isadora Wing forgives and accepts herself. Moreover, Isadora describes her extramarital affair with a levity that would be unthinkable in earlier American writers. While Hawthorne's treatment of adultery is solemn, reticent, and dignified, *Fear of Flying* takes the reader on a raucous trip through numerous sex scenes, all described with zest and wit.

Even though contemporary literature is more cynical than the literature from America's past, love and marriage remain as positive goals to be sought by healthy human beings. Isadora Wing, that modern and yet traditional woman, declares: "I only know that if I stop hoping for love, stop expecting it, stop searching for it, my life will go flat as a cancerous breast after radical surgery" (1979: 278).

Isadora believes firmly in the concept that a "good" marriage is the best way of achieving love in the modern world: "Two people holding each up like flying buttresses. Two people depending on each other and babying each other and defending each other against the world outside. Sometimes it was worth all the disadvantages of marriage just to have that: one friend in an indifferent world" (1979: 162)

The modern note in the above passage is in the last sentence. Adultery is less shocking to modern authors because they see the successful marriage as the exception not the rule. Indeed, at the book's start Isadora has already been divorced once, and the conclusion of the book does not offer any certainty that her second marriage will last.

The conflicts between passion and honor, love and society that moved the tragic lovers of the past have given way to psychological conflicts. Isadora is torn by the conflict between her need for security and stability and her desire to experience more freedom and excitement than marriage seems to allow.

Until humans learn how to achieve both freedom and commitment, stability and yet adventure, the conflict between the desire for a good marriage and the temptation to stray from marriage through adultery will probably always be found in human society. And adultery will likewise be a theme in the literature which holds a mirror up to society in hope of clarifying and transforming human value systems.

REFERENCES

Albee, Edward. (1962) 1981. *Who's Afraid of Virginia Woolf?* New York: Atheneum.

Carpenter, Frederic. (1944) 1978. "Scarlet A Minus." In *The Scarlet Letter*, edited by Bradley Beatty. New York: W. W. Norton.

Cather, Willa. (1923) 1972. New York: Vintage.

Chase, Richard. 1951. *Emily Dickinson.* Westport, Conn.: Greenwood.

Chopin, Kate. (1899) 1976. *The Awakening.* New York: W. W. Norton.

Cooper, James Fenimore. 1851. *Leather-Stocking.* New York: G. P. Putnam.

Dickinson, Emily, 1960. *The Complete Poems of Emily Dickinson,* edited by Thomas Johnson. Boston: Little, Brown.

Dreiser, Theodore. (1900) 1970. *Sister Carrie.* New York: W. W. Norton.

Faulkner, William. (1940) 1964. *The Hamlet.* New York: Vintage Books.

———. 1957. *The Town.* New York: Random House.

———. 1959. *The Mansion.* New York: Random House.

Fiedler, Leslie A. 1966. *Love and Death in the American Novel.* New York: Dell.

———. 1968. *Return of the Vanishing American.* New York: Stein and Day.

Fitzgerald, F. Scott. (1925) 1953. *The Great Gatsby.* New York: Charles Scribner's Sons..

———. 1934. *Tender Is the Night.* New York: Charles Scribner's Sons.

Griswold, Rufus. 1856. *The Female Poets of America.* Philadelphia, Pa.: Parry and McMillan.

Hawthorne, Nathaniel. (1850) 1978. *The Scarlet Letter.* New York: W. W. Norton.

Hemingway, Ernest. 1966. *The Short Stories of Ernest Hemingway.* New York: Charles Scribner's Sons..

James, Henry. 1903. *The Ambassadors.* New York: Harper.

———. (1897) 1936. *What Maisie Knew.* Garden City, N.J.: Doubleday.

———. (1881) 1951. *The Portrait of a Lady.* New York: Random House.

———. (1904) 1962. *The Golden Bowl.* New York: Grove.

Johnson, Thomas. 1955. *Emily Dickinson: An Interpretive Biography.* Cambridge, Mass.: Harvard University Press.

Jong, Erica. 1973. *Fear of Flying.* New York: New American Library.

Lawrence, D. H. 1923. *Studies in Classic American Literature.* New York: New American Library.

Lewis, R. W. B. 1955. *The American Adam.* Chicago: University of Chicago Press.

May, Caroline, ed. 1848. *The American Female Poets.* Philadelphia, Pa.: Lindsay and Blakiston.

Melville, Herman. 1851. *Moby Dick.* New York: Harper.

Miller, Arthur. (1949) 1958. *Death of a Salesman.* New York: Viking.

Pizer, Donald. 1976. *The Novels of Theodore Dreiser: A Critical Study.* Minneapolis, Minn.: University of Minnesota Press.

Reardon, Joan, 1978. "Fear of Flying: Developing the Feminist Novel." *International Journal of Women's Studies,* 1: 306-320.

Rougement, Denis de. 1940. *Love in the Western World.* New York: Harcourt Brace.

Tanner, Tony. 1979. *Adultery in the Novel.* Baltimore: Johns Hopkins University Press.

Twain, Mark. 1884. *The Adventures of Huckleberry Finn.* New York: Harper.

Warren, Robert Penn. (1946) 1971. *All the King's Men.* New York: Bantam.

Watts, Emily Stipes. 1977. *The Poetry of American Women from 1632 to 1945*. Austin, Tex.: University of Texas Press.
Wharton, Edith. 1920. *The Age of Innocence*. New York: D. Appleton.

6

R. J. Connelly
PHILOSOPHY AND ADULTERY

Until the late 1960s, it was almost impossible to find evidence indicating professional philosophers in the United States had any thoughts about sexuality. *The Encyclopedia of Philosophy,* published in 1967, contains no entries for "sex," "marriage," or "adultery." The cumulative edition of *The Philosopher's Index* of the same year is also silent on these topics. What little research had been done on sexuality by Christian philosophers does not appreciably add to our stock of resource material. It is fair to conclude that, until very recently, U.S. philosophers had ignored a major field of human interest, leaving to poets and popular essayists and, later, clinicians the serious task of understanding human sexuality.

BACKGROUND—WESTERN TRADITION

The whole of Western tradition reveals the same myopic condition among philosophers. The major sources of philosophical thinking concerning adultery, meager as they are, derive from Plato, St. Paul, Augustine, Aquinas, and Martin Luther. In these streams of thought the ideal of sex evolves from the Greek notion that sex was a natural nonmoral function to the Christian belief that sex was a necessary evil. The latter view developed as more emphasis was placed on human spiritual immortality and its corollory, the depreciation of the body and the physical world generally. Or, when the focus was turned on this world, the future well-being of the species was seen to be more important than the purpose of any individual or group of individuals. In this climate, sex enjoyed for its own sake became associated with selfishness and sin. Consequently, sex was understood to be redeemed only to the extent that it served as a means of participating in the divine creation of new life. Procreation, therefore, was the primary end of sex, and marriage was deemed the appropriate institution to sanction procreation and provide for the upbringing of children. The resultant traditional idea of monogamous marriage continues to exert strong influence on contemporary views of sex and marriage.

Professor Buford (1984: 41) lists six characteristics of the stereotypical traditional model of monogamous marriage:

1. *Ownership of the other person.* The husband and wife are in "bondage" to each other. ("You belong to me!") This is different than belonging *with* someone.
2. *Denial of oneself.* Once the marriage contract has been entered into, you have sacrificed yourself and your individual identity to the other person. This is particularly true of the woman, who takes the name of her husband, moves where he chooses, encourages him in his occupation, and takes care of "his" home and children.
3. *Maintenance of the "couple front."* The marriage is your "identity card." You would be lost without it. You must always present yourselves as a couple.
4. *Rigid role behavior.* The roles of the man and the woman are set along predetermined lines, usually according to sex-role stereotypes. The man is to be the leader—aggressive, protective, and knowledgeable. The woman is to be the follower—compliant, supportive, and receptive.
5. *Absolute fidelity.* The marriage contract coerces you to be bound to the other person both physically and psychologically. Neither of you may touch another woman or another man.
6. *Total exclusivity.* All others are excluded by your contract. This is thought valuable because enforced togetherness will preserve the union.

In sum, the traditional view prohibits one from engaging in sex with any person other than one's marriage partner. The integrity of the marriage union, including continuity of the family and its role as the ideal means of rearing children, requires the absolute prohibition of adultery.

In the modern period, most of the philosophers who write on sexuality only play variations on the traditional theme of monogamous marriage. For example, David Hume (1711-76) looks to current social custom and determines that the consequences of such practices as polygamy, divorce— and by implication, adultery— would be undesirable. He does not explicitly deal with the adultery issue. In commenting on the duration to be assigned a marriage union, Hume (1882: 239) rejects the idea of voluntary divorce. "[N]othing is more dangerous than to unite two persons so closely in all their interests and concerns, as man and wife, without rendering the union entire and total. The least possibility of a separate interest must be the source of endless quarrels and suspicions." Presumably, this also rules out adultery, which could be viewed as an extreme case of separate interest which could easily lead to "endless quarrels and suspicions." Such undesirable consequences are the primary reason Hume would reject adultery as well as voluntary divorce.

Immanuel Kant (1724-1804) dismisses arguments based on consequences and concentrates on the unique character of the marriage union itself in order to determine what is moral. Marriage is a unity of concord and will between two persons. It is the only means of overcoming the inherent limitation of sexual love. Sexual love turns persons into dehumanized objects of appetite and fails to acknowledge and respect the status of all persons as ends in themselves, who should never be treated simply as means. Marriage is the only legitimate way to combine sexual love with human love. Human love respects the other as a subject, as a rational agent. In marriage two persons create a new reality, as it were, a unity of will. (Kant, 1963: 166-9)

Because marriage is a unique contract, it places special responsibility on the partners. Adultery constitutes a contradiction of the very meaning of this unity of will. According to Kant, then, adultery is always morally wrong, regardless of circumstances or consequences. At the same time, however, Kant reflects the secularization of the idea of marriage since Luther in his attitude that while marriage binds for life, adultery undermines this human contract and may render it void.

A contemporary of Kant, Johann Gottlieb Fichte (1762-1814), analyzes the nature of the marriage union itself, and is the first philosopher to make explicit the idea that the marriage relationship has intrinsic value apart from the end of procreation, or any other end. It is its own end.

> The marriage relation is the true mode of existence of grown persons of both sexes, required even by nature. In this relation all man's faculties develop; but out of it many, and among them the most remarkable faculties of man, remain uncultivated. Precisely as the whole existence of man has no relation to any sensuous end, so neither has its necessary mode, marriage. (Fichte, 1869: 406-407)

He also concludes that adultery is contrary to the nature of this union. A woman gives herself to one man in marriage and consequently her whole dignity requires that she belong only to this one. As far as the man is concerned, Fichte comments that it is not possible for one man to conform to the contradictory wishes of many women.

Soren Kierkegaard (1813-1855) develops one of the most detailed modern accounts of monogamous marriage. Human perfectability involves progression through three stages, esthetical, ethical, and religious. Sensual immediacy is the orientation of the first stage. In *Either/Or* (1959), Kierkegaard illustrates the limitations of this stage in the life of Johannis the Seducer, who moves from woman to woman seeking only momentary pleasure. Monogamous marriage epitomizes the virtues of the ethical state. Kierkegaard (1945: 98, 107) goes so far as to remark that a successful married life equates with moral perfection, which is the goal of human existence. Consequently, he goes to great lengths to show the necessity of faithfulness in married life. But Kierkegaard does not develop a connection between marriage and the religious sphere of existence. "Faith alone can make man whole" is the point of the religious stage of life. To illustrate this stage, however, Kierkegaard does not refer to married life but uses examples of individual exceptions to law and reason such as Abraham's willingness to sacrifice his own son Isaac at God's command. It is not clear from this discussion how Kierkegaard would relate the faith of an Abraham to married life.

The nineteenth century also witnesses the emergence of strong opposition by philosophers against monogamy in its traditional form. Arthur Schopenhauer (1788-1860) condemns monogamy as an unnatural institution. Sex is primarily an instinct which manifests the operation of the blind, irrational, and universal causal force Schopenhauer calls Will. The only aim of sex is procreation and thus survival of the species. Women, inferior to men in every respect, "exist in the main solely for the propagation of the species, and are not destined for anything else. . . ." (Schopenhauer, 1928: 450). Monogamy, however, unfairly elevates women to a position of equality and also denies certain benefits to unmarried women. Men, therefore, do themselves an injustice by entering a traditional marriage. More important, monogamy contradicts the naturally polygamous origin of man's sexuality and frustrates the operation of Will in its drive toward maximum propagation of the species.

With this world view, the practice of adultery is one sign that monogamy is corrupt and bound to fail. Schopenhauer, however, does not address the question as to whether adultery would or should retain any meaning in a polygamous society.

Karl Marx (1818-1883) and Friedrich Engels (1820-1895) also herald the end of monogamous marriages as they knew them. In their writings, they identify economic forces as determining the shape of all social institutions. Private property, in particular, leads to class divisions and monogamous marriage. "Monogamy arose from the concentration of considerable wealth in the hands of a single individual—a man—and from the need to bequeath this wealth to the children of that man and no other. For this purpose, the monogamy of the woman was required, not that of the man, so this monogamy of women did not in any way interfere with open or concealed polygamy on the part of the man" (Engels, 1942: 67). Monogamous marriage in microcosm exhibits the same opposition and contradictions which affect capitalist societies as a whole. There is a natural antagonism in marriage between the man's exclusive supremacy and the woman's servile role. Such inequality inevitably breeds the concomitant institutions of adultery and prostitution.

Only the abolition of private property and the class system of capitalist production can redeem the institution of marriage, Engel argues. By transforming the means of production into social property, the need for male supremacy in marriage will be eliminated.

By removing the economic reasons for marriage, men and women will have no other motive to join together than mutual inclination. After "the revolution," marriage will still be monogamous because "sexual love is by its nature exclusive" (Engels, 1942: 72). Authentic state monogamy will provide no reason for adultery or prostitution. "As people marry for love so they will separate when love is gone. But as long as it lasts marriage will tend to be monogamous, and now for the first time for men as well as women."

In the twentieth century, sexuality began to receive intense scrutiny from philosophers. On the continent, from the late 1930s on, existentialist philosophers and psychoanalysts attempted to integrate the idea of sexuality with other concerns of philosophy, much of the seminal work of Ortega y Gasset, Sartre, Simone de Beauvoir, Jaspers, Merleau-Ponty, Paul Ricoeur, and Buber became available in English translation during the 1950s and 1960s. The first half of Ruitenbeck's book *Sexuality and Identity,* published in 1970, presented a selection of existentialist approaches to sexuality. In 1972, D. P. Verene's *Sexual Love and Western Morality* for the first time included under one cover selections from philosophers from ancient to modern times. But very little in the above material dealt explicitly with adultery.

American philosophers for two-thirds of this century have managed to ignore completely the topic of sexuality along with many other relevant and controversial issues of the day. This is in large part due to the influence of the analytic tradition in the U.S. The narrow, specialized, and scientific focus of language analysis is at odds with the more traditional aproach which recognizes the validity of developing a systematic world view including a philosophy of human nature and ethics. A philosophy of sexuality could logically (if not easily, historically speaking) grow out of these interests, as happened on the continent. The analytic tradition seems to have held up this development in English speaking countries.

ARGUMENTS AGAINST ADULTERY

Prior to the late 1960s, the only work in sexual morality that appeared in the United States was Peter A. Bertocci's pioneering *Human*

Venture in Sex, Love, and Marriage (1949) written in response to the fragmentation in our understanding of sex and love occasioned by recent developments in the sociological, psychological, and biological sciences. The Kinsey study, for example, restricted itself primarily to biological behavior of the human male and thereby ignored qualitative and holistic aspects of sex and love. Bertocci set himself the task of developing a more balanced and realistic "philosophy" of sexual morality.

> This is not a psychology of sex and love although it leans heavily on what are deemed to be psychological truths. It is concerned primarily not with the pattern of behavior individuals are exhibiting in our or other cultures, but with the paths of action worth following if life is to realize the highest values in sex, love, and marriage. This, then, is a philosophy, that without neglecting the physiological, psychological, and sociological facts, sees sex and love in the context of life as a whole; it is an essay in right and wrong. (Bertocci, 1949:11)

Bertocci contends that human sex gains its ultimate significance through association with other life values. The greatest satisfaction is to be derived when sex is integrated as part of a "love progression."

> Loving, therefore, is a kind of growing. Love inspires all to live with at least one other person in mind. The circle of self-enjoyment grows into an ellipse in which the two poles are included. But, as Plato long ago reminded us, love is a suffering yearning for what one does not possess completely. The individual must refocus his mind and body, re-form his ideas and dreams, so that the good he wants for himself and for his sweetheart may be realized. Love means growth; it means work; it means moral progress. Thus love, inclusive of sex, needs marriage to protect and nourish its values. And marriage, to be a most fruitful and inclusive experience which protects and nourishes the values of both love and sex, must be put to work in building a family and a society. This is the inner progression of love. (Bertocci, 1949: 51)

In his later book, *Sex, Love and the Person* (1967), Bertocci examines the same basic theme, but with greater emphasis on the concepts of personality and creativity. He responds to the recent influence of Albert Ellis, Hugh Hefner, and Joseph Fletcher.

> My thesis is not that sex is crucial to the development of personality.
> My thesis is that sex cannot live as a refreshing and creative ex-
> perience outside the commitment of love, marriage, and home (and
> all that stands for). There are no short cuts to creativity for either
> sex or romantic love. Persons cannot live the fragmented lives that
> sex and love alone involve without finding that the springs of cre-
> ativity in sex and love are likely to run dry because they do not
> reach the deeper tributaries provided by the other values in their
> lives. (Bertocci, 1967: 131-2)

By "home" Bertocci means a creative environment in which persons
continue growing and strive to reach their maximum potential as
human beings. Monogamous marriage is the best alternative we
know of for building such an environment.

Because Bertocci aims both of his books at young people, their
parents, and those who work with them, he concentrates on the
problem of pre-marital sex. He does remark that his arguments also
apply to extramarital sex. The arguments below all emphasize bad
consequences which inevitably follow from extramarital relations.

First, adultery is a sign of lack of self-control over one's sexual
impulses. Learning quality sex control is necessary over the long run
to protect the emotional safety and moral security of the spouse.
True love seeks to protect marriage partners from experiences which
could lead to loss of self-confidence or uncertainty. By implication,
the non-marital sex partner is also compromised by what usually
turns out to be a short-term sexual relationship, even when love is
present.

Second, adultery in another way compromises long-term values
for the sake of temporary values of immediate self-interest. Extramarital sex does not tend to promote the continuous growth and
creativity of the married couple. Sex outside marriage tends to
trivialize its role in contributing to the long range objective of developing two personalities to the fullest. "If sex is to play a continuing creative role in our lives it needs the continuing support of our
whole being" (Bertocci, 1967: 161-162). In this sense, Bertocci contends that marriage takes sex seriously, which adultery fails to do.

Third, other pragmatic concerns make adultery an immoral option. Bertocci implies that extramarital sex frequently leads to the
breakup of a marriage relationship. In addition, there is always the

possibility that an unwanted pregnancy could result from extra-marital sex. Because of these circumstances, eventually such sex causes negative and destructive feelings in all parties involved.

In conclusion, Bertocci offers us a contemporary version of the traditional view of monogamous marriage. What is new is his attempt to work out a philosophy of sex taking into consideration perspectives from the behavioral sciences, especially humanistic psychology. But in pressing consequential arguments against adultery, Bertocci lays himself open to the charge that we are dependent on empirical evidence to prove conclusively that adultery is always or most of the time damaging to the personality development of the marriage partners. At this point in time we do not have the evidence we need from the behavioral sciences to establish this. The larger issue, of course, is whether adultery is to be faulted for undermining personality development or whether the traditional view of monogamous marriage itself is the problem.

Bertocci's approach is also relatively novel in its emphasis on what is now called the companionship model of marriage. This model underscores the importance of personal and relational growth and development, and thus avoids many of the excesses associated with the evolution of the traditional stereotypical view of marriage, such as authoritarianism and inequality.

In his article "Marriage, Love, and Procreation," Michael D. Bayles also argues in favor of the companionship mode of marriage (Bayles, 1975). He is primarily interested in determining along utilitarian lines what is in the best interests of society to promote and regulate by means of legislation. He concludes that a monogamous marriage of intentionally indefinite duration is a unique and valuable institution that deserves special attention and protection from society.

Bayles begins by citing Aristotle's definition of the good life as consisting in large part of strong interpersonal relationships of affection. Twentieth century mass society may have an even greater need for such relationships because of widespread alienation and the loss of a sense of close community. Personal love is one of the most valuable of interpersonal relationships one which requires a great deal of intimacy in order to cultivate quality communication and deep sharing between two persons. Intimacy, in turn, presumes privacy or at least nonintrusion to protect a relationship which necessarily makes two people more vulnerable because of the personal information shared. One of the most common ways of expressing the feelings and attitudes which make up a love relationship is sexual intercourse. Monogamous marriage, or a relationship intentionally of indefinite duration, is the most conducive to developing a significant interpersonal love and trust relationship.

Bayles claims that a marital relationship that is intentionally entered into for only a definite period of time is of lesser value than one of indefinite duration. The latter symbolizes a strength of commitment not usually found in pre-marital or adulterous relationships, for example. Therefore, society is justified in preferentially promoting and protecting marriage of indefinite duration over other alternatives.

This does not mean that divorce and adultery should be legislated against. The growing incidence of such practices may indicate that the ideal of monogamous marriage of indefinite duration is deteriorating. Bayles suggests that many people may not be suited to a monogamous relationship and should never marry. Others, he points out, get married for the wrong reasons. Consequently, society must make provisions for divorce but not encourage it. By implication, Bayles argues that adultery threatens the intimacy, privacy, and depth of sexual sharing presupposed by a marriage of indefinite duration. He might further argue that the average person could not maintain a personal relationship of love and trust and all that such a commitment entails with more than one person at a time. Bayles does not seem to be in favor of legally prohibiting adulterous relationships. On the other hand, society should not promote or protect such relationships.

Adultery could also be criticized if it jeopardizes society's interest in protecting the welfare of children. Bayles acknowledges that modern technology has enabled us to disassociate reproduction from sex and marriage. Nevertheless, he believes that monogamy is the best institution we have for controlling procreation and providing for the rearing of children.

Marriage has traditionally been the central social institution concerned with procreation. Consequently, if society is to exercise some control over procreation in the future, it would involve the least change in conditions to do so through marriage. Moreover, there is considerable evidence that the disruption of family life contributes to juvenile delinquency. Whether divorce or marital breakdown (with or without divorce) is a prime cause of such delinquency does not matter. The point is that the disruption of home life does seriously affect the development of children. The chance of such disruption outside of a marriage that is intentionally of indefinite duration is higher than for that within. Moreover, there is some reason to believe that the presence of mother and father is instrumental in the psychological development of children. In any case, the presence of two people rather than one provides the security that there will be someone to care for the children should one of the parents die. Generally, children are better off being with one parent than in a state orphanage, but better off still with both parents. Hence, for the welfare of children it seems best that procreation and child rearing primarily occur within the context of marriages intentionally of indefinite duration. (Bayles, 1975: 200-1)

An adulterous relationship could threaten the overall development of children. Such a relationship with its own demands on time and attention could distract from the responsibility persons have to a child of their own marriage. Children out of wedlock may present a more serious problem both legally and morally, because the chances of there being a detrimental effect on the development of these children may be greater.

In conclusion, Bayles's paper represents a reaction against what he calls "vulgar" hedonism and the way it elevates sexual liberation to a level of first priority. Bayles tries to return to a concept of the good life which places sexual pleasure in its proper perspective as only one contributing element.

Another form of argument against adultery asserts that extramarital sex is seriously wrong because it involves the breaking of a promise. One of the most basic promises at the heart of monogamous marriage is that two individuals agree to refrain from sexual relationships with third parties after they are married. According to a consequential analysis, if an adulterous relationship becomes known to the other spouse, unjustifiable harm results.

To begin with, it may have been difficult for the nonadulterous spouse to have kept the promise. Hence that spouse may feel the unfairness of having restrained himself or herself in the absence of reciprocal restraint having been exercised by the adulterous spouse. In addition, the spouse may perceive the breaking of the promise as an indication of a kind of indifference on the part of the adulterous spouse. If you really cared about me and my feelings, the spouse might say, you would not have done this to me. And third, and related to the above, the spouse may see the act of sexual intercourse with another as a sign of affection for the other person and as an additional rejection of the nonadulterous spouse as the one who is loved by the adulterous spouse. It is not just that the adulterous spouse does not take the feelings of the nonadulterous spouse sufficiently into account; the adulterous spouse also indicates through the act of adultery affection for someone other than the nonadulterous spouse. (Wasserstrom, 1975: 210-11)

Thus, according to Richard Wasserstrom, breaking the promise of sexual exclusivity can lead to "the intentional infliction of substantial pain" on one spouse by another.

It may be argued that an adulterous relationship is immoral even if it is covert or kept a secret. A consequential theory might stress that the breach of this most serious promise of sexual exclusivity could lead to the growth of a certain callousness and disregard for other lesser promises. If a pattern of promise-breaking should develop, then both spouses will suffer negative consequences and the marriage relationship will inevitably deteriorate.

Deontological (i.e., duty-based and nonconsequential) theories also have application here. A Kantian approach, for example, would dictate that a chosen action has moral worth only if done with the proper motive, that is, for the sake of duty or just because it is the right or rational thing to do. This eliminates feelings, inclinations, circumstances, and consequences as possible justifications for our actions. But how do we identify what is our duty? Kant himself offered the categorical imperative as a means of testing the moral worth of proposed actions. This principle commands that we should act in such a way that we could wish the maxim of our action to become a universal law. We can describe the proposed maxim of the adulterous spouse this way: "I will make promises, but I will also break them when it is in my best interests to do so." This cannot be conceived as a universal law, however, because if everybody shared such an attitude, then promises would never be honored. The very nature of a promise is contradicted by a law that allows promise-breaking. Even if desirable consequences resulted from breaking a promise, Kant would say such action is still wrong because it contradicts our rational nature which prescribes universal moral laws. In sum, breaking a promise is always wrong.

A second formulation of the categorical imperative may also apply to adultery. Kant says that as rational creatures we all possess an inherent moral worth that deserves utmost respect. This version of the imperative commands that we always act so as to treat ourselves and others as ends in themselves and never solely as means to an end. An adulterous relationship has the potential for turning others into means, into mere objects of sexual satisfaction. To the extent that such relationships tend to be fleeting, there is reason to suspect that adulterers cannot relate in such a way that each person is respected. We may also question whether the nonadulterous spouse can be treated as an end in him or herself, rather then being reduced to mere bread winner, homemaker, parent, socializing partner, or sex object, for example.

In conclusion, the promise-breaking argument against adultery is based on the premise that monogamous marriage is defined in part by the reasonable expectation of sexual exclusivity. This premise, of course, can be challenged. Wasserstrom asks us to consider the implications of what has been characterized as an "open marriage" relationship. From the beginning of their marriage, both partners may agree to engage in extramarital relationships under certain circumstances and with full knowledge of the other partner. With an original agreement of this sort could there be a case for promise-breaking? Other moral considerations would be involved, of course, such as being discreet, caring for the feelings of all involved, and under what circumstances, if any, a couple would have children out of wedlock. But extramarital sex *per se* would not seem to necessarily imply wrongdoing. Another way of challenging the above premise is to consider the implications of actual or imaginary cultures which might permit extramarital relationships under various circumstances. If commitment of sexual exclusivity is culturally relative, then we can question whether it is a necessary and sufficient condition for the existence of a marriage. In sum, the promise-breaking argument against adultery requires that we accept as necessary the connection between the nature of monogamous marriage and sexual exclusivity.

A related argument against adultery emphasizes the inevitable connection between adultery and deception. It is a reasonable expectation of those who enter marriage that such a close relationship demands a maximum of truth-telling, especially as regards intimacy in relationships outside marriage. Acts of adultery, it is assumed, go beyond what is legitimate and moral. Consequently, there is usually an effort made to conceal the adulterous relationship from others, including the spouse. It seems unavoidable that deception will be necessary to secure the secrecy of the extramarital relationship. And because deception is wrong, especially in close relationships like marriage, adultery is also wrong.

One common form of deception is lying. Active lying may be used to divert attention away from the increasingly complex way of life the adulterous spouse must assume to accomodate marital responsibilities as well as the needs and demands of the extramarital relationship. Outright lies and half-lies may serve to conceal facts about the actual use of time and the whereabouts of the adulterous spouse. The avoidance of direct lying may still involve lies of omission. That is, if no questions are asked and the information about the extramarital relationship is not volunteered and brought to the attention of the other spouse, a "lie" is still involved in the sense that the spouse in fact is deceived as to the actual state of the present marital relationship and the expectation of sexual exclusivity.

We must believe that deception results in marital harm if we presume that sexual intimacy is a primary source of those feelings of love and affection we associate as necessary to marriage.

> For given this way of viewing the sexual world, extramarital sex will almost always involve deception of a deeper sort. If the adulterous spouse does not in fact have the appropriate feelings of affection for the extramarital partner, then the adulterous spouse is deceiving that person about the presence of such feelings. If, on the other hand, the adulterous spouse does have the corresponding feelings for the extramarital partner but not toward the nonparticipating spouse, the adulterous spouse is very probably deceiving the nonparticipating spouse about the presence of such feelings toward that spouse. Indeed, it might be argued, whenever there is no longer love between

the two persons who are married to each other, there is deception just because being married implies both to the participants and to the world that such a bond exists. Deception is inevitable, the argument might conclude, because the feelings of affection that ought to accompany any act of sexual intercourse can only be held toward one other person at any given time in one's life. And if this is so, then the adulterous spouse always deceives either the partner in adultery or the nonparticipating spouse about the existence of such feelings. Thus extramarital sex involves deception of this sort and is for that reason immoral even if no deception vis-a-vis the occurrence of the act of adultery takes place. (Wasserstrom, 1975: 213)

In conclusion, this argument against adultery is based on the premise that monogamous marriage is defined in part by the reasonable expectation of non-deception. The argument also presumes a necessary connection between marriage and sexual exclusivity. In addition, we must affirm a necessary connection between the feelings of marital love with those of sexual intimacy. As with breaking promises, consequential or deontological arguments can show that deception is morally wrong. But, Wasserstrom's challenges above also are relevant to deception. In an open marriage where adultery is consensual there would be no need for deception. Further, Wasserstrom might question whether sex has to be connected necessarily with the kind and degrees of feelings we associate with the closest of relationships—marriage. Perhaps more good than harm would result from separating sex from love and affection. Then sex could be treated as a good in itself, to be enjoyed for its own sake, which is a prominent theme in many arguments supporting adultery.

ARGUMENTS FOR ADULTERY

In 1969, Thomas Nagel published his pioneering work in philosophy of sexuality, "Sexual Perversion." This article provoked numerous responses in the literature and deserves consideration here even though adultery *per se* is not discussed. However, we can make inferences from this literature relevant to our topic.

Before taking stock of commonly classified perversions, Nagel first sketches out a psychological theory of sexual desire according to its various functions— economic, social, and altruistic. He is especially concerned that we avoid the trap of thinking that sexual desire is only properly thought of as an expression of some other attitude such as love.

In his phenomenological analysis, Nagel adopts a Sartrean model to develop a view of sex as a complex form of interpersonal awareness. He describes how sexual desire is typically communicated on a variety of levels with his paradigm case of Romeo and Juliet meeting in a cocktail lounge. Romeo notices Juliet and becomes aroused. "At this stage he is aroused by an unaroused object, so he is more in the sexual grip of his body than she of hers" (Nagel, 1969: 11). Next, Romeo notices Juliet sensing him. "This is definitely a new development, for it gives him a sense of embodiment not only through his own reactions but through the eyes and reactions of another." This relating becomes even more complicated.

> But there is a further step. Let us suppose that Juliet, who is a little slower than Romeo, now senses that he senses her. This puts Romeo in a position to notice, and be aroused by, her arousal at being sensed by him. He senses that she senses that he senses her. This is still another level of arousal, for he becomes conscious of his sexuality through the awareness of its effect on her and of her awareness that this effect is due to him. Once she takes the same step and senses that he senses her sensing him, it becomes difficult to state, let alone imagine, further interactions, though they may be logically distinct. If both are alone, they will presumably turn to look at each other directly, and the proceedings will continue on another plane. Physical contact and intercourse are perfectly natural extensions of this complicated visual exchange, and mutual touch can involve all the complexities of awareness present in the visual case, but with a far greater range of subtlety and acuteness.

Nagel intends this schema or structure to define the norm of sex: "it involves a desire that one's partner be aroused by the recognition of one's desire that he or she be aroused" (1969: 12).

A perversion, then, would be any form of sexual relating which is an incomplete version of the above configuration of reflexive mutual recognition. In analyzing two-party heterosexual intercourse, Nagel concludes that, "In general, it would appear that any bodily contact between a man and woman that gives them sexual pleasure, is a possible vehicle for the system of multi-level interpersonal awareness that I have claimed is the basic psychological content of sexual interaction" (1969: 15). This would seem to imply that adulterous sex does not count automatically as a perversion. It is possible to complete the above structure of sex in relationships with two different people at different times, while being married to one. Whether this makes adultery morally right or at least neutral is another question. Nagel refuses to associate the concept of perversion in itself with either what is moral or immoral. Morality involves a different kind of analysis and evaluation of behavior. We may infer that Nagel would assume a utilitarian stand and deny that all adulterous relationships necessarily involve harmful consequences. Adultery, therefore, would be permissible if it gives pleasure to the two parties and does not harm anyone involved in the situation.

Robert Solomon responds to Nagel in his 1974 article "Sexual Paradigms." Solomon contends that Nagel concentrates on the form of interpersonal communication involved in sexual relationships to the exclusion of content. Nagel says, in effect, that what is communicated is sexual arousal itself. Solomon complains that "arousal," as Nagel uses it, is too broad a notion to be clearly understood. Nagel doesn't answer these key questions: What is aroused? Why? To what end?

Solomon employs Sartre's definition that sexuality is interpersonal communication using the body as its medium. What, then, is communicated through body language during sexual activity? Body language is used to express feelings and attitudes. Sexual expression may communicate the feelings of tenderness, trust, domination, and passivity better than love. "Love, it seems, is not best expressed sexually, for its sexual expression is indistinguishable from the expressions of a number of other attitudes" (Solomon, 1974: 344).

Perversion, then, according to Solomon, is more a matter of deviance in *content* in sexual communication than, as Nagel states, in the *form*.

> But it seems to me that the more problematic perversions are the semantic deviations, of which the most serious are those involving insincerity, the bodily equivalent of the lie. Entertaining private fantasies and neglecting one's real sexual partner is thus an innocent semantic perversion, while pretended tenderness and affection that

> reverses itself soon after orgasm is a potentially vicious perversion. However, again joining Nagel, I would argue that perverse sex is not necessarily bad or immoral sex. (1974: 345)

Solomon does not specifically refer to adultery in this context but perhaps we could infer that extramarital sex with sincerity would be possible. Whether it is also moral would seem to depend on circumstances and related feelings and attitudes.

Seven years after the above essay was written, Solomon published his book on romantic love, *Love: Emotion, Myth, Metaphor* (1981). After attempting to demythologize much of the thinking about love that has occurred in Western tradition, Solomon presents his own existentialist theory of love. Again, there is no explicit mention of adultery, but we may draw pertinent inferences.

Love, according to Solomon, is just an ordinary emotion.

> Love is an emotion, nothing else. But emotions are not—traditional linguistic usage and certain current popular songs aside—"feelings." Our emotions are neither primitive nor "natural," but rather intelligent constructions, structured by concepts and judgments that we learn in a particular culture, through which we give our experience some shape and meaning. And it is not only love that gives meaning to life but all emotions—hatred, anger, and envy too. But if emotions are primarily judgments, ways of shaping the world, then one might say that we do not "fall in" love at all. Quite to the contrary, the fall is rather a creation, which we have been taught to make by a thousand movies, stories and novels; its most essential ingredient— too often hidden in the language of "spontaneity" and "chance"—is personal *choice*. (1981: xxvii)

An emotional construct is more than a reaction to our experienced world. It is a way of projecting ourselves into a world of meaning of our own making. In the case of love, what is created is a shared identity, a "loveworld." Two individuals, while maintaining their unique individualities, fantasize together and act their way into a relationship which is more than simply a combination or conjunction of the two. This novel reality is a kind of synthesis characterized by a mutual sense of identity. This means that love inevitably involves tension.

> Love is a *dialect,* which means that the bond of love is not just shared identity—which is an *impossible* goal—but the taut line of opposed desires between the ideal of an eternal merger of souls and our cultivated urge to prove ourselves as free and autonomous individuals. No matter how much we're *in* love, there is always a large and non-negligible part of ourselves which is not defined by the loveworld, nor do we want it to be. To understand love is to understand this tension, this dialectic between individuality and the shared ideal. To think that love is to be found only at the ends of the spectrum—in that first enthusiastic "discovery" of a shared togetherness or at the end of the road, after a lifetime together—is to miss the loveworld almost entirely, for it is neither an initial flush of feeling nor the retrospective congratulations of old age but a struggle for unity and identity. And it is this struggle—neither the ideal of togetherness nor the contrary demand for individual autonomy and identity—that defines the dynamics of that convulsive and tenuous world we call romantic love. (1981: 147)

Love is a dialectical process of mutual creating. But the process continues only as long as the two individuals at every moment reaffirm their will to love each other. Voluntary choice is the foundation of romantic love. Because love is a continuous series of decisions it is logically distinct from a commitment. Love is an emotion of the moment. A commitment is a promise, or accepted obligation, or expectation that binds over a period of time. Solomon notes, "If you're in love, you don't need to make a commitment; if you need a commitment, it has nothing to do with love" (1981: xxxiii).

If love and commitment are separable, then we should be able to make a case for adultery being moral under certain circumstances. A marriage must involve commitment and, one hopes, love. There seems to be nothing in Solomon's theory which would exclude simultaneous extramarital love relationships.

> Our exclusivist view of love—"you can only love one person (at a time)"—is at least thrown into serious question by comparison with other emotions, since exclusivity is clearly not required in order to be "truly" angry at someone, or envious. (1981: 51)

That multiple love relationships would complicate a person's life goes without saying. At the same time, the creation of more than one shared identity could be an enrichment of a person's experiencing. Other factors would be relevant in assessing the morality of such relationships. Presumably, Soloman's existentialist approach would demand that a person's autonomy and freedom be respected above all else. An extramarital relationship could be moral, therefore, if it did not violate or jeopardize the autonomy and freedom of the various parties involved.

In a 1977 article titled, "Plain Sex," Alan H. Goldman complains that Nagel and Solomon do not go far enough in separating sex from other considerations. Both of these theories still represent examples of means/ends analyses. That is, they attribute a necessary external goal or purpose to sexual activity. More traditional approaches, for example, tied sex as means to reproduction, or as an expression of love and affection between partners. Nagel and Solomon commit the same mistake in viewing sex as a means to interpersonal communication.

> To analyze sex as a means of communication is to overlook the intrinsic nature and value of the act itself. Sex is not a gesture or a series of gestures, in fact not necessarily a means to any other end, but a physical activity intensely pleasurable in itself. (Goldman, 1977: 276)

> Sexual desire is desire for contact with another person's body and for the pleasure which such contact produces; sexual activity is activity which tends to fulfill such desire for the agent. (1977: 268)

Goldman remarks that sex is more like music than language. That is, music can be aesthetic and pleasing in itself; it is not merely or best conceived of as a vehicle for expressing other specific feelings and attitudes.

Goldman prefers a Kantian approach to determining right and wrong in sexual relationships. In particular, he focuses on the second formulation of the categorical imperative which prohibits using persons solely as means to private ends. This principle, however, does not involve an absolute prohibition on using others as means.

> Many human relations, most economic transactions, for example, involve using other individuals for personal benefit. These relations are immoral only when they are one-sided, when the benefits are not

mutual, or when the transactions are not freely and rationally endorsed by all parties. The same holds true of sexual acts. The central principle governing them is the Kantian demand for reciprocity in sexual relations. In order to comply with the second formulation of the categorical imperative, one must recognize the subjectivity of one's partner (not merely by being aroused by her or his desire, as Nagel describes). Even in an act which by its nature "objectifies" the other, one recognizes a partner as a subject with demands and desires by yielding to those desires, by allowing oneself to be a sexual object as well, by giving pleasure or ensuring that the pleasure of the acts are mutual. It is this kind of reciprocity which forms the basis for morality in sex, which distinguishes right acts from wrong in this area as in others. (Of course, prior to sex acts one must gauge their effects upon potential partners and take these longer range interests into account.) (1977: 282–283)

His last sentence reveals that Goldman favors a mixture of deontological and consequential theory. Recognition of a person's subjectivity is a constant. But there are different ways to respect this idea in practice. If the persons involved in extramarital relations treat each other with such respect and reciprocity and no unnecessary harm were done to any of the parties involved, then extramarital sex would be moral.

The same conclusion follows from Goldman's analysis that separates sex from other external ends such as reproduction, love, affection, or communication. Sex in itself simply satisfies desire and gives pleasure. In this sense, "Sex desire . . . is desire for another which is nevertheless essentially self-regarding" (1977: 284). This is why "sex affords us a paradigm of pleasure, but not a cornerstone of value" (1977: 283). Sex offers us a needed outlet for desire and is one of the most satisfying forms of recreation. But it is not an essential value and should not be elevated to a position of prominence in a person's rational plans for the good life. Nor is it conceptually connected with those more important values like love or marriage which are altruistic in nature and do bear significantly on what we mean by the good life. Extramarital sex, therefore, in theory, has nothing to do with marriage and should not, in itself, constitute a threat to marriage.

One year after Nagel's landmark essay, Richard Taylor published his book on ethics, *Good and Evil* (1970). In his chapter,

"Eros, or the Love of the Sexes," Taylor also attempts to isolate the concept of sexual passion from love in particular. He claims that sexual passion has almost nothing to do with love.

> Clearly, it is no form of love at all, beyond the fact that it happens to be called by that name, and it has almost nothing to do with love, in any sense in which this is of special moral significance. Eros, or the attraction of the sexes, is found in virtually everything that lives and appears to differ in men only in certain accidental details. Men, for example, are aware of this drive, can formulate and act on deliberate plans with respect to it, can to some degree at least understand it, and can forsee its consequences; but none of these things changes its essential nature. It is in us as irrational, blind, and unchosen as in any insect; it is something that is simply thrust on us by nature, we then have to act out our response to it. The fact that we know what we are doing and are aware of what is going on does not change this in the least, for no more did any man ever choose not to be impelled by its urging, than did any ever choose to be so impelled. One could not aptly describe a pair of copulating grass-hoppers, or mice, or dogs, as making love; they are simply cop-ulating. The expression is no less inept when applied to people—except that here we feel some euphemism is needed, and this one serves.
>
> Love, as a sentiment, expresses itself naturally in sympathetic kindness, even sometimes in a kind of identification of oneself with the thought, feelings, and aspirations of another. It is compatible with sexual passion, but it by no means rests on it nor, contrary to what so many would like to believe, does it find its highest expres-sion there. This is made obvious by a number of things; for example, by the natural love of parents for their children, and by the fact that sentiments of genuine love and friendship can exist and sometimes persist through a lifetime among persons of either sex, wherein the erotic element is entirely absent. And on the other side, it is notori-ous that sexual passion can be kindled by one for whom one cares nothing at all, and equally, that one may have a friend who is truly beloved who nevertheless stirs this passion not in the least. Looking at it from still another point of view, it is obvious to anyone having a knowledge of human affairs that genuine love, as St. Paul put it, "never fails"; that is to say, it is inseparable from loving kindness in action, and absolutely ennobles everything that it touches. The erotic passion, on the other hand, left to itself seldom succeeds, for it is a notoriously fertile source of folly, of madness, sometimes of human degradation, and very often of cruelty and unspeakable crime. (Taylor, 1977: 205)

Taylor deals explicitly with the topic of adultery in his recent book, *Having Love Affairs* (1982). Here, his focus is not casual sex without love. Rather, he uses first person accounts and case studies to examine the phenomenon of extramarital "romantic love" or "passionate love." He defines a love affair as "an intense, passionate, and intimate relationship between a man and a woman, at least one of whom is married to, or cohabits in a marriage relationship with, someone else" (Taylor, 1982: 17). The purpose of the book is to have the reader gain a better understanding and be more tolerant of such relationships. Pragmatically speaking, such relationships will always be with us.

> Love affairs are like wars: Everyone finds them exciting, yet everyone knows they carry with them the risk of untold destruction. But just as wars are not going to be stopped by piously intoning "Thou shalt not kill," neither are people going to stop falling in love and acting on those deep and beautiful feelings just because someone says "Thou shalt not commit adultery." Wars and the kinds of "moral equivalents" that people find in prize fights and football can be made less destructive, and so can love affairs, together with such substitutes for these that people find in fantasy and literature. We really need no barren, spiritless, and negative prohibitions, here or anyplace else. (1982: 188)

Taylor's primary defense of love affairs rests on his contention that passionate love is an ultimate good.

> If love and affection are good—and they are, indeed, the ultimate good, exceeding wealth, honor, and everything else in the joy they bring to their possessor—then the free expression of passionate love cannot be bad, except in its effects. (1982: 49–50)

Nothing in human experience, Taylor notes, except perhaps the ecstasies of religion, rivals the fulfillment to be found in passionate love. Fame, power, and wealth are but poor substitutes for the warmth of genuine affection such love entails. Love affairs, therefore, are good insofar as two people find great satisfaction in loving each other intensely, intimately, and freely. In a love affair, two people share their love as a gift rather than an obligation. Since the ulterior motives for love and affection in marriage are not present, their love relationship may seem all the more authentic. The primary reason for falling in love is simply the passionate love the two persons feel for each other.

Taylor is not arguing that love affairs are better than marriage, since in the long run they rarely provide as much overall satisfaction as a good marriage. Rather, love affairs are to be taken seriously because they involve depths of feeling and affection often missing from marriage relationships. In any case, love affairs are valid ways of relating because of the satisfaction they bring two individuals.

Further, Taylor argues that love is basically a private matter best left in the hands of the individuals involved.

> However inadvisable it may be to seek love outside the conventional restraints, the right to do so is about as clear as any right can be. For we are here dealing with what is ultimately personal and private, with that realm into which no one else can step without trespassing. Everyone has a right to be in any one's arms he chooses. (1982: 48)

The only qualification is utilitarian. This libertarian view of adultery demands that we seek to minimize the bad effects of such a relationship. The major part of *Having Love Affairs* is devoted to the project of developing such an ethic for love affairs.

> Love affairs should be taken with the same seriousness as marriage. Instead of pretending that they do not exist, which is plainly false and hypocritical, or pretending that something so common ought not to exist, which is ethically naive, we should set before us some guiding principles, some dos and don'ts, that begin with the love relationship itself and then seek, instead of simply abolishing or diminishing it, to minimize its power to cause damage and destruction, thus increasing its power to yield fulfillment to those involved. (1982: 62)

The ethics of love affairs consists of a set of rules for husbands, wives, and lovers. Taylor proposes three rules to guide the actions of those who suspect or know their partners are having an affair. Taylor first assumes that the marriage relation is good and should not be destroyed. Given this assumption, the first three rules are: Do not spy or pry, Do not confront or entrap, Stay out of it. These rules are a reasonable extension of the idea that love affairs are good. Given this assumption, then, the nonadulterous partner has an obligation to respect and even protect the privacy of such a relationship. To refuse this obligation would occasion more negative results and jeopardize the marriage relationship over the long run. Three additional rules govern the feelings of spouses and to the same end. These also are rules of avoidance: Stop being jealous, Stop feeling guilty, Don't give it away. Taylor recommends such rules on the strength of their reasonableness in fostering the least amount of negative consequences for all involved.

Another set of rules serves as guidelines for the love affair partners. The first rule recognizes the fact that the mutual fulfillment of individual needs is the primary reason for a love affair and what keeps it together: Be aware of the needs of the other. Taylor articulates five more rules which, in effect, encourage extramarital fidelity. The rules address the issues of truth, discretion, accomodation, trust, and constancy: Be honest, Do not exhibit and boast, Never deliver ultimates, Do not betray, and Do not abandon.

In sum, Taylor tries to fill a need occasioned by recent trends in the liberalization of attitudes about sex. Attitudes have changed, but philosophers have mostly concentrated on debating the virtue of monogamous marriage and the legitimacy of extramarital or other sexual arrangements. Taylor is the first to see the need for taking another step and spelling out moral rules for adulterous love, or stated more positively, moral guidelines for the expression of passionate love. For the traditional "Thou shalt not," Taylor substitutes "Thou shalt love, freely, honestly, tenderly, joyously, generously, and unselfishly" (1982: 50). The novelty in Taylor's approach deserves more attention. As yet, no reviews of the book or other responses have appeared in philosophical literature.

A onetime student of Taylor, Russell Vannoy, published his major work, *Sex without Love: A Philosophical Exploration,* in 1980. We can use this work to illustrate both a development upon the theme of Taylor's earlier essay and an implicit critique of his book on love affairs. Vannoy's general conclusion is that "on the whole, sex with a humanistic non-lover is far preferable to sex with an erotic lover" (Vannoy, 1980: 49). The concept of erotic love seems equivalent to Taylor's passionate or romantic love.

Much of Vannoy's book presents a valuable analysis of the concept of erotic love. Taylor does not analyze his own concepts of passionate or romantic love. Vannoy tries to show that it is almost impossible to arrive at a single definition of erotic love. Indeed, the conception of erotic love seems to be self-contradictory. For example, there is a conflict between a person's wanting to develop a sense of identity, of oneness with another person, and the desire to remain free and independent. Oneness serves our needs for security and stability. Freedom is necessary for experiencing adventure and variety. Vannoy concludes that there can be no successful resolution of such conflicting desires; the search for erotic love causes endless mental torture. He reaches the same conclusion by examining other conflicts such as ecstasy versus endurance, altruism versus self-interest, choice versus emotion, security versus insecurity, opposites attract versus like attracts like.

To say that love, or sex with love, does not result in increased contentment and peace of mind seriously challenges Taylor's vision of the satisfaction to be derived from extramarital love, not to mention love in marriage. On the other hand, if Taylor's moral rules could apply even when his definition of passionate love does not, Vannoy might agree that such rules could help guide the conduct of the type of person he describes as a "generous, considerate, and sexually adept non-lover committed to humanistic principles" (1980: 218).

Vannoy cites other reasons for separating sex from love, and by implication provides the elements for a defense of adultery. For one thing, some recent studies in psychology cast love in a negative light. Lawrence Casler, for example, argues that the need for love is symptomatic of a deficient sense of self-worth or personal insecurity. Such a need is based on sexual craving and social norms which seem to condemn those who are unloved.

Vannoy quotes feminist writers who view love in a historical context and argue that love is a self-deluding act by which women masochistically glorify their male oppressors. He cites a 1969 article by Ti-Grace Atkinson:

The most common escape (from their imprisonment in the female role and the denial of their humanity) is the psychopathological condition of love. It is a euphoric state of fantasy in which the victim transforms her oppressor into her redeemer: she turns her natural hostility against herself—her consciousness—and sees her counterpart in contrast to herself as all powerful (as he is by now at her expense). The combination of his power, her self-hatred and the hope for a life that is self-justifying—the goal of all living creatures—results in a yearning for her stolen life—her self—that is the delusion and poignancy of love. "Love" is the natural response of the victim to the rapist. (Vannoy, 1980: 25)

Another reason for separating sex from love is that the stereotypical view of sex without love ignores the possibilities for a fulfilling experience in such contacts. Vannoy describes a hypothetical situation in which sex without love appears every bit as rich and positive an experience as that traditionally associated only with sex with love.

Is sex without love superficial, as compared with the unity of heart, mind, and body that is claimed to exist between sex and love? Suppose that at a San Francisco night club I find myself overwhelmed by an attraction for someone in both a sensual and sensuous sense. Such a person's beauty need not, of course, be physical. There are many things about this person which may stir my emotions, even though I may have no desire to become emotionally involved with her in the sense usually meant by erotic love. The experience is enriched by the beautiful setting, by the hopes of sharing an evening with her, by memories of previous encounters with such charming individuals, by the prospects of meeting her or someone like her again, by the thought of having sex with an utter stranger with whom I may have a unique and fresh experience of her and my sexual abilities, by the fact that she has been sensually aroused and has responded to my stare, and so forth. Is this merely a description of a ludic playboy on the prowl for a sex object? It could be, but it need not be. For people who are concerned with persons as persons can experience such rich complexity of thought, emotion, and sensuality as much as anyone else; and so long as the object of one's affections shares one's views, an evening may be spent together that can be totally free of mutual exploitation.

It can be an evening of sensuous eroticism that may continue for hours and include all the foreplay, afterplay, kisses and caresses that actual lovers enjoy, perhaps done simply out of deep mutual

admiration for each other's sensuous qualities and out of gratitude
for having been chosen by the other for such an evening. Yet the
pair may go their separate ways in the morning and never see each
other again, perhaps because they prefer their own independence
and singlehood to permanent emotional involvement and marriage.
The claim, then, that sex with love is a rich, complex phenomenon
and sex without involvement is a mere sensation in the groin is a
fallacious dualism. (1980: 26)

This case shows that sex with a non-lover is not necessarily superficial, crude, selfish, or animalistic. "Sex can be a loving act and . . .
even loveless sex can be fun under certain circumstances" (1980: 27).
Vannoy distinguishes between a loving act, or series of acts, and sex
within the context of marriage, commitment, and emotional involvement. Sex can be a loving act if care and consideration of the
other person are present, and if there is a shared point of view about
the use of sex for mutual pleasure.

Vannoy suspects that those who attack "sex without love" have
a deep-seated aversion to sex itself. For someone who believes that
sex is basically dirty or evil, can sex even with a loved one ever be
completely open, spontaneous, and guilt-free? "Only someone who
can first enjoy sex for its own sake can really provide his beloved
with a joyous experience" (1980: 28).

Vannoy lists a number of more practical advantages that accrue
to his position of sex without love or sex for sex's sake.

There is the fun of seducing someone. One does not seduce a lover.
    One need not feel obligated to perform sexually except when
one feels like it. But lovers often feel that they owe their beloveds the
satisfaction of each other's needs even when they are not in the
mood for sex.
    One can experiment with new partners or with new sex tech-
niques without feeling guilt or fear of offending one's beloved. Furthermore, if sex is an appetite, as many claim, it seems odd to think
that one could go through life satisfying an appetite in only one
way. One's appetite for food cannot be permanently satisfied by
hamburger, no matter how many different ways one tries to prepare
it. Could not the same thing also be true of the sexual appetite? Isn't
there a need for a variety of partners, and isn't our claim that we can
be satisfied with one person forever a product of social conditioning
used to preserve and protect the institution of marriage?

One need not fear performing inadequately, ejaculating prematurely or not having an orgasm with a stranger whom you'll never see again. But if these things happen too often with a lover, one will feel that one has failed the loved one. This can be quite disheartening even if the lover is forgiving of one's faults.

Perhaps the most basic difficulty of using sex to express love is that one is often merely using sex as a means to an end: expressing love, rather than enjoying sex for sex's sake. The focus tends to be on the emotions of love rather than lust itself. The sensual aspects of sex thus tend in many such cases to be sacrificed to tenderness, something which has its own worth and beauty, to be sure, but which may not be the central focus many sexual partners would prefer. (1980: 56)

Sex for sex's sake, then, means that individuals engage in sexual activity to enjoy certain uniquely sexual feelings which give pleasure. An act has sexual significance, therefore, if it is motivated by a desire for or yields such feelings. This motive is the key to understanding what defines an act as sexual or not. Sex may serve other purposes with different motives.

Defenses of adultery tend to accept monogamous marriage as a given in our society and then show why alternative forms of sexual relationships are also valid. John McMurty, in a widely-publicized article from 1972, "Monogamy: A Critique," develops a Marxist attack against the institution of monogamous marriage itself. By implication he encourages adultery as a form of guerrilla warfare which, in the long run, may contribute to the downfall of the institution of marriage as we know it

McMurty argues that sexual exclusivity, which is supposed to promote the growth of intimacy and affection, actually inhibits personality growth and alienates the marriage partners from each other. On the whole, sexual exclusivity is more harmful than beneficial.

Formal exclusion of all others from erotic contact with the marriage partner systematically promotes conjugal insecurity, jealousy and alienation by:

(a) Officially underwriting a literally totalitarian expectation of sexual confinement on the part of one's husband or wife: which expectation is, *ceteris paribus*, inevitably more subject to anxiety and disappointment than one less extreme in its demand and/or cultural-juridical backing;

(b) Requiring so complete a sexual isolation of the marriage partners that should one violate the fidelty code the other is left alone and susceptible to a sense of fundamental deprivation and resentment;

(c) Stipulating such a strict restraint of sexual energies that there are habitual violations of the regulation: which violations *qua* violations are frequently if not always attended by (i) willful deception and reciprocal suspicion about the occurrence or quality of the extramarital relationship, (ii) anxiety and fear on both sides of permanent estrangement from partner and family, and/or (iii) overt and covert antagonism over the prohibited act in both offender (who feels "trapped") and offended (who feels "betrayed"). (1972: 593)

There are other disadvantages.

The sexual containment and isolation which the four principles together require variously stimulates such social malaises as:

(a) Destructive aggression (which notoriously results from sexual frustration);

(b) Apathy, frustration and dependence within the marriage bond;

(c) Lack of spontaneity, bad faith and distance in relationships without the marriage bond;

(d) Sexual phantasizing, perversion, fetishism, prostitution and pornography in the adult population as a whole. (1972: 594)

The underlying issue is that the restrictions of monogamous marriage reduce sexuality to a dimension of private property.

The ground of our marriage institution, the essential principle that underwrites all four restrictions, is this: *the maintenance by one man or woman of the effective right to exclude indefinitely all others from erotic access to the conjugal partner.* . . . In other words, the four restrictions of our form of monogamous marriage together constitute a state-regulated, indefinite and exclusive ownership by two individuals of one another's sexual powers. Marriage is simply a form of private property. (1972: 594-5)

Consequently, marriage is not really intended to promote directly the good of the marriage partners or even their children. Rather, marriage is a linchpin of our present social structure and is indispensable to the continuation of capitalism. Here, we will look at just one of McMurty's arguments supporting this thesis.

> Because the exclusive marriage necessarily and dramatically reduces the possibilities of sexual-love relationships, it thereby promotes the existing economic system by:
>
> (a) Rendering extreme economic self-interest—the motivational basis of the capitalist process—less vulnerable to altruistic subversion;
>
> (b) Disciplining society's members into the habitual repression of natural impulse required for long-term performance of repetitive and arduous work tasks;
>
> (c) Developing a complex of suppressed sexual desires to which sales techniques may effectively apply in creating those new consumer wants which provide indispensable outlets for ever-increasing capital funds. (1972: 598)

It is not surprising, therefore, that while in the eyes of many, monogamous marriage may be justified as in the best interests of society as a whole, nonetheless, it causes enormous harm to individuals by suppressing their need and interest in exploring a variety of sexual relationships. McMurty implies that adultery may help to offset the oppressiveness of the traditional institution of marriage. But more often than not, adulterous relationships simply "imitate and culminate in the marital mold," rather than pioneering a real alternative (1972: 599). Thus, adultery constitutes only a mild form of protest against the capitalist order of society and does not break the stranglehold of private property over sexuality.

Numerous criticisms have been lodged against McMurty's portrayal of monogamous marriage. In his 1975 article, "The Consolation of the Wedded," David Palmer protests that McMurty's view is historically and sociologically shortsighted. McMurty seems to contend that monogamous marriage is inherently evil and this in turn causes other social ills. Palmer suggests the facts may better support the idea that marriage has been surrounded and negatively influenced by a variety of other evil institutions and practices. Michael D. Bayles (1975) would concur. He believes that McMurty attacks an outdated view of marriage, one that prevailed a century ago. His arguments carry much less weight today when the companionship mode of marriage is more prevalent. Palmer also challenges Mc-Murty's claim—that marriage has disastrous psychological consequences for the individuals involved—as mere speculation without the requisite backup of empirical evidence. Indeed, McMurty makes no reference to psychological and sociological literature for such evidence.

THE FUTURE OF ADULTERY IN PHILOSOPHY

Thus far in American philosophy the topic of sex has turned out to be something less than a burning issue. The single most influential resource in the field of philosophy of sexuality is still Nagel's 1969 article on perversion. For example, the longest chapter in Vannoy's 1980 book on sex without love updates the controversy over this issue and then develops its own theory on perversion. This emphasis in the literature will probably continue, presuming, for one thing, that the gay rights and feminist movements keep pressing society to acknowledge the legitimacy of homosexual relationships. The challenge of grappling with the problems associated with such relationships may have been one of the stronger forces in the 1960s that inspired Nagel's article.

The second most influential resource in American philosophy in the last two decades seems to be McMurty's 1972 essay condemning the institution of monogamous marriage. The future of such radical critiques is dubious. If anything, conservative trends in society in the 1980s will probably reaffirm the value of marriage and spawn more negative reactions to McMurty's thesis.

Where does this leave the topic of adultery? As we have shown in our survey of the literature in this chapter, very few philosophical publications in the United States have directly addressed the topic. Richard Taylor's 1982 book, *Having Love Affairs*, is the first sustained book-length treatment of adultery. It is questionable, however, whether Taylor's book will have much influence on mainstream philosophy. It is written in a popular style geared more to a general audience rather than to fellow professionals. This is not a new trend. The 1960s stimulated interest among philosophers in the practical and concrete applications of their theories including philosophy of sexuality. Adultery, however, has never been a major focus in this area. This is unfortunate since the pollsters indicate adultery is a common and pervasive fact of contemporary life and will remain so in the future. Taylor's book recognizes this fact. But it is unlikely that this topic will receive its due from other philosophers in the immediate future.

REFERENCES

Alexander, W. M. 1970. "Philosophers Have Avoided Sex." *Diogenes*, 72: 56-74.

Bayles, Michael D. 1975. "Marriage, Love and Procreation." In *Philosophy and Sex*, edited by R. Baker and F. Elliston. Buffalo, N.Y.: Prometheus.

Bertocci, Peter A. 1949. *The Human Venture in Sex, Love and Marriage*. New York: Association Press.

————. 1967. *Sex, Love and the Person*. New York: Sheed and Ward.

Buford, Thomas O. 1984. *Personal Philosophy: the Art of Living*. New York: Holt, Rinehart and Winston.

Cohen, Carl. 1975. "Sex, Birth Control and Human Life." In *Philosophy and Sex*, edited by R. Baker and F. Elliston. Buffalo, N.Y.: Prometheus.

Elliston, Frederick. 1975. "In Defense of Promiscuity." In *Philosophy and Sex*, edited by R. Baker and F. Elliston. Buffalo, N.Y.: Prometheus.

Engels, Friedrich. 1942. *The Origin of the Family, Private Property and the State*. New York: International Publishers.

Fichte, Johann Gottlieb. 1869. *Science of Rights*. Philadelphia, Pa.: Lippincott.

Goldman, Alan. 1977. "Plain Sex." *Philosophy and Public Affairs*, 6: 267-287.

Gray, Robert. 1978. "Sex and Sexual Perversion." *Journal of Philosophy*, 75: 189-99.

Held, Virginia. 1973. "Marx, Sex, and the Transformation of Society." *Philosophical Forum*, 5: 168-84.

Hume, David. 1882. *The Philosophical Works*, vol. 1, edited by T. H. Green and T. H. Grose. London: Longmans, Green.

Kant, Immanuel. 1963. *Lectures on Ethics*. Trans. Louis Infield. New York: Harper and Row.

Kierkegaard, Soren. 1959. *Either/Or*, vol. 2. Trans. W. Lowrie. New York: Anchor.

————. 1945. *Stages on Life's Way*. Trans. W. Lowrie. Princeton, N.J.: Princeton University Press.

Margolis, Joseph, and Clorinda Margolis. 1977. "Separation of Marriage and Family." In *Feminism and Philosophy*, edited by M. Vetterling-Braggin, F. Elliston, J. English. Totowa, N.J.: Littlefield, Adams.

McMurty, John. 1972. "Monogamy: A Critique." *Monist*, 56: 587-599.

Mill, John Stuart. 1970. *The Subjection of Women.* Cambridge, Mass.: M.I.T. Press.

Moulton, Janice. 1976. "Sexual Behavior: Another Position." *Journal of Philosophy,* 73: 537-546.

Nagel, Thomas. 1969. "Sexual Perversion." *Journal of Philosophy,* 66: 5-17.

Norton, David L., and Mary F. Kille, eds. 1971. *Philosophies of Love.* San Francisco, Calif.: Chandler.

Palmer, David. 1975. "The Consolation of the Wedded." In *Philosophy and Sex,* edited by R. Baker and F. Elliston. Buffalo, N.Y.: Prometheus.

Rapaport, Elizabeth. 1973. "On the Future of Love: Rousseau and the Radical Feminists." *The Philosophical Forum,* 5: 185-205.

Ruitenbeek, H. M., ed. 1970. *Sexuality and Identity.* New York: Delta.

Schopenhauer, Arthur. 1928. *Essays on Women.* New York: Simon and Schuster.

Shaffer, Jerome. 1978. "Sexual Desire." *Journal of Philosophy,* 75: 175-189.

Singer, Irving. 1974. *The Goals of Human Sexuality.* New York: Schocken.

———. 1966. *The Nature of Love: Plato to Luther.* New York: Random House.

Solomon, Robert. 1981. *Love: Emotion, Myth, Metaphor.* New York: Doubleday.

———. 1974. "Sexual Paradigms." *Journal of Philosophy,* 71: 336-345.

Taylor, Richard. 1977. "Eros, or the Love of the Sexes." In *Social Ethics,* edited by T. A. Mappes and J. S. Zembaty. New York: McGraw-Hill.

———. 1982. *Having Love Affairs.* Buffalo, N.Y.: Prometheus.

Vannoy, Russell. 1980. *Sex Without Love: A Philosophical Exploration.* Buffalo, N.Y.: Prometheus.

Verene, D. P. 1975. "Sexual Love and Moral Experience." In *Philosophy and Sex,* edited by R. Baker and F. Elliston. Buffalo, N.Y.: Prometheus.

———. 1972. *Sexual Love and Western Morality: A Philosophical Anthology.* New York: Harper and Row.

Wasserstrom, Richard. 1975. "Is Adultery Immoral?" In *Philosophy and Sex,* edited by R. Baker and F. Elliston. Buffalo, N.Y.: Prometheus.

7

Philip E. Lampe
ADULTERY AND
THE BEHAVIORAL SCIENCES

Sexual behavior has been viewed from three major perspectives: moralizing, medicalizing and normalizing. Within the Western culture heritage the moralizing perspective, viewing sex in terms of moral and immoral behavior, is the oldest and probably most widespread. This was followed by the medicalizing perspective, wherein sexual behavior is viewed in terms of medical causes and effects. Most recently sexual behavior is interpreted in terms of normal social behavior. It is the normalizing perspective which now is identified with the scientific approach and is deemed to be the most appropriate perspective for the behavioral sciences.

Sexual taboos in the Western culture and the immaturity of the behavioral sciences impeded the development of the scientific study of sexual behavior. Earliest attempts tended to take the form of individual case studies usually carried out by a health care professional utilizing patients. The first major organization for the study of sex was the *Institut fur Sexualwissenchaft* which was established in Berlin in 1897. This institute continued until 1933 when it was destroyed by the Nazis. Five years later the second major organization for the study of sex was founded. In 1938 Alfred Kinsey began the Institute for Sex Research at Indiana University. Until this time most of the scientific knowledge of sex available in the United States came from Western Europe from such European writers as Sigmund Freud, Havelock Ellis and Richard von Krafft-Ebing. They were also largely responsible for fostering an open discussion of sex and thereby paving the way for the acceptance of the study of sexual behavior and the dissemination of sexual information in the United States.

STUDY OF ADULTERY

Adultery is not a commonly used term in the behavioral sciences because it has a long tradition of usage in religious literature and is identified with the moralizing perspective. The word comes from the Latin *adulterare,* which means to go beyond the limits (i.e., legal or natural); to corrupt or ruin; to pollute. Consequently, the word is inextricably related to a moral judgment in the minds of the people. The more popularly used terms—"infidelity," "unfaithfulness," and "cheating"—are also avoided because of their judgmental nature. Because science attempts to be objective and nonjudgmental, it prefers to utilize neutral terminology. In an effort to accomplish this, the expressions "extramarital relations," "extramarital sex," "extramarital affair," and "swinging" are but some of the many substitutes which have been used.

In recent years there seems to have been an increase in the number of scientific books, articles, talks and seminars which have been presented on extramarital sexual relations and related topics. One obvious reason would be that there is now more data available than ever before. Another important and related reason is mentioned in the prologue of a recent book on the psychoanalytical aspects of extramarital sex: "Because there has also been an immense change in what is permissible to say and print, sociologists and other professionals have been studying and reporting on all forms of sexual behavior, including extramarital sex" (Strean, 1980: xiii).

Nonscientific treatments of extramarital sexual relations, or adultery, have also abounded but have been basically propagandistic in nature, intended to promote certain ideologies, whether pro- or anti-adultery. Not surprisingly, the terminology employed often varies with the point of view propounded, with those opposed generally using the term "adultery." In the United States the most common example of such a genre is religious writing, which intends to convince its audience of adultery's immoral nature and the potentially harmful effects it could have, in this life as well as the hereafter. This perspective, derived from the Judeo-Christian tradition, which has been prevalent in the United States, is based on faith and is concerned with spiritual salvation. Pro-adultery literature is also based on a kind of faith, i.e., a firm belief in something for which there is no proof. Ironically, this approach, no less than the anti-adultery approach, also tends to be concerned with salvation, although it is a humanistic or natural rather than a supernatural salvation. Individual freedom, psychological growth and personal fulfillment are the promised rewards (see Mazur, 1973). Among the advocates of this pro-adultery faith are some therapists who encourage premarital sex and extramarital sex as a means to achieve and/or maintain self-fulfillment and mental health (see Fine, 1975).

Whereas the nonscientific approach is based on ideals, logic and speculation or authority and/or tradition, the scientific approach is based on the collection and analysis of empirical data. The scientific approach is nonpromotional; it takes neither a proscriptive nor a prescriptive attitude toward adultery. Science is concerned merely with understanding and explanation. Hence, adultery is studied as a type of social behavior.

Social scientific studies of sexual behavior have fallen into one or more of the following categories: (1) The ecology and styles of sexual behavior as a physical act; (2) The individual and/or social meanings of the act; (3) The norms and standards that govern the act and/or the factors which implement or impede the social norms and standards; (4) The history of sexual behavior and/or sexual norms; (5) The incidence of such behavior.

PRE-KINSEY ERA

Much of the early work on sexual behavior was at best pseudo-scientific, containing a mixture of moralizing and value judgments. Even this type of work met with resistance in the English-speaking countries, which were under Victorian influence. At its most extreme, Victorianism led to such bizarre practices as separating books on library shelves by sex of authors, and covering the legs of pianos for the sake of modesty. As a result, non-English-speaking Western countries, particularly Germany, provided the United States with much of its ideas regarding sexual behavior. *Psychopathia Sexualis,* written by Dr. Krafft-Ebing in 1906, was especially influential after its translation was published in the United States in 1933. Krafft-

Ebing believed that "Man has beyond doubt the stronger sexual appetite of the two. From the period of pubescence he is instinctively drawn toward women. . . . Woman, however, if physically and mentally normal, and properly educated, has but little sensual desire. If it were otherwise, marriage and family life would be empty words" (1933: 14). "Woman's mind," he claimed, "certainly inclines more to monogamy than that of man" (1933: 15). Today such ideas are no longer tenable and appear blatantly sexist. They do, however, clearly represent the spirit of the times. Perhaps the major contribution of Dr. Krafft-Ebing is that he helped to bring many forms of sexual behavior into the open.

One of the earliest pioneers of the more scientific studies of sex was Havelock Ellis, an English physician. His seven-volume work *Studies in the Psychology of Sex* (1933) was first published in German. Its arrival in the United States so offended the public morality of the times that legal proceedings were brought against it. The judge hearing the case stated that the claim the work was of scientific value was merely a "pretense, adopted for the purpose of selling a filthy publication." Consequently, until 1935 the work was legally available only to members of the medical profession. Ellis, unlike Krafft-Ebing, attempted to describe differences in sexual behavior without being judgmental. Thus, he helped to introduce the concept of individual and cultural relativism to the study of sexual behavior.

Because of the cultural climate of the times, early social scientists generally did not study extramarital sexual behavior in any in-depth, systematic manner. One of the more common obstacles encountered was the reticence of individuals to admit to this type of socially and morally proscribed behavior. This same problem was reported by several of the early researchers, including Kinsey, Pomeroy and Martin in their famous landmark study of male sexual behavior in the 1940s. Respondents appeared to be more cooperative in answering questions regarding virtually all other types of sexual experiences. Besides making studies difficult, the reported unwillingness to openly discuss adultery has made the accuracy of the findings questionable.

Extramarital sex was not the exclusive or primary focus of early research. It was often an almost incidental, although useful, by-product of the primary purpose of a study. One of the more notable examples of this was the research done by the psychiatrist Gilbert Hamilton who, along with Ellis, is often regarded as one of the pioneers in the study of sexual behavior. In the early 1920s he was given an invitation and financial support by the National Research Council's Committee for Research on Problems of Sex to undertake research into the problems of sex in the marital relation. The resulting study was to become a widely quoted reference. Among his findings it was reported that 28 of the 100 men and 24 of the 100 women who were interviewed had experienced extramarital sexual relations.

Interestingly, however, a higher percentage of both men (29 percent) and women (41 percent) reported they had had extramarital *love* affairs. Obviously, not all of these love affairs were consummated. It was also found that more of the men and women who had engaged in extramarital sex had sexual experience prior to marriage. The positive correlation between premarital and extramarital sexual experience has been raffirmed in subsequent studies.

In attempting to explain the overall results of his study, Hamilton said that the findings "are suggestive of the possibility that a tendency to have a relatively large number of love affairs is likely to be associated with a relatively inferior capacity for finding satisfaction in marriage" (1929: 224). Later he expressed what appears to be an ideological cause for extramarital sexual relations. "In fact it seemed to me that the majority of the young wives who had indulged in adulterous sex relations had done so more out of loyalty to a belief in spousal sex freedom than in response to anything suggestive of an overwhelming sex urge" (1929: 540).

That same year the largest and most ambitious of the studies of sex was published by the United States Bureau of Social Hygiene. The sociologist Katharine Davis had studied 2,200 women for the stated purpose of providing more adequate data on the physical and mental aspects of the sex life of normal individuals. This was important because much of the previous data concerned "abnormal" subjects. It was hoped that the study would reveal not only what people did, thought, and knew about sex, but, just as importantly, what they did *not* know.

Respondents were asked whether a husband was ever justified in having sexual intercourse with a woman who was not his wife. Twenty-four percent answered affirmatively and 76 percent negatively. Further findings reported a surprising lack of a double standard. Twenty-one percent said there could be justification for a wife having sexual intercourse with a man not her husband, while 79 percent said there couldn't. Commenting on the findings, Davis observed that "Of the 248 who consider that a husband is warranted in having extramarital relations, 170 (72.6 percent) practiced masturbation, 142 (60.1 percent) admitted homosexual feelings or practices, and 69 (29.7 percent) had indulged in sexual intercourse" (1929: 354-355). She went on to say that the figures were approximately the same for those who consider a wife justified. It is not clear whether this information was meant to describe or discredit these respondents. Regardless of the intent, the result may well have been the stereotyping, in the mind of the reader, of all persons who had condoned extramarital sexual relations as being sexually deviant and/or immoral.

In explaining reasons for the positive responses Davis wrote, "Extra-marital relations for either are justified by the affirmative group on a number of grounds: unsatisfactory relations between husband and wife, from whatever cause; separation or divorce, or when divorce is desired but cannot be obtained. A few regard the husband's or wife's love for another as justification; or the unsatisfied desire for children" (1929: 353).

Almost a decade later, the psychologist Lewis Terman reported on his study of 792 married couples which was concerned with discovering the psychological and psycho-sexual correlates of marital happiness. Although many questions regarding sexual behavior were asked, the respondents were not queried regarding extramarital intercourse. The reason given was that the researchers were "doubtful about the possibility of securing truthful answers" from respondents who believed they might suffer serious legal consequences were their infidelities ever discovered (1938: 335). A question was included, however, which asked "Do you frequently experience desire for intercourse with someone else than your wife (husband)?" Terman found that 72 percent of the 769 husbands who answered indicated that, on occasion, they had experienced a desire for extramarital sexual intercourse. Only 27 percent of the 770 wives who answered the item indicated a similar desire.

Unfortunately, it is not entirely clear how serious all of these "desires" were. One may, for example, experience desire for extramarital intercourse without acting on it, just as one may desire to be somewhere else at a particular time but be unwilling to make the trip. This may be especially true of the 29 percent of the husbands and 15 percent of the wives who indicated they only rarely experienced the desire. Such desires may range from being idle wishes to powerful—but resistible—temptations. On the other hand, a desire may spark an actual adulterous act. So the usefulness of Terman's information is, at best, limited.

Perhaps more useful is the information that the desire for extramarital intercourse was inversely related to the spouses' marital happiness. Respondents who indicated that they never, or only rarely, desired extramarital intercourse reportedly had happier marriages than those who indicated more frequent desire. Finally, consistent with the findings of Hamilton, premarital sexual experience was found to be positively correlated, for both men and women, with admitted frequency of desire for extramarital intercourse.

Terman presented some possible explanation for his finding that more husbands than wives desire extramarital sex. First, he mentioned, but indicated he did not endorse, the widespread belief that women are by nature more monogamous than men. Subsequently, he stated:

> Apart from the possible effect of differential culture pressure—the so-called double standard—we doubt whether this interpretation is justified. Perhaps the figures reflect chiefly the sex difference in strength of the sexual drive. Wives, as we have seen, prefer intercourse less frequently than men and are rated appreciably less passionate than their husbands in 50.2 percent of cases, as compared with 7.6 percent who are rated as more passionate. A majority of wives have as much sex as they want (or more) from their husbands, while approximately one-third of the husbands have less from their wives than they want. (1938: 336-337)

Two years later the psychologist Carney Landis and colleagues published the results of a study of 153 normal females and 142 female psychiatric patients. It was discovered that a significantly higher percentage of the abnormal women (24 percent) than the normal (4 percent) had extramarital experience. "One possible explanation of this difference is that more of the abnormal women were poorly adjusted in marriage and, hence, went outside of the marital relationship in attempts to gain sexual satisfaction" (1940: 98), an observation that supported the previously cited findings of both Hamilton and Terman.

It has generally been assumed that a person who does "wrong" will feel guilt. Landis' study examined the correlation between guilt feelings and extramarital sex and discovered that a larger number of respondents expressed guilt feelings concerning premarital than extramarital sex. Although not discussed by Landis, it may be stated that while lack of guilt cannot be considered a cause of extramarital sexual relations, it may be seen as a contributing factor. Guilt resulting from premarital sexual relations would have to be worked through and neutralized if the behavior was to be continued. Once sex before marriage has been justified and/or accepted, the same reasons or rationalizations may later be used to apply after marriage to extramarital sex. Guilt has been mentioned in other studies as one of the factors which causes individuals to refrain from, or terminate, extramarital sex relationships.

Up to this time most major studies of sex were conducted by physicians, psychologists or psychiatrists. These studies tended to share the same basic weaknesses. They used relatively small, non-random samples of self-selected white, middle-class individuals who were often patients of the researchers. Not only does this raise the question of the representativeness of the data to the general population, but it also tends to place the studies in the medicalizing perspective. Regardless of the way these researchers approached the topic, the fact that they were health care professionals may have strengthened the notion in the minds of the readers, if only by implication, that there were medical reasons for what was commonly considered to be deviant sexual behavior.

In 1948, Alfred Kinsey, a zoologist by education, published the first of his famous studies, *Sexual Behavior in the Human Male*. Its subsequent widespread popularity is not only a tribute to the quality of the work but also an indication of the extent of the public's desire for accurate and complex sexual information. This study, together with its companion study of females, is generally considered to be a watershed work. The review which appeared in the *Library Journal* was typical of other reviews at the time. It hailed the work as "unique in breadth of scope and objectivity from all previous studies in the area." Although it has since been criticized, especially for its nonrandom sampling, it not only continues to be referred to today but is the standard against which all other studies of sexual behavior are measured.

The study contained many questions which concerned extramarital sex. In the section dealing with extramarital intercourse, he wrote: "There seems to be no question but that the human male would be promiscuous in his choice of sexual partners throughout the whole of his life if there were no social restrictions. This is the history of unrestrained human males everywhere. The human male almost invariably becomes promiscuous as soon as he becomes involved in sexual relations that are outside of the law" (1948: 589). Based on this assumption, his findings that only 37 percent of the respondents had extramarital sexual experience were somewhat surprising. However, he attributed this low figure to a lack of honesty on the part of the respondents and estimated that, allowing for the presumed cover-up, the real figure should be approximately 50 percent.

Kinsey went into greater detail than his previously-mentioned predecessors in analyzing data. He noted the existence of an inverse relationship between religiosity and extramarital sexual relationships. Devout church members are far less likely than the inactive members to engage in such behavior. Nevertheless, these differences are "nowhere near so great as the differences between social levels. The community acceptance or non-acceptance of extramarital intercourse is much more effective than the immediate restraints provided by the present-day religious organization. But since sex mores originated in religious codes, it is, in last analysis, the Church which is the origin of the restrictions on extramarital intercourse" (1948: 589).

The greatest differences, then, were related to socio-economic status, particularly as measured by formal education. Males with little education were the group found to have the most premarital as well as extramarital sexual experience. Like the previous studies mentioned, Kinsey and associates discovered that there was a relationship between premarital and extramarital intercourse. It was explained, however, that the apparent relationship between the two types of sexual experience was probably to be found in the basic attitudes of the individuals involved regarding sexual behavior. That is, rather than seeing premarital sexual experience as the *cause* of extramarital sexual experience, both pre- and extramarital sexual experience should be seen to be caused by a liberal sexual attitude regarding sex and marriage.

Although the less educated respondents generally had more extramarital sexual experience than members of other groups, they tended to seek such experience less often as they grew older. Well-educated males, in contrast, became more involved in extramarital sexual relationships as they aged, so that by age 50 they were actually more involved than their less-educated counterparts (27 percent to 19 percent). At every social level most males were forced to engage in extramarital intercourse only sporadically. In most cases a number of female partners were used for relatively short periods of time, with the interval between each partner varying from weeks to years. Once again, however, a class difference emerged: higher class males were likely to have fewer partners but longer lasting affairs. Prostitutes were found to be a relatively rare source of extramarital sexual gratification for the average male, supplying only between 8 to 15 percent of all extramarital intercourse.

Lower class wives appeared to expect more extramarital sexual behavior on the part of their husbands and were consequently more tolerant of it than middle class wives. However, such behavior was generally done more discretely in the upper classes and therefore resulted in fewer marital problems. Nevertheless, it often caused marital discord and divorce when known or discovered. Finally, Kinsey reported that wives, at every social level, were more accepting of adulterous husbands than were husbands of adulterous wives.

In attempting to explain why males are more adulterous than females, the opinion was expressed that females have less desire for a variety of sexual partners, before or after marriage. The easy expla-

nation—females are basically more "moral" than males—is specifically rejected by Kinsey. More likely explanations, he believed, could
be found in the differences in the sexual responsiveness of males and
females, as well as in the differences in the conditionability of the
two sexes. Human females are aroused by fewer stimuli than males
are—a pattern also found among lower mammals—and they also
tend to find less sexual excitement in psychic associations and non-
tactile stimulations. So Kinsey theorizes that males more frequently
engage in extramarital intercourse because of certain physical, psychological and social differences. Especially important in this regard
is the male's desire for a variety of experiences. Thus, concludes
Kinsey, extramarital intercourse may occur irrespective of satisfactory sexual relations within the marriage.

Sociologists Ernest Burgess and Paul Wallin collaborated in a
1953 study of young engaged couples. The study, hailed at the time
as "an important and outstanding book" and "the finest research yet
achieved in the field," explored possible justifications for extramarital
relations. They discovered that 55 percent of the 223 men and 49
percent of the 216 women who responded indicated that husbands
were justified to seek extramarital sex under certain conditions. In
considering whether there was ever justification for wives seeking
extramarital sex, 48 percent of the men and 38 percent of the women
answered affirmatively. We can note that more women than men
upheld the so-called double standard. While women were almost
evenly divided in their opinions on husbands' extramarital behavior
(49 percent saying it was justifiable sometimes, 51 percent saying it
never was), they were more clearly against any such justification for
such behavior among wives (38 percent to 63 percent). Even so,
when we compare these responses with those obtained almost a
quarter of a century earlier by Davis, we can discern that women's
attitudes in this matter were becoming much more "permissive."

In an attempt to identify the specific conditions which would
provide justification for one's own possible extramarital behavior,
this question was asked: "If you were not considering divorce or
separation, under which of the following conditions would you, as a
husband [or wife], permit yourself extramarital relations?" (1953:
401). In response, 48 percent of the 225 males and 73 percent of the

225 females who answered indicated they would not engage in such behavior under any condition. Therefore, there appeared to be more acceptance of extramarital relations engaged in by others than by oneself. Of the 118 men and 61 women who indicated they could envisage such a possibility, the following were the five most frequently selected conditions: for men—frigidity of wife (52 percent), repeated unfaithfulness of wife (44 percent), wife's chronic illness (23 percent), general dissatisfaction with wife (20 percent), and strong affection for another woman (18 percent); for women—repeated unfaithfulness of husband (49 percent), unsatisfactory sexual response from husband (25 percent), strong attraction to another man (23 percent), general dissatisfaction with husband (16 percent), and husband's chronic illness (10 percent). The remaining reasons given were: spouse's temporary illness, a single act of unfaithfulness by the spouse, wish for variety, wanting to arouse the spouse's jealousy, spouse's frequent absence, and wife's pregnancy.

An important distinction was made by both men and women regarding repeated and one-time unfaithfulness. One-time unfaithfulness was found to be much more acceptable to most respondents. On the other hand, repeated unfaithfulness was given as a leading justification for one's own adultery. This may indicate a motive of revenge or retaliation. A similar, though less dramatic, distinction was made between chronic and temporary illness, with the former providing more of a justification for seeking sexual satisfaction elsewhere. Commenting on the reasons "chronic illness," "frequent absence," and "unsatisfactory sexual response," the authors said that "the excess of men over women in all three categories can be interpreted as signifying that the men in looking forward to marriage think of themselves as less capable of enduring sexual frustration than do the women" (1953: 402). However, both men and women revealed that it is preferable to rely on prudence rather than on one's ability to resist temptation. Thus, better than nine out of ten of the 1,000 men and women who were asked indicated that they would object if their spouse asked to go out with a former friend of the opposite sex.

That same year, Kinsey published the second of his studies, *Sexual Behavior in the Human Female*. Because of the unexpected success of his earlier study, this work received unprecedented pre-publication publicity for a scientific study. Like the earlier work, this one was dedicated to a wide-ranging study of sexual phenomena, including adultery. Although the literature on sexual behavior continued to grow, Kinsey nevertheless commented that "There is a surprising paucity of any open and frank discussion of extramarital coitus in the serious literature (1953: 430).

As in the earlier study, reference was again made to the importance of our mammalian background in understanding what is regarded as man's desire for a variety of sexual partners. Kinsey argued that "It is widely understood that many males fail to be satisfied with sexual relations that are confined to their wives and would like to make at least occasional contacts with females to whom they are not married" (1953: 409). He added, however, that this is not to say that all men will necessarily seek intercourse with other partners. Many husbands will refrain from engaging in such behavior because they consider it to be morally and/or socially unacceptable. Nevertheless, even these individuals will be able to understand that sexual variety might provide satisfactions which can no longer be found within a marriage. Variety, whether it be in books, music, recreation, friends, or sex, is desirable. It appears to stimulate and so counteract psychological fatigue, which is a prime source of difficulty in maintaining a strictly monogamous relationship.

This desire for sexual variety, however, is not as prevalent among women. Kinsey stated that "many females find it difficult to understand why any male who is happily married should want to have coitus with any female other than his wife" (1953: 409). His data supported the fact that most women have not engaged in sexual intercourse with someone other than their husbands. Only 26 percent of his sample had experienced extramarital sex by the age of 40. Moreover, among these, 41 percent reported they had had only one extramarital sexual partner, and 44 percent reported they did not intend to repeat the experience. An additional 16 percent of the married women admitted they had engaged in extramarital petting without engaging in coitus.

Females were more likely to engage in extramarital sexual activity when they were in their mid-thirties and early forties, often becoming involved with younger men. College-educated females were more likely to have had extramarital experience than those who had less education. Religion was found to be an important factor in controlling sexual behavior. Once again, there were correlations between premarital and extramarital sex. Twenty-nine percent of the females who were not virgins at the time of their marriage had had extramarital experiences as compared to only 13 percent of the premarital virgins. Kinsey expressed the opinion that there was an increase in the acceptance of sexual activity after the turn of this century, and that sexual activity itself increased after World War I.

The desire for extramarital sexual experience, Kinsey suggested, was prompted by: the search for variety of experience with new and sometimes superior sexual partners; the conscious or unconscious attempt to acquire social status through socio-sexual contacts; the accommodation of a respected friend who desires sex; the assertion of independence from the spouse and/or of the social code; the retaliation against the spouse's adultery or nonsexual mistreatment, real or imagined; and the search for a new source of emotional satisfaction.

Possible consequences of extramarital sexual experience included: the development of emotional relationships which could interfere with relations with one's spouse; the improvement of sexual relations with one's spouse; immediate and/or long-range marital problems; pregnancy; and divorce. In regards to this last point, males rated their wives' extramarital sexual activities as prime factors in their divorces twice as often as wives cited husbands' sexual activities. Finally, Kinsey mentioned that a spouse was sometimes *encouraged* to engage in extramarital relationships; as an excuse for his/her own adultery; to participate in mate swapping; for surreptitious observance; to obtain homosexual contacts; for sadistic satisfaction in forcing the wife to have sex with others; and to offer the spouse the opportunity for greater sexual satisfaction.

An important appraisal of the Kinsey reports, entitled *Sexual Behavior in American Society,* appeared in 1955. Kinsey's studies were credited by the sociologist Ernest Burgess as being the first satisfactory approximation of the extent of extramarital sexual behavior in our society. Although the central point of interest in his work was biological, Kinsey had, to a surprising extent, adapted a sociological explanation for sexual behavior. In discussing the study of adultery, Burgess expressed the opinion that a sociologist would assume that extramarital behavior varies according to a person's profession. For example, teachers, who are usually more conventional and subject to strong community controls, would probably exhibit a low incidence, as would ministers. Lawyers would be lower than physicians, and both would be below the level found among musicians and actors, who tend to have the more bohemian standards. Because of high mobility and relative freedom from social controls, occupations such as sailors, traveling salesmen and aviators would also have high rates of extramarital intercourse.

Burgess went on to state that according to his own studies there were five important factors which could lead to extramarital sexual behavior among husbands. First, some men get married with little or no expectation of confining their sexual activity to their wives. These are the "Don Juan" types. Second, some men marry without being deeply in love with their wives, or their love for them fades away. These husbands often look for love elsewhere. Third, some men are separated from their wives for prolonged periods of time and seek female companionship during their absence. Fourth, some men have occupations which cause them to be very mobile and experience frequent but short separations from home. While away, some of these act as though they were not married. Fifth, certain occasions, such as celebrations, conventions and parties may cause a relaxation of conventional controls. Thus, some men take advantage of these moral holidays.

THE POST-KINSEY ERA

A decade after publication of the last of the Kinsey reports, there was a general increase in both the number and quality of studies which dealt with extramarital sexual relations. By the end of the 1960s there was a growing body of relevant research as studies began to focus exclusively on this topic. Changes had occurred in society which facilitated a deeper, more extensive probing of this area. Among these were: changes in the divorce laws; the frequency and explicitness of the sexual material to which the public has been exposed through movies, television, books, magazines and even courses in schools; the diminution of the strength and unanimity of organized religion's moral pronouncements; the number of married women in the work force together with the types of jobs held by them and the length of time (hours per day and years per career) spent outside of the home; the increased personal mobility which served to weaken community censure; and the increasing spirit of individualism and felt need for personal fulfillment. Conditions were favorable not only for the collection of extramarital sexual information, but also for its dissemination. Individuals were willing to discuss personal sexual experiences and eager to read about those of others.

As a consequence, in the post-Kinsey era of the late 1960s, the amount of research in this area had reached such proportions that several professional journals were initiated which specialized in reporting the findings of sexual studies, and the books on the subject continued to multiply. In 1965 two sociologists, John Cuber and Peggy Harroff, published the results of a study of 211 middle and upper class married couples. Based on their findings, the researchers identified five distinct types of marriages and briefly discussed each type's susceptibility to what they termed "infidelity." The five types are: (1) Conflict habituated, which is characterized by a great deal of tension and intermittent conflict; (2) Devitalized, in which a once full, happy, close relationship becomes lifeless and apathetic; (3) Passive-congenial, a relationship which from the beginning is marked by a lack of vitality and romance; (4) Vital, in which there is a genuine sharing and togetherness resulting in feelings of mutual satisfaction; (5) Total, the closest, most satisfying of marriages, based on the sharing of important values and interests. The couple are best friends and lovers as well as spouses.

According to the authors, infidelity occurs in each type of marriage—even in the "total"—but the reasons it occurs are quite different. Infidelity may be nothing more than another outlet for hostility in the conflict-habituated marriage, whereas in the passive-congenial marriage the spouses may be trying to break the boredom of an empty, mechanical conjugal relationship. A devitalized marriage may cause a husband or wife to become unfaithful in an attempt to recapture a spirit or mood which is no longer present in his or her own home. In the vital marriage some infidelity may be due to the emancipation of the spouses, while in other cases it is just accepted by them as a fact of life or a source of mutual, albeit vicarious, gratification. Such behavior produces different reactions in each different type of marriage. Because of the rich and deep relationships found in both the vital and total marriages, deception and insincerities are more likely to be detected by the spouses than in the other types, and the reaction may be more serious. Divorce may result when the partners are unwilling to accept anything less than the full, deep, complete partnership that has existed from the beginning.

Gerhard Neubeck, who was president of the American Association of Marriage Counselors, edited a book entitled *Extramarital Relations* in 1969. Included were two articles worth noting because they added something new to the relevant literature. The first study conducted by Neubeck and Schletzer utilized a small sample of 40 couples and yielded the following information. Those individuals who were found to score low in "strength of conscience" appeared to become more sexually involved outside of marriage than those exhibiting a stronger conscience. The former group, however, did not appear to become more emotionally involved nor did they fantasize about extramarital involvement to a greater degree. When classifying individuals according to marital satisfaction, those scoring low tended to seek greater involvement outside of marriage through fantasy rather than emotional or sexual involvement.

A second article, entitled "Adultery: Reality Versus Stereotype," by John Cuber, reported the findings of a study of 437 respondents. The author was able to categorize the relationship between the adulterous behavior of the respondents and their marriage. Three types of relationships emerged: Type I, in which the adulterous relationship simply compensates or substitutes for what is seen to be a defective marriage. Sometimes the adulterous relationship in this case is similar to a good marriage in terms of the psychological dimensions; Type II, in which the adulterous relationship results from the physical separation of the spouses, for whatever reason, for a period of time. Such relationships tend to be short-term and nonmeaningful. These are not considered to pose a real threat to the marriage; Type III, in which what is called a bohemian mentality is exhibited by one or both of the spouses wherein a monogamous commitment is not accepted. This typology supports previously mentioned findings.

The effects of the extra-marital relationship on the marriage vary. Important considerations include (a) whether it is covert or is known to the spouse; (b) whether it is consensual or nonconsensual; (c) whether only one or both spouses participate in such behavior; (d) whether condonement by a spouse is genuine and is based on principle or is merely the result of an ultimatum by the offending partner. A comparison of the sexual relationships between spouses before and after an adulterous relationship shows that sometimes the marital sexual relationship improved, sometimes it deteriorated and sometimes it remained unchanged. The same is true of the overall marital relationship. Thus the author concluded, "Perhaps the most important theoretical overall generalization which our study supports is the great heterogeneity masked in the monolithic word 'adultery'" (1969: 195).

Two additional findings of Cuber are worth noting. The first is that the "other woman," the female who is sexually involved with a married man, experiences negative feelings of "second class" status. The second is that while adulterous relationships are generally less enduring than marriage, long-term relationships are, on average, more psychologically fulfilling than marriage. Marriages are expected to endure but affairs are not. Therefore, if an affair does last it is for reasons intrinsic to the pair itself.

That same year Morton Hunt, a free-lance writer who frequently ventures into the realm of the social sciences, published a book entitled *The Affair*. What makes this book noteworthy is that it is concerned exclusively with extramarital sex. It was based upon data gathered from 360 questionnaires, 91 interviews, and various diaries of a non-random sample of white middle-class respondents. At the beginning of the book Hunt wrote that "To date there is still only one major source of sound statistical information on extramarital sexual activity in the United States—the first and second volumes written by Alfred Kinsey and his associates . . ." (1969: 10-11).

Reporting his own findings, Hunt noted that a large majority of the respondents indicated that they always or usually disapprove of adultery. Even a majority of those who themselves had had extra-marital affairs were generally disapproving. There are many ways in which an affair may come about. Sometimes a married couple takes a "conjugal vacation," or has a "summer divorce," in order to freely pursue personal sexual fancies. (Recall Burgess's idea of "moral holidays.") A number of married individuals engage in what Hunt calls "brinksmanship." This is a game in which novices at infidelity stop short on the brink of sexual activity. Some players are able to remain on the brink for an indefinite period of time without discomfort or frustration. Others cannot and either consummate the relationship or terminate it. Although there is some degree of physical and/or emotional involvement inherent in brinksmanship, many players do not consider themselves really unfaithful as long as they do not fall. Others, however, experience some degree of guilt and have at least some sense of infidelity. Hunt believes that as many as one-quarter of all middle class wives and between one-tenth and one-eighth of their husbands may engage in this game. This estimate roughly agrees with the previously mentioned finding of Hamilton that many more wives than husbands have nonconsummated love affairs.

Regarding extramarital relationships, it was found that between one-tenth and one-twenty-fifth of first affairs last only one day, a little over one-tenth last more than one day but less than a month, almost one-half last more than a month but less than a year and that about one-fourth last two or more years. Very few, however, endure four or more years. He noted that these findings appear to contradict Kinsey's impression that the most common affair was only of one- or two-days duration. They also challenge Cuber's feelings that the fairly long-term or even lifelong affairs were relatively infrequent. In fact, most middle class affairs last between several weeks to several years, with the participants meeting weekly.

Several classes of problems were expressed by participants in relation to their affairs. Communication was often a problem; lovers dared not arouse anyone's suspicions. A meeting place also presented a problem. Meetings in one's own home was dangerous because of the possibility of being seen by family, friends, and neighbors, while meetings at motels were a sure sign of an affair to anyone who might recognize the couple or his or her car. In addition to the problem of a meeting place, there was that of a meeting time. A suitable time had to be worked into the schedules of both parties, and for those who had both family and steady employment this could be very difficult. Another problem is that the individuals had to remain sexually active both at home and away. A decrease of sexual interest with the spouse could arouse suspicion and/or displeasure.

Hunt said that one in six spouses knew for sure of the other's first affair. In later affairs the number increased to one in three. Approximately three-fourths of those who discover the affair reacted in the traditional fashion: rage, jealousy, humiliation, and depression. Over one-third of those who subsequently divorced indicated it was a direct result of the affair. If a divorce does occur, only about one in ten of the ex-spouses will marry the person with whom they were amorously involved. In those cases in which they do marry, about one-half will themselves subsequently get divorced.

Hunt published a second book on sexual behavior in 1974, entitled *Sexual Behavior in the 1970's,* based on a study commissioned by *Playboy* magazine to describe the sexual activity of male and female Americans. Although the data was obtained from 982 respondents, making it much larger than his previous study, it once again utilized a non-random sample of primarily white middle-class individuals. Unlike the other work, this book covered a wide range of sexual activity, with only one part devoted to postmarital and extramarital sex. A general observation was made that "While most Americans—especially the young—now feel far freer than formerly to be sensation-oriented at times, for the great majority of them sex remains intimately allied to their deepest emotions and inextricably interwoven with their conceptions of loyalty, love and marriage" (1974: 253).

It was found that 41 percent of the white male sample had experienced extramarital coitus. Data indicated that while males began extramarital sex at an earlier age than was true for Kinsey's sample, the overall incidence was similar. Furthermore, no increase was found among women from Kinsey's time except in the "under 25" age category. There was no important difference found based on socioeconomic status or education, but those who later got divorced reported having started extramarital relationships much earlier in their marriage. Approximately one-tenth of the males and females limited their extramarital sex to petting.

Hunt also found that more females experienced orgasms in marital than in extramarital intercourse. For some people the physical shortcomings of extramarital sex appear to be outweighed by the psychic rewards, such as a sense of personal desirability, an illusion of recaptured youth, and a rediscovery of passion. A few people find in an extramarital relationship an untarnished peak experience, others find it to be a sordid exercise in meaningless sensuality, while most experience a mixture of satisfactions and frustrations that, on balance, add up to less overall pleasure than they experience in marriage.

During the past generation there has been almost no measurable increase in the number of American husbands, and only a slight increase in number of wives, who have ever had an extramarital experience. The only significant change in this regard is found among those, especially females, who are under 25 years of age. Likewise, there has been virtually no change in attitude toward such behavior. In a series of questions dealing with the acceptance of extramarital activity by one's own mate, answers ranged from 80-98 percent against it. In contrast to earlier studies, such as those of Baber (1939) and Kinsey (1948), females were no more accepting of such behavior on the part of their husbands than were males on the part of their wives. The primary change regarding adultery which seems to have occurred is the reduction of the acceptance of the double standard.

According to Hunt, his findings contradicted popular opinion and the perception of the mass media. There has been no sexual revolution, he claims, with regard to adultery. Some people may believe that his respondents were not truthful, as has been suspected in several of the earlier studies. However, Hunt thought this to be unlikely and speculated that although the majority of individuals desire and/or fantasize about extramarital relationships, "most people continue to disapprove of such behavior because they believe that when it becomes a reality rather than a fantasy, it undermines and endangers the most important human relationship in their lives" (1974: 256).

Hunt remarked that,

> Even though the words "adultery" and "infidelity" have become
> somewhat unfashionable among sexual liberals because of their
> moralistic overtones and their inapplicability to mutually sanctioned
> extramarital acts, the evidence of our survey indicates that nearly all
> extramarital activity is still adulterous and unfaithful in the emo-
> tional sense; that is, by far the largest part of extramarital activity is
> secret and furtive, violative of the emotional entente existing be-
> tween the spouses, productive of internal conflict and guilt feelings
> on the part of the one engaging in such acts, and anywhere from
> infuriating to shattering to the other if he or she discovers the truth.
> (1974: 226-267).

A study of extra-marital sex was conducted by the sociologist
Lewis Yablonsky with the help of other sociologists and their stu-
dents. In the first of a proposed two-part study, 771 men from across
the country answered questionnaires regarding extramarital sex, and
50 gave in-depth interviews. The results of the study were published
in 1979 under the title *The Extra-Sex Factor*. Like most of his
predecessors, Yablonsky failed to use a random sample, thus limit-
ing the applicability of the findings to young or middle-aged, college
educated, middle-class whites. In describing his research, Yablonsky
stated that he found, for reasons similar to those mentioned by
Kinsey, that married men are still somewhat reticent about revealing
their extramarital sexual behavior.

Data revealed that the percentage of males who have engaged in
"extra-sex," approximately 50 percent, has not changed since Kinsey's time. Nevertheless, there has been a noticeable change in the
frequency and number of sexual partners. The average adulterous
male has had at least seven partners, and about 65 percent of the
time his female partner is single. The most active males reportedly
have averaged 20 affairs, with most being one or two night stands.
Only about 16 percent last beyond a year. The results support Kinsey's observation that most affairs have a short duration.

Nine out of ten adulterous men indicated they want to maintain
their marriage. Since they feared that the marriage could be damaged
if the wife found out, over 80 percent of the affairs were covert.
Yablonsky feels that in many cases the wife maintained what is

called an "ostrich posture"; she feared that she would feel compelled to do something that would destroy the marriage were she to discover her spouse's adultery. It is therefore probable that in those cases where the husband has not maintained secrecy, he has decided to end the marriage.

In indicating their personal reasons for extra-sex behavior, 48 percent explained that they enjoy heterosexual relationships, including sex; 40 percent said they like variety; 34 percent gave absence from home as a reason; 31 percent stated it was for more sex than the wife was willing to give. Other reasons, in order of frequency, were: "fun," "desire," "put romance in life," "sex with wife boring," "it is the 'in' thing," "anger and/or revenge," and "open marriage." The author expressed the opinion that "the data strongly suggests that most men have extra-sex for the purpose of exploring their personal emotional identities and enlarging their human contacts and relationships beyond the primary family situation" (1979: 26).

A unique feature of Yablonsky's study was the questioning of nonadulterous males for their reasons for not engaging in extra-sex. Seventy-three percent of the husbands reported they had remained faithful because they loved their wives and honored their marriage contract, nine percent gave "religious beliefs" as a reason, another nine percent said they had not had an opportunity to be unfaithful, six percent cited fear as a reason, and the remaining three percent responded with a variety of other reasons. More than eight out of ten nonadulterous husbands voluntarily refrained from extramarital sexual relations for what may be considered positive reasons (i.e., love, honor, religious conviction) rather than negative ones (i.e., fear, lack of opportunity).

CONCEPTUAL DEVELOPMENT

Science is built upon empirical data, and, as is evident from the preceding material, many empirical studies have been conducted during the twentieth century which have contributed to our knowledge of extramarital sexual behavior. Science also requires definition of terminology, clarification of concepts, and development of explanatory theories. This stage in scientific development usually begins on a large scale only after there is a body of empirical data to explain. There is not always a clear-cut distinction between these two stages and, in reality, many studies incorporate both, as was the case with many of those presented. Some, however, are much more clearly concerned with the interpretation (often of someone else's data) and conceptual development. The following studies are examples of this type.

In 1949 Kingsley Davis wrote a book in which he showed how, in the United States, jealousy was a common reaction to adultery. He explained how sexual property (people) is different in form, but in some respects similar to, economic property (things); relations to each are institutionally defined and regulated. He identified four attitudes toward property: (1) Need, when an object of property satisfies some organic requirement; (2) Vanity, when an object is valued for the response it elicits from others; (3) Pride, when the object represents some form of accomplishment for the owner; and (4) Love, when the owner wants affection from the object. Since affection is a phenomenon of the will, the question of possession is largely under the control of the object one wishes to possess. Jealousy results, Davis believed, when an owner fears rivalry for or loss of the object of his love, pride, or vanity.

Using this framework it may be seen that a spouse could be perceived as one's property and, as such, each of the four attitudes may apply. A husband or wife helps satisfy the organic need for sex. In addition, a successful or attractive spouse may be valued because of the response he or she elicits from others. Consequently, the spouse may also be valued because he or she represents an accomplishment, much like a trophy, in having won out over all the competitors, real or imagined. Finally, affection is commonly bestowed by the spouse. Whether adultery is viewed as a threat will depend on the specific society in which it occurs. Of special importance in this regard is the form of marriage which is socially approved and the relevant norms which are promoted. Davis wrote, "Jealousy is an emotion which has a function as a part of the institutional structure. Not only is it normatively controlled but it gives strength to the social norms as well" (1949: 192). Thus, it may be that our institution of monogamy causes adultery to be resented and therefore creates jealousy, rather than, as Westermarck (1922) believed, jealousy being that which creates monogamy.

Almost a decade later Albert Ellis, a clinical psychologist, published a book which has less value as a scientific contribution than as an example of an ideological statement concerning changing sexual mores. His book *Sex Without Guilt* carried the following dedication: "Dedicated to the countless men and women who have fought the lonely battle against guilt for doing those sexual things which are neither harmful to themselves nor to others." "Many of the old grounds for opposing adultery," he writes, "are just as senseless, in today's world, as many similar grounds for combating premarital sex affairs" (1958: 54). For example, many modern men and women do not consider adultery sinful, and therefore the act gives them little or no guilt. Furthermore, contraceptive techniques have lessened the dangers of illegitmate pregnancy, and prophylactic measures can eliminate venereal infection. And in at least some social circles, reputations may be enhanced rather than harmed by such behavior. Adultery need no longer be committed under the sordid and/or non-loving conditions of the past, especially when one considers that the Kinsey research has shown that adulterous affairs which are covert may actually enhance and preserve one's marriage. It may be said with little fear of scientific contradiction, that literally millions of men and women who engage in adulterous affairs thereby gain considerable adventure and experience, become competent at sexual pursuits and practices, are enabled to partake of a high degree of varietism, and have substantial amounts of sexual and nonsexual fun that they otherwise would doubtlessly be denied" (1958: 55).

Paradoxically, however, he advised his readers that in this country it is usually better *not* to commit adultery. Ellis offered many reasons for this opinion. In our society individuals are socialized to feel that adultery jeopardizes their marriages and indicates a lack of love. Once an individual is raised to feel these things are true, Ellis wrote, they tend to *become* true. Because individuals believe adultery is inimical to marriage, those who engage in adulterous relations generally do so covertly. This dishonesty, as any dishonesty, may prove harmful to the marital relationship. Because of the pervasive cultural belief that sexual satisfaction should be limited to marriage partners, the adulterer's sexual interest may actually be diminished; his or her spouse may then become sexually deprived and maritally discontented. Since most individuals have but limited financial resources, time, and energy, an adulterous person may deprive his or her spouse in these non-sexual ways as well. Ellis suggested that for individuals who have good all-around marriages, such behavior is foolhardy when it risks destroying the marriage. Ideally, Ellis explained, decisions which may affect the marriage should be made jointly, and since the decision to engage in adultery is generally made individually, adultery can destroy the mutual trust and confidence of a working partnership.

Ellis concluded by saying that "Today's adulterer need not feel evil or wicked. But, from the standpoint of impairing his own marriage, he may well be acting irrationally and neurotically. If he thinks of adultery not in terms of sin but in terms of the possible *adulteration* of his marital happiness, he should be able to make wiser choices in this connection" (1958: 59).

In 1970, the sociologist Jessie Bernard published an article, "Infidelity: Some Moral and Social Issues," in a book on marriage. She stated that the institution of marriage in our society presently requires both exclusivity and permanence. But these two requirements may be incompatible with our desire to continue to be attractive to members of the opposite sex. A choice may have to be made between exclusivity and permanence. The current trend seems to be for an emphasis on exclusivity over permanence in the younger years but on permanence over exclusivity in the later years.

Bernard believes there is a difference between infidelity and adultery. The former refers to a violation of promises or vows, such as those included in the wedding ceremony. She said the clearest example of infidelity is an action which violates a marital vow and results in deprivation for the spouse of any or all of his or her marital rights. However, Bernard questions whether extramarital behavior which does not result in any emotional, financial or sexual deprivation for the spouse can be considered infidelity.

Extramarital relations are of many kinds. Seven different classes are identified by Bernard based on a review of the literature. The first and least significant, morally and socially, is the relationship which takes the form of coquetry and flirtation. It may include embracing and petting. Second is a somewhat more serious relationship which tends to be transient and takes the form of sex-as-play. Third is the "matinee." This is a sexual relationship between co-workers which is not allowed to become too serious. Fourth is a quasi-matinee form found among high-status individuals and is described as a "cocktail-lounge" model. This is semi-serious, semi-committed, and semi-stable, usually carried on between older business or professional men and younger single women. Fifth is a form of infidelity which is similar to conventional marriage in that it has both commitment and endurance, is monogamous, and sometimes continues even after it has lost appeal. Sixth is fantasized infidelity, wherein one has relations with an imagined partner or has imagined relations with a real person. This is more common than acted-out infidelity. A form of this is thinking of someone else while having sex with one's spouse. The seventh and final form is one that may never be a sexual union. It is a deep, lasting emotional union where there is a profound sharing of oneself with someone other than one's spouse. This form may not be termed adultery, but it may be a case of infidelity.

Finally, Bernard stated that despite the high incidence of the several forms of infidelity, society continues to give lip service to marital exclusivity. Nevertheless, there are certain signs of change. There is an increasing emphasis by researchers on some of the positive functions of extramarital relations, and greater tolerance has been exhibited by some theologians for sexual behavior, including extramarital sex. Also, divorce laws have changed to such an extent that adultery, which was at one time virtually the only universally accepted grounds for divorce, is not even accepted as a sufficient reason in some places. Finally, it appears that there has been, and will continue to be, an increase in the incidence of extramarital sexual relationships among younger women.

Gordon Clanton continued the line of questioning begun by Bernard (1970) and Hunt (1974). Clanton stated that "adultery by definition seems to involve impurity, infidelity, and lack of virtue" (1977: 114). Nevertheless, a growing number of people include extramarital sex, with the knowledge and consent of their spouse, as part of their lifestyle. He raised the question whether such extramarital experiences were really adulterous. The answer given was both yes and no. "Yes" in that they are sexual relationships with partners outside of the marriage, but "no" in that they are thought neither unchaste nor deceptive by the spouses. Therefore, the term adultery should be neutral to meet the realities of today. The use of new terms to replace the term adultery have only added to the confusion because of their newness and lack of agreement.

Clanton proposed a typology of adultery based on the extent to which the spouse knows and approves of the relationship. "Clandestine adultery" is that in which the adulterous spouse is fearful of letting his or her spouse know of the relationship, and thus it is both unknown and unapproved (covert and nonconsensual). This is what adultery frequently connotes for most people. "Consensual adultery" is that in which the spouse both knows and approves of the partner's extramarital sexual behavior. Hence, the marital partners do not view the action as infidelity. "Ambiguous adultery" is that in which elements of both of the above types are present (i.e., covert-consensual or overt-nonconsensual). A spouse may know but not approve of his or her partner's extramarital behavior, or may approve of the general idea of sexual freedom but not know about the actual relationships. In some cases a spouse finds he or she is unable to accept the behavior after all.

Clanton noted that most studies have been concerned with clandestine adultery and that more research was needed regarding consensual and ambiguous adultery. For example, Clanton noted that not all consensual adultery is alike. There are three subtypes based on the degree of commitment to and the probability of permanence of the relationship. (1) *Group marriage* is a social and sexual agreement linking at least three persons, two of whom are married. Thus, it is a form of consensual adultery which exhibits a high degree of commitment and expectation of permanence. (2) *Open-ended marriage* is based on an understanding between spouses that each may have friendships with the opposite sex which may include sexual intimacy. The expectation is for a significant friendship-type commitment relatively close and relatively long-lasting. (3) *Recreational adultery* is a general category which includes "swinging." It is characterized by expectations of minimal emotional involvement in a very transient, sexual relationship.

Finally, Clanton believes that people who engage in deviant forms of behavior, such as adultery, need some form of support to minimize the negative effects. Without this support the deviants experience feelings of alienation and anxiety. If they are not able to receive these feelings of support and shared experience from other people, they may find them in works of fiction. The popularity of fiction which deals with adultery, he argued, may be due in part to the support it lends to those who are themselves engaged in such behavior. It also seems likely that it serves as a source of vicarious enjoyment for some who are not themselves adulterous.

In 1979 Judith Bardwick, a psychologist, published a book in which she discussed the sexual revolution. She stated that it really took place in the 1920s rather than the 1960s or 1970s. The revolution occurred with the passing of the Victorian era. Since then there has been a consistent rise in the percentage of males and females who have had nonmarital or extramarital sex, and the age at which they start has consistently declined. Contrary to the findings of Hunt, Bardwick believes that there has also been an increase in the sexual activity of middle aged women. It appears that many women begin affairs looking for excitement or approval when they enter their mid-thirties. While the percentage of men who have had extramarital sexual experience seems to be about the same as it was in Kinsey's day, the percentage of women has increased greatly and is now approaching that of men. This, claimed Bardwick, is probably the most revolutionary development of the current sexual revolution.

Bardwick said that today we are all affected, to some degree, by the "playboy" fantasy promoted by the mass media. This fantasy extolls pleasure, variety, and experimentation. According to images presented by the media, autonomy has replaced emotional interaction, freedom has replaced fidelity, and sex has replaced love. Sex has become separated from commitment, recreational sex has been glorified, and the idea that sex must be legalized in order to be enjoyed is seen as ridiculous. But this fantasy has also been the source of a new stress. People now wonder if they are missing some important sexual experiences and if they are enjoying their experiences as much as they should.

A major problem with the search for new sexual experience,

Bardwick claimed, is that most people feel betrayed and hurt when someone with whom they are sexually and emotionally intimate becomes sexually and emotionally intimate with someone else. When people are raised with the ideal of fidelity it is very difficult for them not to be sexually and emotionally possessive.

> Behavior is easier to change than emotion, which is not so easily legislated by logic. Reason may tell us that sex has no particular significance, that two people can never be all things to each other, that monogamy is an arbitrary and outmoded rule, or that no one has the right to limit another's experiences. But most of us want to feel that we have the monogamous affection of those whom we love sexually. A monogamous commitment is a sign that our love is really reciprocated (1979: 99).

The psychoanalyst Herbert Strean published a book in 1980 entitled *The Extramarital Affair,* the object of which was to assess the causes and results of such behavior. The work was based on a selective review of the literature, the author's own personal experience with patients, and reports from psychoanalysts with whom he worked. Strean believes there has been a sharp rise in the incidence of extramarital affairs in recent years. But, he observed, an adulterous person rarely breaks up his or her marriage in order to marry or live with a lover. There appears to be a large cluster of men and women in our society who want to preserve their marriages and at the same time engage in extramarital relationships. It is this group of individuals with which he is primarily concerned.

Strean has cited many case studies, and through psychoanalysis has arrived at reasons for the affairs. These were expressed in terms such as Oedipus complex, sadomasochism, latent heterosexuality (or latent homosexuality), and continuing adolescence into adulthood. He noted that the conclusions of the research of others reveal that the experts are in disagreement about the emotional health or maturity of those engaged in extramarital affairs. His own opinion is that "an extramarital affair is never a healthy or mature act. . . . Although I believe that an occasional one-night stand or short-term extramarital affair can sometimes be viewed as a harmless regression, a prolonged extramarital affair always implies that the adulterer is involved in a conflicted marriage and therefore is a conflicted person who probably can profit from psychotherapy" (1980: 202-203). Thus, we see that the medicalizing perspective is still alive and not all social scientists have been able to successfully adopt the normalizing perspective.

CONCLUSION

This brief survey of the relevant literature has excluded all journal articles and, obviously, some books. An attempt was made to select works from different time periods so that the reader would be able to judge what, if any, changes have been occurring in society regarding adultery. Although there were many differences evidenced in terms of concerns, techniques, depth of probing, as well as size and composition of samples, some rather consistent findings were evident. First, adultery is found throughout society, in every geographic region, country, socioeconomic class, religion and adult age category. Second, males are more adulterous than females, although the discrepancy between them has been decreasing. Even so, it appears that, contrary to what some may believe, over half the married population has never had an adulterous experience. Third, the incidence of adultery is much higher for individuals who had premarital sexual experience. Fourth, for females, adultery seems to increase when they are in their thirties and forties. Fifth, most adulterous relationships are short-lived and can be measured in terms of days, weeks, or months. Rare are those which are measured in terms of years. Sixth, most adultery is covert. The adulterous spouse conceals his or her sexual activities, and, it appears, the other spouse prefers it that way. Seventh, if the adultery is discovered, the marriage is affected. Although a few marriages are reportedly improved, most are damaged. Eighth, most adulterous spouses want to preserve their marriages. Ninth, when divorce results from the adultery, the adulterous spouse rarely marries his or her lover. If they do marry, they will probably get divorced.

Finally, as analyzed and defined in chapter 2, it appears that most adultery is heterosexual, nonconsensual, and volitional, with low visibility. While much adultery is based on affection, adultery without affection appears to be even more common, based on the frequency of short-term liaisons. As it is commonly defined, adultery is comsummated. Nevertheless, many of the aforementioned studies indicate there is much sexual behavior which stops short of actual coitus, but which would be considered sexually unfaithful by the spouse. And while most individuals are probably aware their relationships are adulterous, there are some who are not conscious of the fact that their sexual partner is married.

FUTURE STUDIES OF ADULTERY

In the 1980s a number of books written by non-scientific writers have begun to appear, some of which are ideological in nature. The authors have drawn upon scientific studies to varying degrees and tend to be highly selective in their representation of the facts. An obvious attempt is made to influence the reader in a specific manner. In addition to books which attempt to justify or condone extra-marital sexual behavior, several are concerned with the prevention of adultery.

Behavioral scientists, meanwhile, continue to study the behavior in order to determine what, in fact, *is* occurring. Since society is a living, changing entity, scientists can be expected to demonstrate an ongoing, active interest in sexual behavior in general and extra-marital relationships in particular. As can be seen in the preceding review of the literature, not only are more scientists showing an interest in adultery, but they are representing an increasing number of disciplines. Also evident is the fact that although the moralizing and medicalizing perspectives persist, the normalizing perspective is increasingly utilized.

Each discipline has its own special questions, methods and concerns. What is of interest to the biologist is not necessarily of interest to the sociologist. Even when they are interested in the same phenomenon, they are interested in it for different reasons. Each discipline— anthropology, sociology, psychology, and more recently sexology— collects and interprets its own data on adultery leading to its own particular insights. Altogether a larger and more complete body of knowledge results.

Science is generally characterized by a period of data collection followed by a period of hypotheses formulation and testing. It appears that the Kinsey studies ushered in the much-needed period of systematic and scientific collection of empirical information regarding the sexual behavior, including adultery, of men and women in the United States. If history is any guide, we can now expect to see, in addition to a continuation of data collection, a period of synthesizing the material, together with the formulation of hypotheses and theories which attempt to explain and unify the data. Future studies will be guided by these theories and will be designed to test the hypotheses.

Many questions remain to be answered. Among them are the following: (1) What type of relationship exists between premarital and extra-marital sex? Is the former an independent or intervening variable? (2) Why has the sexual revolution affected the incidence of adultery among women more than men? Has the incidence among housewives also risen, or only that of working women? (3) Is the incidence among Blacks and Hispanics similar to that of whites? For males and females? (4) How much homo-sexual adultery exists? Is it more common among males or females? Does it affect the marriage differently than heterosexual adultery? (5) Do members of religions who do not believe in divorce see sex among divorced individuals as adulterous? Is a distinction made between the behavior of members and nonmembers?

In answering these and other relevant questions there needs to be a number of studies conducted by trained behavioral scientists using nation-wide random samples. The resulting data must then be analyzed in an objective manner to seek explanations rather than justifications of ideological positions. There has been a lamentable lack of such research in the past. It is hoped that this situation will be remedied in the future.

REFERENCES

Baber, Ray. 1939. *Marriage and the Family.* New York: McGraw-Hill.
Bardwick, Judith. 1979. *In Transition: How Feminism, Sexual Liberation, and the Search for Self-Fulfillment Have Altered America.* New York: Holt, Rinehart and Winston.
Bernard, Jessie. 1970. "Infidelity: Some Moral and Social Issues." In *The*

Psychodynamic of Work and Marriage, edited by J. Masserman, 131-146. Orlando, Fla.: Grune.

Burgess, Ernest. 1955. "The Sociologic Theory of Psychosexual Behavior." In *Sexual Behavior in American Society,* edited by J. Himelhoch and S. Fava, 12-28. New York: W. W. Norton.

Burgess, Ernest, and Paul Wallin. 1953. *Engagement and Marriage.* New York: Lippincott.

Clanton, Gordon. 1977. "The Contemporary Experience of Adultery." In *Marriage and Alternatives: Exploring Intimate Relationships,* edited by Libby and Whitehurst, 112-129. Glenview, Ill.: Scott, Foresman.

Cuber, John. 1969. "Adultery: Reality Versus Stereotype." In *Extramarital Relations,* edited by G. Neubeck, 190-196. Englewood Cliffs, N.J.: Prentice-Hall.

Cuber, John and P. Harroff. 1965. *The Significant Americans.* New York: Appleton-Century.

Davis, Katherine. 1929. *Factors in the Sex Life of Twenty-two Hundred Women.* New York: Harper.

Davis, Kingsley. 1949. *Human Society.* New York: Macmillan.

Ellis, Albert. 1958. *Sex Without Guilt.* New York: Lyle Stuart.

Ellis, Havelock. 1933. *Studies in the Psychology of Sex.* New York: Random House.

Fine, R. 1975. *Psychoanalytic Psychology.* New York: Jason Aronson.

Hamilton, Gilbert. 1929. *A Research in Marriage.* New York: Lear.

Hunt, Morton. 1969. *The Affair.* New York: World.

———. 1974. *Sexual Behavior in the 1970's.* Chicago: Playboy Press.

Kinsey, Alfred, et al. 1948. *Sexual Behavior in the Human Male.* Philadelphia: W. B. Saunders.

———. 1953. *Sexual Behavior in the Human Female.* Philadelphia: W. B. Saunders.

Krafft-Ebing, Richard Von. 1933. *Psychopathia Sexualis.* Brooklyn, N. Y.: Physicians and Surgeons Book Co.

Landis, Carney, et al. 1940. *Sex in Development.* New York: Paul B. Hoeber.

Mazur, Ronald. 1973. *The New Intimacy: Open-Ended Marriage and Alternative Life-Styles.* Boston: Beacon Press.

Neubeck, Gerhard and Vera Schletzer. 1969. "A Study of Extramarital Relations." In *Extramarital Relations,* edited by G. Neubeck, 146-152. Englewood Cliffs, N.J.: Prentice-Hall.

Strean, Herbert. 1980. *The Extramarital Affair.* New York: Free Press.

Terman, Lewis. 1938. *Psychological Factors in Marital Happiness.* New York: McGraw-Hill.

Westermarck, Edvard. 1922. *The History of Human Marriage.* New York: Alberton.

Yablonsky, Lewis. 1979. *The Extra-Sex Factor.* New York: Times Books.

8

Philip E. Lampe
ADULTERY AND
THE TWENTY-FIRST CENTURY

In 1805 an edition of the Bible was printed which caused frowns and consternation among the faithful and probably more than a few smiles among the faithless. Due to a printer's error the sixth (or seventh) commandment read "Thou shalt commit adultery." This edition quickly became known as the "Wicked Bible." If the same error were to occur in 2005 the reaction may be very different. Some cynics may say that it would probably lead to a general return to reading and quoting the Bible.

Many important changes have obviously occurred in the last two centuries. The eighteenth century was characterized by a rural-agrarian, family-centered society. All social institutions tended to be male-dominated. Females found their identity in and through their relationships with males. They were identified first with the father and later with the husband, and their place was in the home. In general, it can be stated that wives and children were considered to be the property of the husband-father. Marriage and children were necessities for members of both sexes. As a result, everyone was expected to get married and have a large family. Romantic love often had little or nothing to do with the choice of a marriage partner. More mundane considerations took precedence, including the size of the dowry. The head and the stomach were more important than the heart. Religion was not just a personal matter, but also a public matter. Religious values were frequently the basis for civil and criminal laws, and religious leaders were often leaders of the community. Church and state were usually not too far apart.

In colonial America, most knowledge of sex came from observation, usually of animals, and personal experience. There was, of course, also the information and misinformation shared among friends. However, there was very little serious information available in written form, other than books which took a moralizing perspective to condemn most sexual behavior. Such books contributed little to the interested reader's understanding. Therefore, information was sought wherever possible. One source which was available is a book of writings, entitled *Aristotle's Masterpiece,* which appears to have originated in medieval Europe. Because it was less moralizing and more medicalizing then most, it was often used as a sex manual. The writings gave a core of sexual information, often false, based on what is now discredited medical theory. They also stated that over-indulgence in sexual activity could affect eyesight, dry up the body and shorten one's life. Nevertheless, overall the book did promote a more positive and accepting attitude towards sex than was common in the eighteenth and nineteenth centuries.

COLONIAL AMERICA

According to Kuhn (1955: 134) the culture of Puritan New England was more influential in shaping our national culture than any other regional or immigrant group, before or since. Many of the basic values of contemporary society originated in New England. Puritan values prevailed for almost three-quarters of a century in the laws of the land (Bell, 1967: 29). Although Puritan values have since been diffused, they have never completely disappeared.

Marriage was considered more of a civil ceremony than a church ceremony. As such, divorce and remarriage were allowed. The Puritan family, as was typical of the time, was patriarchal. The father played a dominant role not only in ordinary family matters, but also in the marriage of his children. In several colonies a young man was required by law to obtain the consent of the girl's father before beginning the courtship. Even if the father did not actually select the mates for his children, he was given veto power over their choices. Disobedience to his wishes was not only viewed as rebellion against one's family but also against one's religion. The father was seen as God's spokesman within the family and the commandment "Honor thy father and mother" was taken very seriously. In fact, disobedience could result in death. A Connecticut law stated:

If a man have a stubborn and rebellious son of sufficient years and understanding, viz. sixteen years of age, which will not obey the voice of his father or the voice of his mother, and that when they have chastened him will not harken unto them, then may his father and mother, being his natural parents, lay hold on him and bring him to the magistrates assembled in court, and testify unto them that their son is stubborn and rebellious and will not obey their voice and chastizement, but lives in sundry crimes, such a son shall be put to death. (Trumbull, 1876: 69-70)

Courtship was generally rather limited due to the lack of free time and the relative lack of importance given to romantic love as a necessary ingredient of a successful marriage. An additional factor was the rural setting with its often considerable distances between families. Not only did this affect the frequency of courtship but also some of the practices of courtship. One of the more interesting of these was known as "bundling." This refers to the practice of allowing the couple to get into bed together at night so they could carry on their conversation after everyone else had gone to bed. Such a situation saved candles and firewood which could otherwise have been necessary. Thrift and frugality were a way of life, and the saying "Waste not, want not" described the prevailing mentality. But if frugality was a virtue so too were discipline and moral concern. In order to ensure that no sexual intimacies would occur, the couple was often required to remain fully clothed and, if an additional safeguard were deemed prudent, a wooden bar placed between them on top of the covers. Bundling was not limited to New England, but was also reported in other sections of the country, including parts of the American frontier (Bell, 1967: 34-35).

Another interesting practice was for a young man to meet a maiden, propose marriage, and obtain legal permission all in the same day. Matrimonial advertisements in the newspapers were sometimes utilized to make contact. It has also been reported that strangers would sometimes knock on someone's door and inquire about the availability of an unmarried girl. No matter how the couple met, it was expected that the courtship would be accomplished "with decent haste and not too much sentiment" (Goodsell, 1934: 372).

Colonial Americans favored both early marriages and large families. This combination tended to reinforce the official hostility to nonprocreative sex which was supported by the Puritan association of sex with the sin of the Garden of Eden (Francoeur, 1982: 4-5). Sexual intimacies were considered appropriate only in marriage; both premarital and extramarital sexual relations were forbidden. However, as Francoeur has pointed out, there were certain "invisible" people such as slaves and servants with or among whom sexual behavior was often overlooked. Thus, there was actually a variety of sexual practices and customs which were often ignored in our history books. Unlike many societies, control over sexual behavior was expected of both males and females. As a result, marriage at an early age was a common occurrence, as was the remarriage of the divorced and widowed. A woman was considered an "old" or "ancient maid" if still unmarried at twenty-five years of age. Adult men who remained unmarried were viewed with disapproval and, possibly, suspicion. Males without mates posed a threat to the wives and daughters of the rest of the males. Thus, in Hartford such men were taxed twenty shillings a week (Calhoun, 1960: 67-68), which undoubtedly was an encouragement to either get married or move elsewhere. The same reasoning led New Haven to order married men separated from their wives to repair their relationships. As long as they were separated the men were a potential threat.

Colonial New England had a strict code of sexual behavior. According to Calhoun (1960: 39), "the Puritan emphasis on sexual restraint was of a piece with the general gospel of frugality so appropriate among a class of people trying to accumulate capital in an age of deficit. Urgent economic interests furthered the novel virtue of male chastity. The necessity of accumulation led the puritan to reprobate all unprofitable forms of sin including licentiousness, that prodigal waster." In addition, succumbing to temptation of the flesh was inappropriate for those who were "chosen" by God. In general, fornication was less severely punished than adultery. A newly married couple who had a child within the first seven months were forced to make public confession of their sin before the whole congregation. Unmarried people guilty of fornication could be enjoined to marriage, be fined, whipped, made to stand in the pillory or branded on the cheek. If the guilty couple was engaged to be married the punishment was usually less severe. However, if a betrothed woman was guilty of fornication with a man not her fiance, they were treated as adulterers.

Adultery was severely punished. It was not only a violation of religious values but was also considered a threat to the family and the community. The laws made no distinction between men and women adulterers. Both were supposed to suffer the same consequences. In fact, however, women were generally treated more harshly (Hunt, 1959: 234). The original penalty for adultery was death. The death penalty was provided in early seventeenth century Jamestown (Willison, 1951) as well as in New England (Haskins, 1960). Such punishment was actually inflicted on some offenders. Usually, however, adulterers were not executed (Howard: 1904). Other punishments included whipping on the bare back, branding on the face, and wearing a badge on the left sleeve for life. Rhode Island specified that anyone guilty of adultery should be ". . . publicly set on the Gallows in the Day Time, with a Rope about his or her Neck, for the Space of One Hour; and on his or her Return from the Gallows to the Goal, shall be publicly whipped on his or her naked Back, not exceeding Thirty Stripes; and shall stand committed to the Goal of the country wherein convicted, until he or she shall pay all Costs of Prosecution" (Howard, 1904: 173). In addition, adultery was considered sufficient grounds for divorce. Everything in society, however, was not uniformly sex negative. There were some mitigating influences which counteracted to some extent the negative attitudes toward sex. More liberal sexual ideas of the Enlightenment reached the United States from Europe. Some well-known Americans such as Benjamin Franklin and Thomas Paine were influenced by them.

A clear illustration of this is found in a letter Franklin wrote to a French lady friend, Madame Brillon: "I often pass by the house. It appears to me desolate. Formerly I broke the commandments by enjoying it with my neighbor's wife. Now I enjoy it no longer and thus I am less a sinner. But when they concern women, these commandments are always inconvenient, and I am annoyed that we are counseled not to break them. If in your voyages you should encounter Saint Peter, ask him to rescind them, as they were given only to the Jews, and are too hindersome to good Christians" (Franklin, 1939: 34).

Another European import which moderated sexual ideas was Romanticism. Romanticism was a revolt against reason, authority and tradition. It also opposed order and discipline. Romanticism manifested itself in social, political and moral reforms. Naturalness, individuality, experimentation, freedom and emotion were exalted. Their expression in art, music and literature brought major innovations in attitudes and perceptions. In literature there was a concern with realism and concreteness which resulted in, among other things, novelists writing about love affairs in minute detail. These movements helped to make people more sexually aware and accepting.

Such was society around the time of the appearance of the "Wicked Bible" in which the printer's error resulted in the commandment which required one to commit adultery. Colonial New England attempted to control sexual behavior, including adultery. Although there is ample evidence to indicate that the attempts were generally not too successful (Morgan, 1978), it is important to note that a sustained effort was made. Hence, based on the material presented in the preceding chapters, it appears that in colonial times adultery was harshly punished by law, religion condemned it as a violation of God's commandments, writers generally avoided direct reference to it, at least as a major theme, unless to illustrate its harmful effects, and philosophers did not consider it a worthwhile topic of debate. The social scientific study of society was still a thing of the future and whatever "facts" were needed or desired could be obtained from authority, religion (usually the Bible), folklore and/or experience.

MODERN AMERICA

At the beginning of the twentieth century Western sexual attitudes were essentially the same as they had been for the past 2,000 years. Beliefs and assumptions about sexuality that had existed in the early Christian church were later expressed in the legal and ecclesiastical thought of the Middle Ages, which has been instrumental in the development of the American tradition. The influence of religion in enforcing the traditional negative attitudes regarding sex declined somewhat with the corresponding decline in the importance of religion itself. However, medical and scientific assumptions together with sexually hostile or repressive laws continued to reinforce the generally anti-sex tradition. Some laws classified many sexual acts as "against nature" or as crimes "not fit to be named." Some changes in attitudes regarding sex began in the early part of the twentieth century. These increased gradually until the second half of the century when they greatly accelerated. During this time there were some attempts, which ultimately proved successful, to take socially deviant forms of sexual behavior out of the category of "sickness," (i.e., to demedicalize sex). An attempt, largely unsuccessful, has been made by some to also take sex out of the category of "sin" (i.e., to demoralize it). One of the ways these changes are attempted is to speak of sexual behavior, at least between consenting adults, as personal options or alternative lifestyles that fall within the range of normal behavior (i.e., to normalize it). Thus widespread positive or at least neutral attitudes toward sex have only recently begun to appear. This change has resulted from a number of basic changes in society.

In contrast to the eighteenth century, the latter half of the twentieth century has been characterized by an urban-industrialized-service society that is individual-oriented. Social institutions still tend to be male-dominated although females have now entered into and have begun to advance within the ranks of every one of them. Females have thereby been able to establish an identity of their own apart from that of males. In some cases they now retain their maiden names even after marriage. Neither marriage nor children are any longer considered a necessary part of a person's life. Each now becomes a separate option. Modern society generally provides alternative means to fulfill the needs that were previously met in matrimony. Meanwhile romantic love has become the most socially acceptable basis for marriage and may even be more or less accepted as justification for living together without marriage. Yet another change has occurred in the realm of religion. Religion has become basically a personal matter, and attempts have been made to eliminate it as a basis for law. A current constant concern is the constitutional requirement of separation of church and state.

A number of significant changes have occurred in marriage and family. The number of viable options has increased. Individuals now choose whether or not to marry, whether to have children and, if so, when and how many. A choice may be made whether to conceive by natural or artificial means. In some cases women are choosing to have children and remain single. In addition, women may now decide whether to have a career (an option selected by more than half of all wives) or remain at home. For those who marry, the possible length of the marriage has been greatly extended due to the increase in life expectancy. Just in the twentieth century life expectancy has increased by approximately 26 years (Horton and Hunt, 1980: 401). This change is related to two additional decisions, that of divorce, which has increased dramatically over the years, and that of adultery, which also appears to have increased. The first often follows the second (Kreitler, 1981).

One of the most obvious areas of change has occurred in relation to the social perception of sexual behavior. It is now generally perceived to be a personal matter, but public discussion of it is acceptable. Classes on sex education are now a common part of a school's curriculum. Sex is a major theme in both the mass media and entertainment media. Government provides birth control aid and abortion to virtually all who wish them. Society also recognizes alternative lifestyles and sexual preferences. Consequently, homosexuality and premarital and extramarital sex are often openly admitted and discussed. Even some religions have accommodated themselves to these facts of life.

READING THE PAST

The historian Vern Bullough (1976) identified four important causes for attitudinal change: (1) the emancipation of women and the acceptance by women of their own sexuality and sex needs; (2) the growth of anti-natal mentality together with the belief that pleasure rather than procreation is the primary purpose of sex; (3) a growing recognition of the variety possible in human sexuality. Contact with foreign ideas and/or countries through reading and travel is an important source of this recognition; (4) organized propaganda for new forms of sexuality. All four of these factors identified by Bullough have been aided by the attention given them by the mass media, which have thereby become an important factor. Thus the attention given to the growing incidence and acceptance of adultery by the media could be added as a fifth cause to the preceding list.

A review of the changes—legal, religious, literary, philosophical, and scientific—that have occurred in the United States in regard to adultery is in order. The section on law (chapter 3) documents the legal changes that have occurred regarding adultery in the United States. Perhaps in no other area, with the possible exception of literature, has as much change occurred as that found in the law. Laws have prohibited extramarital sexual behavior and defined it as a crime. Early punishments included physical disfigurement, whipping, public humiliation, imprisonment, fines, and even the possibility of death at the hands of the offended spouse. Adultery was viewed as an offense against both society and the innocent spouse and could therefore be tried in both criminal and civil cases.

Each state could and did regulate marriage and family matters according to its own particular norms and morals. Typically, a double standard prevailed and women were treated more harshly than men for the same offense. In fact, adultery was often limited to those instances when a married woman was involved. A married man who had sexual relations with an unmarried woman was guilty of fornication.

Over the years changes have occurred in society that have resulted in a higher status for women and a greater tolerance of sexual behavior, including adultery. These changes have been reflected in the law. Not only have punishments undergone drastic changes, but criminal laws regarding adultery either have been eliminated or have become unenforced or unenforceable. Society has, in effect, ceased to be offended by adultery.

A spouse, male or female, may still be offended by adultery and may bring civil suit against an adulterous mate. However, even this legal action is becoming somewhat more difficult and less punitive. Adultery is now less likely to be mentioned in divorce cases because of the widespread use of "no fault" divorce. However, in many states adultery is still considered legally relevant in those cases deciding the custody of children.

Finally, the opinion is expressed by Sue and Philip Hall that changes will continue to occur in the legal definition and treatment of adultery. While it is unlikely that the state or federal government will ever again become involved in the private sexual behavior of consenting adults to the extent that it once did, it is equally unlikely that adultery will become completely acceptable and unpunished and/or punishable under the law.

Chapter 4 reveals that when speaking of religion in the United States and its view and treatment of adultery, it is necessary to make some distinctions. First, a distinction must be made between church members and church leaders. It appears that church members, including some moralists and theologians, have expressed opinions that depart from official, traditional church teaching or doctrine. Married or lay moralists/theologians are more likely to be in the forefront of change regarding sexual morality, including adultery. This does not come as a great surprise since these people will be more affected by such decisions than will the celibate clergy. Situation ethics is often espoused by those advocating change. Adultery, it is argued, may be either moral or immoral, depending on the circumstances. Although a report of the American Catholic Theological Society agreed with the traditional condemnation of adultery, it recommended that "creative growth should be weighed when considering the morality of open marriages or satellite relationships" (Kosnik, 1977: 152-169). These recommendations, however, were rejected by officials in Rome. Church leaders have not been as accepting of situation ethics, but continue to rely on the many apparent scriptural prohibitions as the official position.

Second, distinctions must be made between religious denominations. There appears to be a wide range of views concerning the morality of adultery in present-day churches. One of the most accepting of views is to be found in the Quaker religion, while one of the least accepting is Catholicism. It should be pointed out that the acceptance is qualified or conditional rather than unconditional. Other religions are located somewhere along this continuum of acceptance-rejection of the morality of adultery. Conservative Protestant denominations, along with Catholics, are likely to continue to condemn adultery.

Dr. Beal concludes with the opinion that although individual church members may modify their own view of adultery there will be little change, if any, in the official position of most major Christian denominations concerning the morality of adultery. It will continue to be considered immoral. This may result in an even greater widening of the already existing gulf between those church members who are traditionalists and those who are more liberal. Churches that reaffirm their moral traditions are faced with the problem of relevancy in the minds of some Americans. This may result in greater patience with and understanding of adultery by pastors and religious counselors in private conferences, but not in official, public pronouncements.

Chapter 5 revealed that, while the great writers of Europe had long been examining adultery and making it a central theme, such was not the case in the United States. Rare was the American who wrote of adultery before the twentieth century. When it was dealt with, it was typically done so without detail and in a moralizing manner. Adultery was evil and the result was inevitably one of suffering and punishment. This was the only treatment of the subject that was socially acceptable.

Among the earliest of the Americans to treat the theme of adultery were women. Females were unable to write about the major theme of male authors—the Western frontier. The frontier symbolized freedom, individualism, adventure and self-reliance. These were virtues only for men; they were socially unacceptable for women. Although adultery was also socially unacceptable, it was closer to the socially promoted and approved female role. More important, adultery was only alluded to in their work and was treated as a temptation to be overcome.

In the twentieth century adultery has become much more common and explicit but, paradoxically, much less important as a theme in literature. This is because of the changing status of marriage and family in society. Offenses against monogamous marriage are no longer perceived to be as potentially harmful as in previous centuries. Society's reaction, as depicted by the authors, also underwent a change. Whereas the reaction to adultery before the twentieth century reflected the spirit of the Old Testament, which emphasized punishment, after the turn of the century it was closer to the spirit of the New Testament, which emphasized forgiveness. Dr. Cutting stated that literature can be expected to continue demonstrating our interest in adultery, which is a reflection of that found among the members of society who are searching for love, freedom, and adventure while enjoying the security and commitment of marriage. Such a search can be seen in the widespread popularity of the generic romance novel, which seems to be especially popular among women. Recent studies have found that there are twenty million readers of these novels and approximately 70 percent of the women who read them are married (Pattee, 1985).

In contrast to authors of literature, Chapter 6 indicated that philosophers, especially in the United States, have not shown much of an interest in the topic of sex. Consequently, the prevailing philosophical tradition has been largely derived from earlier philosophers who were closely aligned with religion and tended to take a moralizing perspective in their analysis. It was not until the middle of the twentieth century that American philosophers became involved in a dialogue on sex. The earliest discussions preserved the traditional connection between marriage (or, at least, love) and sex, resulting in a general repudiation of adultery based on its dysfunctional aspects or negative functions. This sparked a reaction, and within a short period of time there emerged those who recognized some of the possible functional aspects or positive functions of extramarital sex. Sex was looked at and defended apart from marriage. Nevertheless, marital sex was generally seen as superior and preferable to sex outside of marriage. Even among some who defended extramarital sexual relations there was a belief that these relationships should be guided by a set of ethical rules. The proposed set of ethics not only applied to the adulterous pair but also to the uninvolved spouse.

There also appeared an attack on marriage and a corresponding endorsement of adultery as an expression of revolt against the idea that a person belonged to his or her spouse. This, in turn, spurred a reaction on the part of several philosophers who came to the defense of marriage. The more traditional views of sex and marriage once more became evident. Dr. Connelly concluded with the opinion that, unfortunately, the lack of interest exhibited by American philosophers in the area of sex in general, and adultery in particular, was likely to continue. Although the immediate future does not appear to offer much chance of a heated philosophical exchange, there has at least been the beginning of a debate. There are now philosophers with positions on both sides of the ethical issues of adultery.

Chapter 7 shows that there has been considerable advancement in the scientific study of adultery in the United States. Until the middle of the twentieth century adultery was not studied as a separate topic, but was usually included among other forms of sexual behavior. Early studies of sexual behavior were typically neither scientific nor American. Those works that existed were written from a moralizing or medicalizing perspective and often came from abroad. The first scientists interested in human sexual behavior as a topic of publication were usually drawn from the health sciences (doctors, psychiatrists, counselors). As such, sexual behavior, especially that which was extramarital and, hence, socially disapproved, tended to be explicitly or implicitly viewed in medical terms.

A major breakthrough occurred when the zoologist Alfred Kinsey and associates studied human sexual behavior. Their approach was much more scientific than earlier studies. Since then there have been several developments worth noting. First, there has been an increasing attempt on the part of scientists to take a more neutral, objective approach to the study of sexuality. This has resulted in the normalizing perspective. Second, specific forms of sexual behavior have been studied in depth. Thus adultery in its various forms has become the exclusive focus of many studies. Third, publishing opportunities have greatly increased. Several new professional journals have appeared that are dedicated to studies of sexual behavior. Finally, the study of sex has become an accepted and respected profession. One result has been the emergence of sexologists.

Results of the studies indicate that a change in the incidence of adultery has occurred. There appears to have been an increase among women, but not among men (at least since the time of Kinsey). Consequently, the traditional double standard has lessened but not disappeared. Contrary to popular perception based on the entertainment media, most Americans have never been adulterous.

Another change appears to be the greater openness in the discussion of adultery. This should not be confused, however, with a greater social and/or personal acceptance of it. Most respondents continue to disapprove of adultery, especially on the part of their own partners. Thus, while people may talk of adultery openly, most of those who engage in it do so covertly.

ANTICIPATING THE FUTURE

Based on the preceding, it is tempting to predict a continuing increase in the incidence of adultery. Indeed, this is the common forecast. In a recent book entitled *All the Good Ones are Married,* Marion Zola has suggested that, because of the so-called sexual revolution, adultery involving married men and single women will become more prevalent. Women who choose a career are finding that relations with married men can be deeper and more meaningful than those with single men, who, she says, are more often engaged in shallow, sexually exploitative relationships of relatively short duration. This alternative will seem especially attractive for women who do not desire marriage (Zola, 1981).

Social scientists have also predicted an increase in adultery. Dr. Wardell Pomeroy, a successor to Kinsey, estimated that approximately 60 to 65 percent of males and 40 to 45 percent of females have had adulterous relationships, figures that he believes will increase to 65 to 70 percent and 45 to 50 percent, respectively, by 1990 (McGinnis, 1981: 23). Meanwhile, McGinnis, a marriage counselor, believes that the figures will be even higher. He predicted that by 1990 approximately 75 percent of males and 65 percent of females will engage in such relationships. "This, I believe, will be the result of the expanded opportunities for interpersonal relationships outside of marriage—for both men and women, the softening of harsh and punitive attitudes toward people in affairs, the expansion of intimate friendships, the increase in the maturity of marital partners, and the strengthening of marriage itself" (1981: 193).

Such predictions, while plausible, do fail to take several important factors into consideration. First, they assume a continuation of the current trend and overlook the possibility of a reaction. History is full of such examples, and there are indications that a reaction may already have begun. At the beginning of the 1980s a number of publications, books, and magazine articles appeared that advocated sexual abstinence (see Brown, 1980; Bakos, 1981). This reactionary stance has sometimes been referred to as the "New Celibacy" and it is usually seen to be temporary rather than permanent. This reevaluation was articulated by George Leonard, who, in his book *The End of Sex: Erotic Love After the Sexual Revolution,* wrote that we took a wrong turn "Wherever we have split sex from love, creation and the rest of life, wherever we have trivialized and depersonalized the act of love itself" (1983: 26). The sexual revolution, he wrote, caused many people to experiment with sex not because they really wanted to but because they thought they should. Such a practice, he said, was grotesque.

A second reaction to be considered is the success enjoyed by the more conservative religious denominations. In recent years the denominations that have reaffirmed their commitment to the traditional Christian values, including a rejection of adultery, are those that have shown the greatest amount of growth (Hoge and Roozen, 1979). In addition, the last two presidents of the United States, Mr. Carter and Mr. Reagan, have both spoken publicly in favor of a return to more traditional, conservative religious values. And the Moral Majority has enjoyed an increase in power and publicity. Conservative thought appears to be gaining general acceptance nationwide.

In addition, there are long-lasting cultural values that militate against the widespread general acceptance of adultery. The most obvious are religious ones. The Judeo-Christian heritage, so much a part of the culture of the United States, has consistently opposed adultery. From the Old Testament come the commandments "Thou shalt not commit adultery" and "Thou shalt not covet thy neighbor's wife." And the New Testament reaffirms these prohibitions and even extends them. So, to accept the commandments and engage in adulterous behavior at the same time is to experience what has been called "cognitive dissonance." For adultery to reach the proportions projected by Pomeroy and McGuinnis a majority of Christians and Jews would have to commit it, a possibility that is unlikely, according to the research cited in chapter 7.

Many of those not restrained by religious principles will avoid adultery on account of romantic love, a secular value so widely accepted throughout society that it affects even those who are not reached by moral restraints. According to the precepts of romantic love, which were enumerated in chapter 1, no one can love more than one person at a time, and no one who truly loves one person can even desire to be physically united to someone else. Until the idea of romantic love loses its influence, any sexual liaisons outside of marriage will call into question the love between the spouses. Thus those men and women who love their mates will be reluctant to risk the marriage by engaging in adultery. If and when adultery does occur it will tend to be covert.

Finally, since the beginning of the 1980s there has been a nation-wide concern with the possible health risks involved in nonmono-gamous sexual activity. In the early part of the decade national attention focused on herpes. The concern over this recurrent but nonfatal venereal disease led many people to reexamine their sex lives, especially if it included casual or multiple partners. So serious was this concern that a feature article in *Time* magazine declared that the "new scarlet letter"—"H" for herpes—was forcing chastity back into fashion. The watchwords for the 1980s were *caution* and *commitment* (Leo, 1982: 62-66). In the mid-1980s an even greater national and international concern has developed over another sex-ually transmitted disease, AIDS (acquired immune deficiency syn-drome). This as yet incurable venereal disease is considered to be al-ways fatal. Because warnings against indiscriminate sex have been common in the mass media, there has been a reduction in the use of prostitutes and other casual sexual partners, especially those of the same sex. By 1984, health concerns had reached such proportions that the cover of *Time* proclaimed that "The Sexual Revolution is Over" (Leo, 1984). Although this proclamation was undoubtedly premature, it did indicate a change of lifestyle was underway.

After centuries of viewing sexual behavior from the moralizing and/or medicalizing perspectives, the normalizing perspective finally began to be accepted around the middle of the present century—a development that perhaps encouraged the sexual freedom that en-joyed an unprecedented visibility and acceptance in the United States during the 1960s and 1970s. However, the epidemic of venereal diseases of the 1980s, together with the resurgence of religious fundamentalism, may change things. Reports of the physical and emotional suffering of herpes victims has reestablished the link in the minds of many between sex and sickness. The more recent and dangerous AIDS outbreak has fortified this connection, resulting in the reemergence of the medicalizing perspective. Furthermore, some people have begun to see these epidemics as punishments from God for the abuse of sexual behavior. The link between sex and sin has therefore once more emerged in public debate. We may have come full circle, and are now witnessing a return to the moralizing perspective.

In conclusion, the prognostication is for the increase of adultery to level off and begin a moderate but general decline. The twenty-first century should be similar to the twentieth century, with some fluctuations. Continuing differences should remain based on certain sociodemographic variables, such as age, religion, socio-economic class, religion, etc. The sex difference should remain, with fewer women than men experiencing adultery. It is improbable that the percentage of males or females engaging in adultery will remain over 50 percent for a prolonged period of time. Thus, most people in the next century will also be aware that an error has been made if they come across a copy of the Bible that indicates the sixth (or seventh) commandment to be "Thou shalt commit adultery."

REFERENCES

Bakos, Susan C. 1981. "Why Men and Women are Saying No to Sex" "Sunday Woman," *San Antonio Light,* May 17: 3-11.

Bell, Robert R. 1967. *Marriage and Family.* Homewood, Ill.: Dorsey.

Brown, Gabrielle. 1980. *New Celibacy: Why More Men and Women are Abstaining From Sex—and Enjoying It.* New York: McGraw-Hill.

Bullough, Vern. 1976. *Sexual Variance in Society and History.* New York: John Wiley.

Calhoun, Arthur W. 1960. *A Social History of the American Family: Colonial Period,* vol. 1. New York: Barnes and Noble.

Francoeur, Robert. 1982. *Becoming a Sexual Person.* New York: John Wiley.

Franklin, Benjamin. 1939. *Dr. Benjamin Franklin and the Ladies.* Mt. Vernon, N.Y.: Peter Pauper.

Goodsell, Willystine. 1934. *A History of Marriage and the Family.* New York: Macmillan.

Haskins, George Lee. 1960. *Law and Authority in Early Massachusetts.* New York: Macmillan.

Hoge, Dean, and David Roozen. 1979. *Understanding Church Growth and Decline: 1950-1978.* New York: Pilgrim.

Horton, Paul, and Chester Hunt. 1980. *Sociology.* New York: McGraw-Hill.

Howard, George. 1904. *A History of Matrimonial Institutions,* vol. 2. Chicago: University of Chicago Press.

Hunt, Morton M. 1959. *The Natural History of Love.* New York: Alfred A. Knopf.

Kosnik, A., W. Carroll, A. Cunningham, A. Modras, and J. Schulte. 1977. *Human Sexuality: New Directions in American Thought.* New York: Paulist Press.

Kreitler, Peter. 1981. *Affair Prevention.* New York: Macmillan.

Kuhn, Manford H. 1955. "American Families Today: Development and Differentiation of Types." In *Family, Marriage and Parenthood,* edited by Howard Becker and Ruben Hill. Boston: Heath.

Leo, John. 1982. "The New Scarlet Letter." *Time.* (Aug. 2): 62-66.

———. 1984. "The Sexual Revolution is Over." *Time.* (Apr. 9): 74-3.

Leonard, George. 1983. *The End of Sex: Erotic Love After the Sexual Revolution.* Los Angeles: J. P. Tarcher.

McGinnis, Thomas. 1981. *More Than Just a Friend.* Englewood Cliffs, N.J.: Prentice Hall.

Morgan, Edmund. 1978. "The Puritans and Sex." In *The American Family in Social-Historical Perspective,* edited by Michael Gordon. New York: St. Martin's Press.

Trumbull, J. Hammond. 1876. *The True Blue Laws of Connecticut and the False Blue Laws Invented by the Rev. Samuel Peters.* Hartford, Conn.: American Publishing Co.

Willison, George. 1951. *Behold Virginia.* New York: Harcourt, Brace, Jovanovich.

Zola, Marion. 1981. *All the Good Ones are Married.* New York: Times.

INDEX

CONTRIBUTORS

Philip E. Lampe is a Professor of Sociology at Incarnate Word College, San Antonio, Texas. He received his B.A. in philosophy from Conception Seminary, M.A. in sociology from Southern Illinois University (Carbondale), and Ph.D. in sociology from Louisiana State University. Among his approximately fifty publications he has works on adultery, interethnic dating, and husband-wife roles and marital satisfaction.

Tarcisio Beal, a native of Agua Doce, SC, Brazil, made his theological studies with the Franciscan Fathers in Southern Brazil and holds a M.A. and a Ph.D. from the Catholic University of America. He is a Professor of History and Religious Studies at Incarnate Word College, San Antonio, Texas and also teaches Theological Ethics and Scripture in the Permanent Diaconate Program of the Archdiocese of San Antonio. He has written many articles on Latin American history and on liberation theology.

Robert J. Connelly earned his M.A. and Ph.D. in philosophy from St. Louis University. He has twenty-five years of teaching experience and is currently Professor of Philosophy at Incarnate Word College, San Antonio. His publications include *Whitehead vs. Hartshorne, Last Rights: Death and Dying in Texas Law and Experience,* and articles in process philosophy, science and technology, social ethics, and bioethics.

Rose Marie Cutting is a Full Professor at St. Mary's University (San Antonio) where she is the Chair of the Department of English and Communication Arts. She earned her Ph.D. from the University of Minnesota, her M.A. from the University of Michigan, and her B.A. from the College of St. Catherine. She has written *Anais Nin: A Reference Guide, John and William Bartram, William Byrd II and*

St. John de Crevecoeur: A Reference Guide, and articles on women authors and American literature.

Philip A. Hall, Ph.D. is an Associate Professor of Social Work at Our Lady of the Lake University in San Antonio, Texas. He received a B.A. from Cornell University in 1964, an M.S.W. from Washington University in 1966, and a Ph.D. from the University of Chicago in 1980.

Sue M. Hall, J.D. is an attorney in the private practice of law in San Antonio, Texas. She is Board Certified in Family Law and was formerly an Assistant Professor of Law at St. Mary's University School of Law, teaching primarily in the area of Family Law. Her degrees include a Bachelor's degree from the University of Oklahoma, an M.S.W. from Washington University, and a J.D. from St. Mary's University.